100 Nighttime Devotions to
Soothe Your Mind and Rest Your Spirit

Evenings *with* Jesus

Editors of Guideposts

Evenings with Jesus

Published by Guideposts Books & Inspirational Media
100 Reserve Road, Suite E200
Danbury, CT 06810
Guideposts.org

ACKNOWLEDGMENTS

Every attempt has been made to credit the sources of copyrighted material used in this book. If any such acknowledgment has been inadvertently omitted or miscredited, receipt of such information would be appreciated.

Scripture quotations marked (DLNT) are taken from the Disciples' Literal New Testament. Copyright © 2011 by Michael J. Magill.

Scripture quotations marked (ESV) are taken from the *Holy Bible, English Standard Version*. Copyright © 2001 by Crossway Bibles, a division of Good News Publishers. Used by permission. All rights reserved.

Scripture quotations marked (KJV) are taken from the *King James Version of the Bible*.

Scripture quotations marked (MSG) are taken from *The Message*. Copyright © 1993, 1994, 1995, 1996, 2000, 2001, 2002 by Eugene H. Peterson.

Scripture quotations marked (NASB) are taken from the *New American Standard Bible*. Copyright © 1960, 1962, 1963, 1968, 1971, 1972, 1973, 1975, 1977, 1995 by The Lockman Foundation, La Habra, California. Used by permission.

Scripture quotations marked (NCV) are taken from *The Holy Bible, New Century Version*. Copyright © 2005 by Thomas Nelson.

Scripture quotations marked (NIV) are taken from *The Holy Bible, New International Version*. Copyright © 1973, 1978, 1984, 2011 by Biblica, Inc. Used by permission of Zondervan. All rights reserved worldwide. zondervan.com

Scripture quotations marked (NKJV) are taken from *The Holy Bible, New King James Version*. Copyright © 1982 by Thomas Nelson.

Scripture quotations marked (NLT) are taken from the *Holy Bible, New Living Translation*. Copyright © 1996, 2004, 2007 by Tyndale House Foundation. Used by permission of Tyndale House Publishers Inc., Carol Stream, Illinois. All rights reserved.

Scripture quotations marked (NLV) are from the *New Life Bible,* copyright © 1969 by Christian Literature International. Used by permission. All rights reserved.

Scripture quotations marked (NRSV) are taken from the *New Revised Standard Version Bible*. Copyright © 1989 by the Division of Christian Education of the National Council of the Churches of Christ in the United States of America. Used by permission. All rights reserved.

Scripture quotations marked (TLB) are taken from *The Living Bible*. Copyright © 1971 by Tyndale House Publishers, Inc., Carol Stream, Illinois. All rights reserved.

Scripture quotations marked (TPT) are taken from *The Passion Translation*. Copyright © 2016 by Broadstreet Publishing Group, Savage, Minnesota. All rights reserved.

Scripture quotations marked (VOICE) are taken from The Voice Bible. Copyright © 2012 Thomas Nelson, Inc. The Voice™ translation copyright © 2012 Ecclesia Bible Society. All rights reserved,

Cover design by Pat Joyce
Interior design by Pat Joyce and Pamela Walker, W Design Studio
Cover photo by tomertu/Getty Images
Typeset by Aptara

We extend a special thank you to the writers and editors at Guideposts.org and *Guideposts* magazine, whose work we have drawn upon for this book.

We would also like to thank Jennifer Grant and Roma Maitlall for their diligence and contributions to *Evenings with Jesus*.

Printed and bound in the United States of America
10 9 8 7 6 5 4 3 2 1

A Bedtime Prayer

Lord, it is night. The night is for stillness.
Let us be still in the presence of God.
It is night after a long day.
What has been done has been done;
What has not been done has not been done; let it be.
The night is dark.
Let our fears of the darkness of the world
and of our own lives rest in you.
The night is quiet.
Let the quietness of your peace enfold us,
all dear to us, and all who have no peace.
The night heralds the dawn.
Let us look expectantly to a new day,
new joys, new possibilities.
In your name, we pray, Amen.

—NEW ZEALAND BOOK OF
COMMON PRAYER

INTRODUCTION

Many lay restless at night, unable to sleep peacefully because of worries of the day that have their minds churning. Many things pass through the mind during those hours—concerns about things that were done, things that were not done, and things that need to be done. The more that peaceful sleep is desired, the more quickly it flees away, leaving us more tired in the morning than when we went to bed. Does this need to be?

In the Gospels, quite a few important things happen at night.

It is on a quiet, star-filled night when ordinary shepherds hear the distant cries of a newborn baby and, taking the advice of a group of angels, follow the sound (Luke 2:8–20).

It is on a dark, lonely night, many years later, when that baby, now a man, kneels on the ground beneath a grove of olive trees and beseeches His Father for strength (Matthew 26:36–56).

And it is on a fateful, miraculous night, some days after that, when the same man, having been recently killed, appears before His awestruck friends, alive and whole, and exclaims, "Peace be with you!" (John 20:21).

Nighttime is at the very heart of the salvation story. A time of peace and solitude, the evening was often a time when the Savior Himself could retreat to a mountain and pray to His Father (Luke 6:12).

Following Jesus's lead, we, too, are encouraged to take advantage of the opportunity that night offers us to cultivate our spiritual lives and deepen our relationship with God. Aptly titled *Evenings with Jesus*, this book provides us with just the right structure and content to help nurture our spirits before we enter sleep.

Fifteen devotional writers lend their voices to *Evenings with Jesus*. Their profoundly true stories are each designed to ready your body, mind, and spirit for a restorative night's rest in Jesus's able care. Additionally, the relaxing devotions included in this book are complemented by short, related articles, inspirational quotes, scripture, and tips. Every one of them also ends with a brief, intimate prayer—a feature specially included to draw your spirit closer to Jesus's.

Since medieval times, perhaps earlier, Christians have carried on a tradition of evening prayers, sometimes called *complines*, to observe the completion of waking hours. Monastic communities developed special services with specific liturgies for this purpose. The prayers in *Evenings with Jesus* are a continuation of this beloved, age-old tradition—a tradition that has allowed centuries of Christians to grow their faith and strengthen their relationship with Jesus. We are confident that taking the time to pray the prayer included after the evening's devotion will help soothe your mind and ready you for a deep, peaceful night's rest—the same kind of peaceful rest the Lord promises in the Book of Proverbs: "When you lie down, you will not be afraid; when you lie down, your sleep will be sweet" (Proverbs 3:24).

Devotional Practice and Spiritual Well Being

The benefits of daily devotional practice are many and significant. In her doctoral dissertation titled *Lectio Divina: A Contemplative Approach to Intimacy with God*, Dr. Gloria Jean Westerfield discusses a six-week study she conducted to learn whether there exists a positive correlation between daily devotional reading (i.e., *lectio divina*) and spiritual well being. She explains: "The practice of regular [devotional] reading and prayer is as old as Scripture itself. Joshua is enjoined to meditate on the Book of the Law day *and night*, an example followed [also] by the Psalmists" (Westerfield 2014, 27).

Dr. Westerfield ultimately suggests that daily devotional practice does, in fact, positively affect one's spiritual well being. Dr. Westerfield is not alone in reporting the health benefits of religious belief and practice. In a systematic review of the published research literature that covers more than 100 years, soon to be three editions of the *Handbook of Religion and Health* (Koenig et al., 2001; 2012; 2022) document the effects on mental, social, behavioral, and physical health.

Seven Elements of Spiritual Well Being

As one leg of the three-legged stool that supports our existence, our spirits benefit from tending and nurturing—just as our bodies and minds do. To help "tend" your spirit and ease you into a deep, revitalizing sleep, this book identifies and categorizes entries into seven elements that are integral to spiritual well being: Connection, Gratitude, Forgiveness, Positivity, Purpose, Rest, and Values.

Connection: Connection is a vital element of our spiritual well being. Created by God to be social, relational beings, we flourish when we feel connected with God (first), with other people, and with our inner selves.

Gratitude: Practicing gratitude has profound effects on both our mental and spiritual health. Being thankful and showing appreciation for the gifts that God has blessed us with are nourishment for our minds, bodies, and spirits. As Paul the Apostle writes, "Give thanks in all circumstances; for this is God's will for you in Christ Jesus" (1 Thessalonians 5:18).

Rest: Throughout the Bible, God promises to provide His children with rest. "Come to me, all you who are weary and burdened," says Jesus, "and I will give you rest" (Matthew 11:28). Rest allows us to wake up each morning feeling refreshed, renewed, and ready for the new day.

Values: Jesus spent a great deal of His ministry encouraging His followers to do what is good, to love without condition, and to stand up for what is right. Similarly, we are called to adhere to the biblical principles of goodness, love, and integrity. Showing love and kindness toward others pretty much covers all three, and if done consistently throughout the day, can help make sleep deep and restful.

Positivity: Maintaining a joyful, positive attitude is key to fostering a joyous spirit. When you "take delight in the Lord," the Psalmist declares, "He will give you the desires of your heart" (Psalm 37:4). Being positive does not come naturally. It is a decision of the will, and must be made each morning.

Purpose: Having a purpose is what gives our lives meaning and value. As the Bible tells us, we were made by the Creator Himself *with* a purpose and *for* a purpose: "For we are God's handiwork," writes Paul, "created in Christ Jesus to do good works, which God prepared in advance for us to do" (Ephesians 2:10). No matter what happens during the day, that purpose will carry us through and can lead to a peaceful night's sleep. "All things work together for good to them that love God, to them who are the called according to his purpose" (Romans 8:28).

Forgiveness: During His ministry, Jesus preaches and practices radical forgiveness, even going as far as begging God to forgive those who took part in His execution. Following Jesus's lead, we strive to let go of the grudges we might have against the people who have hurt us. Doing so, as the Gospels tell us, will draw us closer to Him and give us peace, joy, and rest. Holding onto grudges will do the exact opposite, driving the mind late into the night, keeping us awake and restless.

In Step with Jesus

After spending the day walking in step with Jesus, we can benefit from putting aside time in the evening to entrust our spirit to Him. After all, there is no one more trustworthy than the One to whom the Psalmist sings: "The day is Yours, and Yours also the night; You established the sun and moon" (Psalm 74:16).

Our hope for you is that the devotions, prayers, and other entries in this book will relax your body, ease your mind, and help you to align your spirit with Jesus's.

Now, we invite you to spend an evening with Jesus.

Harold G. Koenig, M.D.
Professor of Psychiatry & Behavioral Sciences
Associate Professor of Medicine
Director, Center for Spirituality, Theology and Health
Duke University Medical Center, Durham, North Carolina

References

Koenig, H.G., Larson, D.B., & McCullough, M. (2001). *Handbook of Religion and Health*, 1st edition. New York, NY: Oxford University Press.

Koenig, H. G., King, D. E., & Carson, V. B. (2012). *Handbook of Religion and Health*, 2nd edition. New York, NY: Oxford University Press.

Koenig, H. G., VanderWeele, T., & Peteet, J. R. (2022). *Handbook of Religion and Health*, 3rd edition. New York, NY: Oxford University Press, forthcoming.

Westerfield, G. J. (2014). *Lectio Divina: A Contemplative Approach to Intimacy with God*. Wilmore, KY: Asbury Theological Seminary.

HOW TO USE THIS BOOK

There are many ways of approaching the nighttime experiences in *Evenings with Jesus*, and no one way is better than another.

Certainly, you could start with Evening 1 and continue reading each night's entry in consecutive order.

You may wish to read several entries at a time, and we know some of you will read *Evenings with Jesus* in a single sitting or over the course of a short time. Does it need to be read at night? Not at all.

For some people, a particular devotion writer's words will resonate. If so, look up that author in the index and read one writer's work before proceeding on to another.

Alternatively, you may decide to approach this book by considering the spiritual well-being elements one at a time. If you like this approach, on consecutive nights, read entries centered around a particular element, easily identified on the placard at the beginning of each entry. For this approach, you might want to ask yourself a central question concerning the element.

- Connection: How often do you feel a sense of connection with Jesus and the people around you?
- Gratitude: How often do you express gratitude in your words and actions?
- Forgiveness: How easy is it for you to forgive yourself and others?
- Positivity: When you are faced with challenges, how likely are you to think positively?
- Purpose: How often do you feel a sense of purpose in your life?
- Rest: How satisfied are you with the quantity and quality of your rest time?
- Values: How much are your decisions and choices guided by your values?

Lastly, many of our devotional readers like to approach their devotionals in a more random way—maybe even just opening the book at a point and reading that entry. *Evenings with Jesus* can be enjoyed in any order you choose.

However you read *Evenings with Jesus*, may it be an end-of-day journey that brings you comfort and peace and draws you closer to Jesus.

A Peaceful Night

BOB HOSTETLER

Return to your rest, my soul, for the
LORD has been good to you.

PSALM 116:7 (NIV)

I checked into the monastery guest house following a long, taxing season of ministry. I knew I would be entering into a world that was very different from the trappings and rhythms of my usual life. I found my simple room sparely furnished with just a bed, chair, desk, and lamp. I immediately felt the calm of the place, its peaceful quiet. The monks observed the Rule of Saint Benedict and valued contemplative silence, a new experience for me. I knew that the self-guided prayer retreat would last five days and four nights, and I hoped and expected that it might be a restorative time for me. But what I didn't know is that this visit would truly change my life.

I worshiped and ministered in a non-liturgical faith community, but I had also nurtured an appreciation for liturgy. So, on this first visit to a monastery, I decided that I would go to prayer in the sanctuary every time the monks did. They observe the *Opus Dei* (or "work of God") that constitutes the rhythm of their lives. Their day begins with Vigils at 3 a.m. and ends with Compline at 8:45 p.m. They gather for prayer, too, at 5 a.m., 9 a.m., 11:30 a.m., 2:45 p.m., and 6:45 p.m.

Seven times a day.

Every day.

Most of those prayer times lasted no more than fifteen minutes, but I still wasn't sure if I could do it—or if it would do anything for me.

I did. And it did.

During the first couple of days, I discovered how exhausted I was. I'd always worked hard and had taken some healthy *and* unhealthy pride in that fact. But my hard work filled not only my waking hours but also my nights. I would lay my head on my pillow each evening only to toss and turn, my mind racing, my muscles tense. I would eventually fall asleep but would never wake refreshed. Even my "day off" was a whirlwind of activity.

At the monastery, however, I felt my mind and body slowing down, changing tempo. My usual frenzy of activity had ceased. I had no appointments, no meetings, no responsibilities. I didn't even need a watch or clock; I would simply know by the ringing of the tower bell when it was time to eat or go to prayer. Between those times, I took walks, read, or napped. At home I never napped, but at the monastery I found it possible to nap twice a day without these breaks affecting my ability to fall asleep at night. At first it all felt strange, but I began to realize that I was experiencing something new or at least long forgotten: I was experiencing *rest*.

I quickly discovered the differences in the various types of prayer times. For example, the early morning Vigils interrupted the night and Lauds at 5 a.m. greeted the morning. I wouldn't continue these practices once I returned home, but the one "divine office" I learned I couldn't do without was Compline. Compline, from the Latin *completorium*, is the prayer time that "completes" the day. It's a set of prayers that purposefully and effectively prepares the heart, soul, and mind for restful sleep. And in the years since that first visit to the monastery, observing Compline has become an indispensable habit that has repeatedly ushered me into restful, recuperative sleep.

The opening words of Compline—"May the Lord Almighty grant me and those I love a peaceful night and a perfect end"— became precious to me. It cues my spirit that rest is coming soon and that I can confidently "lie down and sleep, for you alone, LORD, make me dwell in safety" (Psalm 4:8, NIV). The confession and plea for forgiveness that soon follows affords the blessing of falling asleep with a clear conscience.

> *In peace I will lie down and sleep, for you alone, LORD, make me dwell in safety.*
>
> PSALM 4:8 (NIV)

The evening psalm (which I sometimes chant in the Gregorian fashion that I learned at the monastery) slows my racing mind and helps me to welcome the Word of God into my head and heart in the last moments of the day.

Other prayers, such as, "Into your hands do I commend my spirit . . . keep me as the apple of your eye and hide me under the shadow of your wings" and the *Nunc Dimittis* ("Lord, you now have set your servant free to go in peace"), fill my mind with better images and ideas than anxiously going over the previous day's unfinished tasks or the coming day's to-do list. And the wonderful words of Augustine's prayer enable me to commit my loved ones and others—and the world, in fact—to God's care before I close my eyes in sleep: "Watch, dear Lord, with those who wake, or watch, or weep tonight, and give your angels charge over those who sleep. Tend to your sick ones, Lord Christ. Rest your weary ones, bless your dying ones, soothe your suffering ones, shield your joyous ones, and all for your love's sake." It's a critical and complete exercise in intercession and trust before I go to bed.

Praying the Compline prayers soothes my mind and spirit, like a loving parent tucking me under the covers and planting a gentle kiss on my forehead. These prayers draw the curtains and turn out the lights on all the activity of the day and hold at bay any concerns for tomorrow. Most of all, they draw me into the arms of God each night.

Jesus, I give thanks this night that You are with me, wrapping Your loving arms around me. Set me free tonight to go peacefully to sleep. I thank You for the comfort and calm You bring.

Friendship Restores My Soul

SUSANNA FOTH AUGHTMON

Though one may be overpowered,
two can defend themselves.
A cord of three strands is not quickly broken.

ECCLESIASTES 4:12 (NIV)

Some of my most solid friendships were born during my college years. I went to a small Christian liberal arts college in the heart of the redwood forest, ten minutes from the ocean. Each school year felt like nine months of summer camp. My friends and I had a lot in common: We loved Jesus, we liked cute boys, and we loved to laugh. We somehow managed to achieve a good education, and our friendships wove us together for a lifetime.

I have three college friends who I still connect with almost daily. We all lived on the same hall during our senior year. Marie France has boundless energy, is passionate about Jesus, and loves to laugh. We became prayer partners during my senior year. She is always up for an adventure. Jane was my go-to in discussing guys and navigating work life. We both worked at the same after-school children's program. I love her no-nonsense take on life and her grounded love of Jesus. She is smart and funny and calls it like it is. Tina and I grew close after we graduated from college.

Both of our husbands were youth pastors. We bonded over the trials and joys of being in ministry. Tina has the best laugh in the world, hands down. Her honesty and her love of nurturing others in their relationship with Jesus shape everything she does. These three make me laugh hard, challenge me, and inspire me in my walk with Jesus.

Following graduation, we attended each other's weddings. We celebrated the arrival of each other's babies—nine boys and three girls in all. Life was busy, but the love stayed strong. We spent the decades after college slipping in and out of each other's lives, connecting when we could.

Five years ago, Jane invited us all to her house for a Christmas party. It was the first time all four of our families had been together in years. It felt like a mini–college reunion. We couldn't stop laughing and reliving memories of dorm life. We could have stayed up all night talking about the good times, life's struggles, and our hopes for the future. There is nothing quite like being in the presence of friends. Sharing laughter, the love of Jesus, and the knowledge that you are deeply and absolutely loved is a beautiful thing.

Over the last few years, our friendship has been galvanized in a new way. With our kids moving into adulthood, we have realized how much we need each other. We went from connecting every few years to texting every few days. Our text thread has been ongoing for six years. It's truly a lifeline. We need each other's wisdom and the connection of deep friendship when life's struggles take us out at the knees. We also like to make each other laugh. We share bits of parenting wisdom and encourage each other over our parenting fails. We cheer on our kids' wins and losses in sports. We rejoice over their college acceptance letters. We empathize with each other over their struggles as they learn and grow. We text each other pictures of home renovation projects. We send each other funny memes and GIFs. We share sermons and song links. Mostly, we pray for each other. Our prayers for each other and our families have solidified our friendship.

Two years ago, before my family moved to Idaho, Jane hosted a going-away party for all of us to get together. It was bittersweet. I was excited for our move but felt the loss of moving far away from my friends. We laughed a lot that night, and I cried a little. In spite

> *Oil and perfume make the heart glad, and A person's advice is sweet to his friend.*
>
> PROVERBS 27:9 (NASB)

of the distance between us, the text thread is still running strong. Their friendship is life-giving.

The most life-giving friendship of all is my friendship with Jesus. His love for me is solid and deep. He reveals the beauty of true friendship on a whole other level. The power of His forgiveness saved me. His Holy Spirit encourages me. His Word offers guidance and wisdom on a daily basis—words of love and truth reaching across the ages. He nurtures me on a daily basis. I don't want to slip in and out of His presence, I want to weave my life into His. In the midst of life's struggles, He is faithful. In my most difficult hours, Jesus offers me light and hope. In my moments of weakness, He shores me up with His mighty strength. Jesus has promised me that I will never be alone. My past is anchored in His grace. He holds my future in His hands. In Him, I am becoming the person I am created to be.

Connection to Her Past

Angela Erdmann never met her grandfather. He'd died in 1946, six years before she was born. She rarely thought of him, until the International Maritime Museum in Hamburg, Germany came calling. "It was very surprising," Angela told *The Guardian*. "A man stood at my door and told me he had post from my grandfather."

Apparently, Angela's grandfather, Richard Platz, had thrown a bottle in the sea in 1913. He was twenty years old at the time. Although much of the postcard in the bottle is indecipherable, Richard's address in Berlin was legible. The bottle, which had been at sea for 101 years, was found by a fisherman in the Baltic and taken to the International Maritime Museum.

"I knew very little about my grandfather, but I found out that he was a writer who was openminded, believed in freedom, and had respect for others," she said. "It was wonderful because I could see where my roots came from."

Jesus, thank You for Your friendship.
As I close my eyes tonight, I know that You will
never leave me or forsake me. I am grateful for
Your faithfulness and love.

A Grateful Heart

JEANETTE LEVELLIE

*Rejoice always, pray continually, give thanks
in all circumstances; for this is God's will
for you in Christ Jesus.*

1 THESSALONIANS 5:16–18 (NIV)

It was a frosty evening here in southern Illinois, the roads icy and the air bitingly cold. It was the kind of night that compels you to drive very carefully and slowly so that you won't lose control of the car. As I turned the heater up and crept along, I spied an elderly man walking in the frozen grass by the side of the highway. Hunched shoulders and gray head bent, his slight frame struggled against the wind.

"I've seen him walking here before, Jesus," I said aloud. "Should I offer him a ride?"

It wasn't a habit of mine to pick up strangers, especially at night. But I had peace in my heart about this guy. And I knew that wind must be knifing right through his thin jacket.

I pulled up beside him and rolled down my window.

"Do you need a ride?" I asked.

He hesitated, then said, "I live two miles that way." He pointed up the road. His beard was unkempt. Most of his teeth were missing. But his eyes were clear and unclouded.

"That's the direction I'm headed," I said. "Come on in!"

The old man moved slowly, finally climbing into the passenger seat, setting his grocery bag on the floor, and arranging his skinny legs in front of him.

"My name is Jeanette," I told him as he buckled his seatbelt.

"I'm Helmut," he said. On the short drive, he explained how he'd lost his job as a pizza deliveryman a few months earlier when the local Italian restaurant closed. He'd used their truck, but now had no form of transportation—except walking.

> *He is a wise man who does not grieve for the things which he has not, but rejoices for those which he has.*
>
> EPICTETUS

When I asked about his European accent, Helmut said he'd emigrated here from Austria as a young man. After saving every spare schilling for years, he'd traveled to the U.S., intent on personally thanking the UCLA professor who'd sponsored him as a young student in Salzburg. Once he arrived in Los Angeles, he discovered the professor had moved to New York. Helmut worked for six months at minimum wage to earn enough money for a bus ticket across the country. As he told me the story, there wasn't a hint of struggle or resentment. He sounded happy to share this history with me.

I looked into those blue eyes, my own moist with wonder.

"Wait! So you came all the way to the U.S.," I asked, my voice trembling, "and then traveled from L.A. to New York City just to say 'Thank you'?"

"Yes, of course!" Helmut said, smiling. His voice was warm with gratitude, and he continued, "He had sent my family money for years so I could attend school and have clothes and food. If it were not for him, I'd be a poor man."

We approached a shambles of a house I'd often noticed many times as I passed it. I'd often wondered who lived there and noticed that it needed paint, a new roof, and a very energetic gardener.

"Right here, this is where I live," Helmut said, pointing at that dilapidated house.

"Do you own this home?" I asked.

"*Ja.* Believe it or not, the previous owner gave it to me when he couldn't keep up with the repairs," Helmut said, shrugging. "That was ten years ago."

I looked at the sagging roof, the dead trees, and the boarded-up windows, and I wondered how Helmut viewed his home. He'd just said in so many words that he was grateful for his life and regarded himself as a wealthy man.

As Helmut thanked me for the ride, stepped out into the bitter cold night, and waved goodbye, I thought about my full closet, my lovely home, and all the material things I enjoyed. I knew all of these good things were blessings from Jesus, and I knew I

About Gratitude

Gratitude is social. It is about, says Pastor Jason Micheli, "presence, participation, and partnership." It is about being *with* one another, *in* life together. It is the thread of nature and neighbor, the seemingly fragile strands of gifts and goodness that weave our lives together.

often took them for granted. Helmut's gratitude convicted me of doing so.

"Lord, forgive me," I whispered. "Thank you for teaching me tonight about true gratitude."

I saw that although I have more possessions than Helmut has, my new friend had just shown me the true riches of a grateful heart.

Jesus, thank You for all the good things you have given me. And thank You for bringing people into my life who remind me to see the world with fresh, grateful eyes and help me to grow in wisdom.

Keep the Music Flowing

NORM STOLPE

*Whoever believes in me, as Scripture has said,
rivers of living water will flow from within them.*

JOHN 7:38 (NIV)

E xcept for me, everyone in my family is musical. My wife,
Candy, spontaneously injects songs into conversations.
Whether chatting with people in the checkout line at the grocery
store or gathering with a small group Bible study, she doesn't
just quote the song, she sings it! Even since her diagnosis with
Alzheimer's about five years ago, she readily recalls songs of
both recent and distant vintage. When we moved from Texas to
Wisconsin to share a duplex with our son David and his family a
year after her diagnosis, we bought a smart TV that connects to
the internet. Candy's gifts and love of music have been transmit-
ted to the next generation in beautiful ways.

Our youngest son, Erik, is also a musician, specializing in
keyboards and bass. He has been active in the music ministry of
his church in Dallas, and he's the Director of Music at Dallas's
"School of Rock." Erik teaches music classes for students from six
years old into their sixties.

David, our middle son, is a schoolteacher and has formed "garage band" clubs that meet after school. These have been especially helpful for students who struggle to fit into their school's social life. David is a self-taught guitarist and song-writer while his son, our grandson Sam, plays cello and mandolin and is a music major in college.

Our oldest, Jon, plays sax and guitar for fun. He loves swapping ideas with his brothers. His son Isaac is a music education major at school, specializing in trumpet and piano.

All three of my sons report that they cannot sit next to me when singing hymns in church because I switch keys unpredictably mid-line, not just mid-song. Nevertheless, I not only love music but draw on it as spiritual fuel. Almost every morning, I sing a praise hymn before I shower and eat breakfast. I am careful to sing only loud enough for God and me to hear. I joke that I make sure Candy is still sleeping, so no human ears are harmed by my singing. For me, giving voice to praise for God to hear is the best way to get the day off to a good start. Often monks and other men and women in religious life spend an hour singing "lauds," or praises, early in the day. When I begin the day in song, the flow of the rest of the day heads in a positive direction, regardless of what challenges may come.

> *The peace of Christ makes fresh my heart, a fountain ever springing!*
>
> ROBERT LOWRY

Yes, the flow of every day will have many turns and eddies, rapids and smooth stretches. Certain songs echo in those rhythms, guiding my maneuvers through what may be unfamiliar to me. I can follow the tune from others who have gone ahead of me, weaving it into my own song. Jesus sings with joy and hope in these melodies.

Whatever may have filled our days, every evening Candy and I wrap up with time focused on each other and Jesus. Our evenings intentionally engage with Jesus before we head to bed for a good night's sleep. We recall how He has been with us through the flow of the day. Most evenings we read from a devotional book, and often these readings will prompt us to go to a hymnal to find a related hymn. If it's familiar to Candy, she will sing the hymn. Though I keep my drone well below her lovely melody, I do enter in. Often the hymn conveys Jesus's presence with more vibrancy than the prose we read. The melody flows into our evening prayers and drifts into our sleep.

Dear Jesus, thank You for being the Rock I cling to, my Living Water, the One who keeps me safe and calm. Thank You for the gift of song and for hearing my songs of praise. Tonight, I thank You for Your presence.

Decisions, Decisions

RANDY PETERSEN

What good is it for someone to gain the whole world, yet forfeit their soul?

MARK 8:36 (NIV)

I thought it was going to be my dream job, but I was wrong. For about a decade, I'd been working as a freelance writer, just eking out a living. Work was steady, but the pay was meager. I managed to pay my bills, but I had a cheap apartment, drove an old car, and couldn't afford to take much of a vacation.

Then I got a call that *seemed* to change everything.

A Christian publisher asked me to create lessons written for Bible study groups. They had created a video series featuring a talented teacher, and I would create printed resource materials to go along with the videos. This was the sort of work I had done often, so I felt confident that I could do it well. They were offering to pay me at least three times what I usually got for jobs like this. We're talking thousands rather than hundreds of dollars!

Immediately I began compiling a mental wish list. Maybe I could make a down payment on a new car. Or could I take a trip to see some old friends? Perhaps I could move to a nicer place.

I told the editor I was interested. He promised to send me a contract, along with transcripts of the videos. My prospects were looking very bright—until I actually read what this person was teaching. My heart fell when I saw his approach to Scripture. I realized that his teaching went against my values. I wrestled with the idea of working on the project. I read through the material several times, and each time I felt Jesus telling me, more and more insistently, "You can't do this."

Visions of my new car and vacation and better apartment began to vanish before my eyes. I didn't give up these visions without a struggle, and I cannot say I've always made the best decisions in these matters. I reasoned with myself: What kind of life would I have if I ditched my soul-level values in exchange for these things? I turned down the job.

> *You make known to me the path of life; you will fill me with joy in your presence.*
>
> PSALM 16:11 (NIV)

Fast-forward about two decades. A friend invited me to stop freelancing and take a full-time job with his company, a Christian nonprofit. He was assembling a team of writers and wanted me to lead it. I knew it would be an adjustment, but the opportunity offered chances to work creatively, hone my leadership skills, and explore the Bible more deeply. And the pay was good. I said yes.

Our offices were in a big city, and I often went out to lunch. Not long after I took the job, I met a man named David who played the saxophone on the corner across the street from our building for much of the day. At first, I would just drop a few bucks in his sax case as I passed by. But after a while, I started talking with him, and soon we became friends.

At some point in our friendship, we figured out that we were both followers of Jesus, and that opened us up to some deep conversations. I learned that this modern-day David was playing psalms of love and praise to the Jesus I loved too.

"It's all about the love, man," he often said. "I'm just out here sharing the love." His music was a gift of love to the city, and all day long he greeted passersby with a nod, a melody, and maybe a kind word. Hot days, cold days, David was on the street corner, sharing Jesus's love with his music.

Unfortunately, after some time, a values conflict began to take hold of me at work, I began to feel that I wasn't growing or best able to use my gifts there. I was stagnating, and worse, my company's view of Scripture interpretation and mine were at odds.

Should I resign? I struggled with making a decision. I had a week of vacation coming, so I used it to drive around New England asking Jesus what I should do. I kept waiting for an answer. Finally, the night before I was due to return to work, I heard a small voice saying, "You should make your decision

The Power of Humility

Humility, the quality or state of being humble, is a lifelong spiritual quest. It is the surrender of our will to God's will. As the Lord's Prayer states, "Thy kingdom come, Thy will be done on earth as it is in heaven." This prayer teaches us to align our will with heaven's will and our heart with the ways of God. Humility is not a sign of weakness. On the contrary, it shows that our strength comes from the Lord and reflects the ways of Jesus.

about work when you're at work. Go back for now, and by the end of the week, I'll tell you what to do."

Monday, I was in meetings all day, discussing strategies and technology—important stuff, but not exactly how I thought I should be spending my time. In my mind, I took one step toward leaving.

Tuesday, I stopped on the corner to talk with my friend David, asking him to pray for me about the decision. "Whatever the Lord tells you to do," he said, "you gotta do." Simple, but profound.

Wednesday, I had lunch with my team to let them know about my dilemma. As I looked around the table, a vision of the possibilities for each of them formed. This one would step into my leadership position. This one would get more writing opportunities. This one would emerge as the spiritual leader of the group. Jesus had just given me a vision of the future! He had a loving vision for each of these individuals, and my leaving would allow them to grow.

By Friday, there was no doubt. I had my answer. I resigned, said a warm goodbye to David, and was able to trust that Jesus had something else for me to do.

Dear Jesus, please continue to help me discern what are your values as I face decisions and transitions in my life. Thank you for the way you've led me and protected me in the past. Thank you for the gifts you've given me that bring true joy and true life!

He Transforms My Small Offerings

ERYN LYNUM

And we know that in all things God works
for the good of those who love him, who
have been called according to his purpose.

ROMANS 8:28 (NIV)

"The lifeblood of the southwest," this creek has been called. Watching my eight-year-old son stand with one foot on each side, it's difficult to believe this trickle carves out the Grand Canyon. We stand at the headwaters of the Colorado River. Not another soul is to be seen. I wonder, hundreds of miles downstream, how many stand at the edge of the Grand Canyon.

At the deepest point in the canyon, the wall stands over 6,000 feet high. Its broadest section stretches an astonishing 18 miles wide. Here, at 10,174 feet of elevation in the Rocky Mountains, is where it all begins—with this meek stream of water my children splash their feet in. The earth here is wet. We cannot know it today, but this whole area will be claimed by a wildfire a year from now. The trees won't last the flames, but the water will. Today we are greeted by vivid colors. Delicate, bright orange petals of wild groundcover flowers blanket the meadow. The soil squishes beneath our sandals, fragrant with wild flora.

Watching my four children skip from one side to the other, I can't fathom the 1,400-mile journey this water will take to the Gulf of California. Great things often begin by humble means—this water does not boast. It only carries out its course.

I think of baby Jesus in this same way. A child humbly arriving in this world, an incredible journey set before Him. With great humility, Christ faithfully carried His Father God's purpose for His life. We read of His unfaltering obedience in Philippians 2:5–8 (NASB), speaking of Jesus "who, although He existed in the form of God, did not regard equality with God a thing to be grasped, but emptied Himself, taking the form of a bond-servant, and being made in the likeness of men . . . He humbled Himself by becoming obedient to the point of death, even death on a cross."

The only One ever to carry out God's plan perfectly is the same One faithfully working within me. I look at my life, and it's easy to feel like that trickle of water—not much to speak of and exhibiting little power or impact. Yet this stream reminds me that Jesus makes much of little. Standing with His Father at creation, Christ took part in the carving of these waterways.

Jesus knows well the potential of these headwaters in etching out the Grand Canyon. He is in the business of transforming small beginnings into glorious testimonies of His power. I can trust the One who perfectly executed God's plans for His life with what feels insignificant in my own. He will take my small offerings, infuse them with His power, and make a powerful impact for His kingdom.

A Vision Board Can Help
You Find Your Purpose

When you are seeking God's purpose for your life, a vision board may help you on your journey.

To make one, cut out images and words from magazines and tack them onto a corkboard or paste them onto posterboard. To decide which words, phrases, and images to choose, think about how you want to feel, who you want to be, and how those things align with who you know God wants you to be.

The vision-boarding process doesn't end once you've attached your cutouts. Hang the board someplace where you will see it frequently. This reminder can help direct your prayers as you ask God to help you to achieve your vision.

When you work on goals that move you toward your life's purpose, the process will renew, enrich, and energize you. When you connect those goals to whom God is calling you to be, you will be more able to tap into the abundant life that He promises.

Dear Jesus, I find in You the perfect example of a purposeful life. You faithfully carried out God's plan in Your birth, life, death, and resurrection. I welcome and trust the work You are doing in my life, and I wait expectantly to watch what wonders You are bringing forth!

Be There for Others

CRYSTAL STORMS

We love because he first loved us.

1 JOHN 4:19 (NIV)

I had the day carefully planned. Because I was leaving for a getaway the following morning, I decided to dedicate the day to clearing out my inbox. The goal was that there would be nothing—*zero* emails!—in my inbox when I departed. I imagined the peace of mind I'd experience on my trip, knowing I hadn't left any loose ends behind.

But the day before I traveled, a thought kept popping into my mind. Just a few simple words, but over and over, I felt a prompt, a reminder in my heart. "Be there for others," it told me. I wasn't sure how it would play out, but I felt an opportunity would present itself to do just that.

I had borrowed my mom's car that week and would return it before reading and deleting emails. I told her I'd pop in quickly to give her the keys. But the more I heard those words, "Be there for others," the less I felt that the day would be my own. I drove to Mom's condo after lunch. My husband, Tim, followed in our car. When we walked into her home, we could see that she needed our help. She was moving at the end of the month, but she had Christmas decorations scattered around the living room that needed to be packed up. I knew this was my chance to be there for *her*, to step in and help her as she has for me so many times over the course of my life.

Instead of resisting the change of plans, I embraced it. I knew I was doing exactly what I was supposed to be doing, and I felt grateful that Jesus had prepared me by whispering those words into my heart that morning. *Be there for others.*

> *When we seek for connection, we restore the world to wholeness. Our seemingly separate lives become meaningful as we discover how truly necessary we are to each other.*
>
> MARGARET WHEATLEY

I brought all the Christmas trimmings to the dining room table, and Mom placed each treasured ornament into its compartment and positioned the nativity scene and wreath in their bins. Then I assembled the remaining stack of cardboard boxes and taped up the bottoms to make them secure. Meanwhile, Tim gathered packed boxes and stacked them neatly against the living room wall.

When we were finished, a few hours later, Mom was encouraged by our progress and very grateful. I reminded her of the many times she had "been there" for me.

Being there for others that day meant letting go of my agenda. Not my plan but His. So, although "inbox zero" wasn't a bad plan, it wasn't what Jesus had planned for me that day.

I thanked Jesus for the prompt to be there for others as Tim drove us home. When we arrived, it would be time to make dinner, and my inbox would not even have one fewer email waiting there than when I woke up that day. But that was OK! We had a quick dinner, snuggled on the couch, and watched a movie together. That night, I drifted off to sleep with a grateful heart, reflecting on all the times others, including my mom, have been there for me.

Jesus, thank You for using me to love others, and thank You for the countless times others have helped, encouraged, and supported me. I am grateful.

Apology Accepted

LOGAN ELIASEN

Then Peter came to Jesus and asked, "Lord, how many times shall I forgive my brother or sister who sins against me? Up to seven times?" Jesus answered, "I tell you, not seven times, but seventy-seven times.

MATTHEW 18:21–22 (NIV)

"Finally, I get to see your bike," Zach said.

I wheeled my bicycle down my driveway where my friends Zach and John stood. I was proud of my bike. I had saved for months during law school, then finally purchased it after I graduated. I had special-ordered the model in matte black and blue. I babied this bike. I kept it clean and maintained, and I hadn't put a single scratch on it. I even stored it in my bedroom for safekeeping.

Zach whistled. "It's beautiful," he said. "Can I try it out?"

I hesitated. I had never let anyone else ride my bike. But Zach was a cyclist, and he knew how to treat a bicycle. I reluctantly surrendered the handlebars to my friend.

Zach eased himself onto the bike, then took off. My heart tightened as he rounded the corner, leaving my sight.

"I'm surprised you let him ride it," John said.

"Well, I'm going to let him drive it to the state park," I said. "I had to start somewhere."

Zach rode back into view. My chest relaxed as he parked the bike.

"It rides so smoothly," he said. "Let's load her up."

Zach and I carefully hefted my bike onto the top of his car. I strapped it into place and double-checked the straps. Zach's own bike was already strapped to the rear of his vehicle.

I grabbed my helmet from my house and met Zach back at the Subaru.

Zach looked at the helmet. "Shoot. I forgot my helmet," he said. "I need to stop back at my house."

"That's OK," I said. "I'll ride with John, and we will meet you at the park."

> *When you forgive, you love. And when you love, God's light shines upon you.*
>
> JON KRAKAUER

A few minutes later, my phone began to ring. It was Zach.

"Logan," Zach said, his voice serious. "I don't know how to say this—I wrecked your bike. I forgot it was on top of my car and when I went home to get my helmet, I attempted to drive into the garage, and, well—"

Ten minutes later, Zach, John, and I stood in front of a crumpled mess of matte black and blue. I thought of the all the effort I had put into saving for and protecting my bike.

"I have insurance," Zach said reassuringly. "I'll file a claim so you can get a brand new one."

My temple pulsed and my mind raced in dismay. Even if I eventually got a check, the claim would likely take weeks to process. Then I would have to special-order a bike again. I didn't even know if the manufacturer still produced the same model. My cycling season was over.

Zach went into the house for a minute, and I stared at my mangled bike, trying to control my emotions.

"Are you OK?" John asked.

"That bike was a big deal to me," I said. "I wish Zach would acknowledge that and give me a full-fledged apology."

"I know," John said. "But did you see Zach's hands when he talked to you?"

"No," I said. I hadn't been looking at Zach. I had been fixated on the ruined bike.

"His hands were shaking," John said. "He was scared. Zach might not be the best at verbalizing his emotions, but he is genuinely sorry."

I thought of Jesus and how He had forgiven Peter. The disciple, His dear friend, had fallen asleep in the Garden of Gethsemane, fled the scene of Christ's arrest, and denied knowing Him three times. Yet the risen Christ had forgiven and restored his friend and follower Peter—no apology necessary.

I knew I had to let it go and forgive Zach. I knew that his friendship was much more valuable than my bike. It became easier when I reflected on all the times Jesus has forgiven me, even when my confessions have been slow to materialize or poorly articulated!

Jesus, You forgave those who were undeserving, just because of who You are. Change my heart to reflect Yours. Help me to forgive others generously as You do.

The Setting of the Sun

RICK HAMLIN

From the rising of the sun to its setting
the name of the LORD is to be praised.

PSALM 113:3 (NRSV)

When night's darkness can be erased with the flip of an electric switch, it's easy to overlook the wonder of the sun, how the Creator illumines our world from dawn to dusk. We also sometimes lose our sense of awe about how the moon, reflecting the sun's light, casts its glow on a clear night so brightly that you can see your own shadow.

I marvel, too, at how the sun marks the seasons, the days getting longer or shorter as the pages of the calendar turn. Starting in November, the sun doesn't reach our breakfast table in the mornings, shielded by trees and buildings as it slides down the horizon, but on the February day when it returns, I want to start celebrating. A beam of light hits the pages of my Bible as I read a psalm or two.

What I've found even more important is marking the end of the day, when the sun sets. Sometimes I can see it from my window, but I like taking a short stroll to a promontory above the

Hudson River that faces west. There I can see the sinking sun's progress along the horizon, moving far to the south at the end of fall and early winter, then moving north as summer approaches.

I cherish watching the colors the setting sun paints in the sky as it goes down. It is an occasion of prayer, gazing at the heavens, full of wonder and joy. Some days I can't see much of anything—too many clouds. But often enough there will be a pyrotechnic display. There are such vibrant colors, gold-encrusted clouds, red fading into magenta, a lustrous blue turning into purple, all of it reflecting in the mirror of the river.

> *There is a time for many words, and there is also a time for sleep.*
>
> HOMER

I live in a city of eight million people, skyscrapers visible to the south, high-rise apartments across the river, cars and trucks crossing the George Washington Bridge. But all of that shrinks and fades when contrasted with God's painting in the sky. Limitless, vivid, bold.

On days that are marked by disappointment or sadness, I'll look up to the sky and wonder what to think. *Where is Jesus in all of this?* Then I'll see something that no artist could possibly create. The sunset. And beyond the clouds, there is light. The presence of the clouds, mirroring the shadow in my soul, can make it especially beautiful, a reminder of how suffering can be an opportunity to know Jesus better, to feel His healing touch, to be lit up inside.

"Look up!" Jesus says, inviting me. *Look up.*

There's always something to see.

3 Types of Rest that Help Us Stay Positive

SLEEP

The Centers for Disease Control and Prevention recommends at least seven hours of nightly sleep for adults over age eighteen. Practice healthy sleep hygiene habits, including keeping consistent bed and wake times, avoiding heavy meals close to bedtime, removing electronic devices from the bedroom, and sleeping in a cool, dark, quiet space.

ACTIVE REST

"Active rest" means slow, deliberate movements; light exercise, such as gentle walking; and good posture when sitting. In a broader sense, "active rest" also means taking time each day to engage in a fun activity, something that brings you pleasure and a break from the "have-tos."

PASSIVE REST

Passive rest is quietly resting while awake. This could mean stretching out on the couch with your eyes closed, relaxing in front of a favorite movie, or sinking into a bath with a good book.

*Jesus, help me to know the light of
Your countenance. When clouds cast shadows,
let me feel Your glow, from dawn to dusk,
sunrise to sunset. Thank You for giving
Your servant rest.*

Training in Thankfulness

LORI HATCHER

Give thanks in all circumstances; for this is
God's will for you in Christ Jesus.

1 THESSALONIANS 5:18 (NIV)

When my husband and I sent our youngest daughter off to college, we supplied her with everything we thought she might need for her new, independent life. A first-aid kit in case she got hurt. A toolkit if she broke down on the road. Multivitamins, cold medicine, and a thermometer. Coins for the laundromat and enough toiletries to last her until Christmas. You name it, we supplied it.

My heavenly Father has been even more generous to me, supplying what I need before I need it. Before my husband lost his job, Jesus led me to a Bible study that taught me the truths I needed to weather that storm. When we hit a difficult spot in our marriage, He led us to a group of likeminded couples who modeled biblical marriage and parenting. When I needed greater depth in my prayer life, our church offered a Bible study that taught me how to communicate with the Lord in a more personal way.

One year, I recorded my spiritual journey in a thanksgiving journal. I captured thoughts and insights from my Bible reading and wrote down three things I was thankful for each day. By the end of the year, I knew I'd have an impressive list of the blessings God had sent my way.

My gratitude list numbered 369 when I entered a very difficult season. Looking back on those days, I realize that the practice of thanksgiving kept my head above water and saw me through.

My favorite swim coach often said, "When you think you can't go any farther, if you've trained well, muscle memory kicks in and carries you to the finish line." The same is true spiritually. If I train well by developing the disciplines of the Christian life, spiritual muscle memory kicks in when I encounter a trial. It holds my head above water when fierce waves try to drown me and carries me through to the finish line. Giving thanks is one of those spiritual disciplines.

> *Let the message of Christ dwell among you richly as you teach and admonish one another with all wisdom through psalms, hymns, and songs from the Spirit, singing to God with gratitude in your hearts.*
>
> COLOSSIANS 3:16 (NIV)

The morning after I received the bad news that would color the rest of my year, spiritual muscle memory lifted me out of bed and down the hall to my office. As I'd done before, I plopped into the soft recliner and picked up my Bible and journal. I tried to read the Scripture, but tears blurred my vision. I opened my journal instead and poured out my heartbreak in a written prayer to God. Closing the journal, my eyes fell on the verse inscribed on the cover, 1 Thessalonians 5:18 (KJV): "In everything give thanks, for this is the will of God in Christ Jesus concerning you."

In everything give thanks.

I opened my journal again, picked up my pen, and set it down again.

There's nothing to be thankful for, I thought.

"In *everything* give thanks," Jesus whispered.

I thought for a long time, sifting through the emotions that dominated my thoughts. Buried under the debris, a glimmer of truth sparkled.

I lifted my pen and wrote, "#370—I'm thankful that nothing is too hard for God."

The shadow that had threatened to engulf me took a tiny step back.

I then wrote, "#371—I'm thankful for Your promise, Jesus: 'I will never leave you nor forsake you.'"

A slice of light split the murky clouds.

Number 372 came easier. "I'm thankful for Romans 8:28, 'And we know that in all things God works for the good of those who love him, who have been called according to his purpose'" (NIV).

By the time I closed my journal again, my tears had stopped. I read the passage in the Bible where my bookmark rested, "'Refrain

Be Grateful for Hard Times

None of us want adversity. But there are plenty of positive insights to be gained from it.

We discover just how resilient we are when dealing with difficulties. Our faith increases even in the midst of doubt and fear. We find that with Jesus's strength, we also gain strength.

Pause and give thanks for the lessons learned, spiritual growth gained, and the people who stood by you. Tough times don't last, but gratitude does.

your eyes from weeping, and your eyes from tears; for your work shall be rewarded,' says the Lord" (Jeremiah 31:16, NKJV).

Nothing about my circumstances changed that morning. The future still felt uncertain, but I knew, somehow, that everything was going to be all right. The discipline of thanksgiving had carried me when my emotions and circumstances threatened to topple my confidence in Jesus's love and care.

I wish I could say I kept my commitment to thanksgiving that year without a struggle, but I can't. Some months, I experienced more difficult days than hopeful ones. But I'd made the commitment be thankful, and I was determined to see it through.

As time passed, my list served as a clear reminder that Jesus had been with me all along. Every gift I catalogued demonstrated His kind heart, unwavering commitment, and daily involvement in my life. When I felt tempted to despair, the mounting list of blessings brought me hope. Before I needed it, Jesus had trained me in the discipline of gratitude, and that practice would see me through life's storms.

On December 31 of that challenging year, I recorded blessings number 998, 999, and 1,000 in my journal. The next morning, I opened the cover of a new blank book. On the first page, I wrote, "#1—I'm thankful for the command to give thanks in *everything*."

*Jesus, thank You for the ways You prepare
me for the challenges and storms of life. I rest in
the grateful knowledge that You are with me and
that You make all things work together for good.
My heart is full of gratitude as I settle down
for sleep tonight.*

A Greater Story

LORI ROELEVELD

Many are the plans in a person's heart,
but it is the LORD's purpose that prevails.

PROVERBS 19:21 (NIV)

My life was on track. Or so I thought. I'm not a person with only one dream, but many. One—that of raising a family and homeschooling my children—was reaching a transition as my youngest was finishing high school. I was ready to write full-time.

My husband supported my plan. I had prayer partners who believed in my work. I had studied my craft, published articles, and won contests. I'd even been contacted by a literary agent. Jesus was confirming my writing talent and my call. Nothing would stand in my way.

Then, our lives caved in. One month after we purchased our first home, my husband's company eliminated his job. Then, he was diagnosed with a disabling illness. God provided for us, but it was through a job offered to me, not him! It matched my education, experience, and skills, but it's not what I had planned. It wasn't what I wanted. It was nothing I had dreamed.

I'd planned to write full-time. This job would be working with families in crisis. Worthwhile, but not the plan. Not my calling.

Not my purpose. I cried. I prayed. I cried again. Then, I went to the interview. As it became clear that the team felt I was ideal for the job, it also became clear to me that Jesus was altering my plans. I made a final appeal to Him. My plan was to write full-time, and I thought that was His plan too. Did I get it wrong?

Just then, the man who would become my boss spoke up.

"There is one thing that usually stops people from accepting this job," he said.

Here it was. My out.

"What's that?" I asked hopefully.

He cleared his throat, and then said, "There's a lot of writing."

That's when I heard Jesus whisper to me, "My plan is for you to write full-time too. Just different writing than you imagined and more full-time than you ever dreamed."

Living a Bigger Purpose

Your bigger purpose could be right under your nose. Maybe it's to touch the lives of everyone you meet by finding your bigger purpose in the here and now.

You may not build libraries around the world, but you can find the bigger purpose in reading to your children. You may not feed the homeless every day, but you can nourish your coworkers and neighbors with a smile or kind word. And consider beginning a charity initiative at work or church. After all, "charity" means "love in action."

When we find and live this purpose, it will provide the ultimate fuel for a meaningful life. Our purpose waits for us to find it and live it.

For nearly a decade, I have met with families in crisis and used my writing skills to tell their stories. My first task is to learn their values, culture, and strengths so people helping them see them as more than a list of their problems. I set their needs in the context of complex and valuable lives. Originally, I'd hoped to write novels that change lives. Instead, I write short stories that impact one hurting family at a time. I even get to do my own personal writing on the side. I wouldn't change a thing.

> *Get your mind so eager, so zestful, so filled with interests that you just cannot be tired.*
>
> NORMAN VINCENT PEALE

Jesus came to us in a way we'd never imagined and yet, now we see how perfectly His ministry, His death, and His resurrection were planned. I had originally imagined my purpose playing out in what I now recognized was a lesser story than the greater one into which God invited me when He upset my initial plans. I hadn't heard His call incorrectly, just incompletely.

I had dreams of impacting people across the world. He saw a purpose for my talent impacting children and parents across town. I had dreams that involved a measure of personal glory. His purpose for me is less glorious but more satisfying and more glorifying for Him. And that is my ultimate purpose and dream, after all.

Jesus, thank You for dreaming greater dreams for me than I ever have. Thank You for giving me a purpose, even if it wasn't my original plan. I'm grateful.

One of Each, Please

LAWRENCE W. WILSON

Give, and it will be given to you. A good measure,
pressed down, shaken together and running over,
will be poured into your lap. For with the measure
you use, it will be measured to you.

LUKE 6:38 (NIV)

In the past, I am sorry to admit, I've underestimated the importance of generosity. I've been known to grumble when Girl Scouts come to the door during their annual cookie campaign. I've left cheap tips at restaurants, mumbling to my wife about the quality of service we'd had. I've passed by panhandlers on the sidewalk, not meeting their gaze and not putting any cash in their outstretched hands or cup. In short, generosity wasn't one of my values. But, I'm glad to say, Jesus has used the people in my life, including my wife and dear friends, to show me a different way. A better way.

I started to become aware of my stinginess one night when my wife and I were on vacation in Kansas City. On an evening stroll around the city, we stopped at one of the many fountains to look at the water. A person, perhaps homeless, approached us and asked whether we could spare any change for a bus ticket. He started to explain his situation, but I interrupted him.

"No," I said, my voice flat. The man walked away.

My wife, surprised by my rudeness, dug around in her purse and jogged after him, giving him two one-dollar bills.

"He'll probably spend that on booze, you know?" I said.

"That's up to him," she said. "What I do is up to me."

Deep down, I knew she was right and loved the spirit of what she said. It was obviously a more loving response than the one I had. It was more like Jesus. I asked myself why I was so resistant to giving. Sure, money had always been tight, especially when we were raising our kids. But we always had enough. More than enough, actually. What accounted for my hesitancy—no, it was more than that—my *resistance* to sharing? I didn't know. I asked Jesus to show me a better way.

> *Always do what is right. It will gratify half of mankind and astound the other.*
>
> MARK TWAIN

Later that summer, we were invited out to dinner by Ron and Karen, friends from church. Beautifully generous, they'd once loaned us their brand-new minivan so that we could take a family vacation in comfort. They were a bit older than we were and had run a successful business for several years. I suspected they had more than enough means to share with others. I was grateful for their frequent hospitality and was never surprised that, when we ate out with them, they always picked up the check.

As the server left the table that night, Ron reached for his wallet. Karen leaned over and whispered, "Now give her a good tip. It's Labor Day, and she's probably got little kids at home."

"I will," Ron promised. I noted that he'd withdrawn a hundred-dollar bill to cover the tab and noticed that he didn't ask for change. He left this generous tip easily, as though it were second nature for him. I saw that Ron and Karen's giving was driven by compassion. They had not always been financially secure, so they could put themselves into the shoes of others who might be struggling to make ends meet. They understood what it was to work hard but not have enough. They did not feel resentful of any opportunity to give and never second-guessed their choice. They gave as Jesus prompted and enabled them to do, and they were content. My giving, on the other hand, had always been about me. Was it *my* responsibility? Did *I* have the money to spare? No wonder the very thought of giving made me anxious.

From that night on, I began to see giving as an *opportunity* rather than an *obligation*. Generosity has truly become one of my values.

And it has some delicious perks. Now, for instance, when I leave the grocery store on spring afternoons and find a group of Girl Scouts setting up camp on the sidewalk, I stop. I find myself face to face with a hopeful kid who is mustering the courage to speak to an adult, hoping to make a sale.

"Sir, would you like to buy some cookies?" she'll ask.

Now, I look her squarely in the eye, and tell her, "Yes! I'll take one box of everything you've got—and make that two boxes of the Thin Mints."

Generosity is delicious!

Jesus, I know that You come to me in many ways—as a beggar in need of food, a single parent trying to provide for her children, or even as a child. May my heart always be open to You.

A Bruised Reed He Will Not Break

BOB HOSTETLER

A bruised reed he will not break, and a
smoldering wick he will not snuff out.

ISAIAH 42:3 (NIV)

I recently spoke at a conference for Christian writers, presenting a workshop I've given several times. I use slides in this talk that define various kinds of writing, including fiction, devotional, magazine stories, and blog posts. In the past, I would turn to the screen behind me to read an example as I taught about differences, nuances, and best practices related to each type of writing.

This time, however, I was in an auditorium where the screens behind me were small and elevated. The room's larger screens were *in front of* the platform. When it came time to share the first slide, I turned to the screens behind me, but the text was too small at that distance for me to make out the words. I stepped off the stage, turned, and looked above me, but I still had trouble discerning the words I needed to read. I made light of my difficulty, and the audience was gracious and laughed along with me.

This little clown show was repeated a few times, until I realized I'd lost any semblance of formal professionalism in my presentation. I'd noticed that on the floor of the platform beside the podium there was a monitor that displayed each slide. So, for the last slide, I dropped to my hands and knees and read aloud from the image on the monitor. The crowd laughed appreciatively—and, I imagine, sympathetically.

I eventually managed to finish, but I wished I'd done some troubleshooting before I got up to speak to make sure the technology worked for me. I felt I'd let the conferees, the conference directors, and myself down by failing to do so.

As I took off my microphone and returned it to the sound team, one of the workshop attendees approached me with a smile.

"When did you become so comfortable in your own skin?" she asked.

My expression must have shown my confusion because she explained her question, saying something like, "You handled that difficult situation so well and even turned it to your advantage with such self-effacing humor. You just seem comfortable with who you are."

I think I responded, "I do?" and went on to attempt an answer. I was so surprised at her gracious perception when I had seen only my clumsiness and inadequacy. In that moment, I thought I also caught a glimpse of Jesus.

The prophet Isaiah, announcing a coming servant who would bring hope and redemption to the world, said, "A bruised reed he will not break, and a smoldering wick he will not snuff out" (Isaiah 42:3, NIV). The first picture is of a slender reed, like one that might be used to make a writing instrument or a simple flute, growing alongside a river or pond. A person, animal, or maybe even the wind has bent or weakened that reed such that it remains upright and stands only by a thread or two. The second picture Isaiah paints is of a twisted wick in an old-fashioned oil lamp. The wick would burn as long as oil remained, but when the oil ran out and the wick began to dry, the flame would flicker and smoke rather than providing light. In each case, of course, the natural thing to do is to snap and pull out the reed or quench the wick. Each of these things is fit only to be tossed aside. But Jesus doesn't toss aside or dispose of us when we are broken or burned out. As the Gospel writer Matthew, applying Isaiah's prophecy to the ministry of Jesus (Matthew 12:20) points out, this servant heals the sick and delivers the oppressed. No one is discarded.

Whoever serves me must follow me; and where I am, my servant also will be. My Father will honor the one who serves me.

JOHN 12:26 (NIV)

Even Peter, who in Jesus's most desperate hour had denied even knowing Him, experienced the gentleness and grace of the Risen Christ. Devastated by his own show of weakness and how he betrayed his dearest Lord and friend, Peter returned to his fishing boat where Jesus had first sought him out and called him to become one of the Twelve. But Jesus, after rising from the dead, pursued Peter again. He appeared one morning to Peter and several other "former disciples" along the Sea of Galilee.

"Friends!" he called. "Have you caught anything?"

For whatever reason—the mist on the water or perhaps something more mystical—Peter and the others didn't recognize Jesus. They answered his question: "No."

Jesus then suggested that they throw the net on the opposite side of the boat. When they did so, the net filled with fish and strained with the weight of their catch. It was then that one of the others recognized Jesus, and said, "It is the Lord!" Impulsive Peter jumped into the water and swam for shore. When the fishermen managed to drag their catch ashore, they found Jesus already making breakfast. He had fish cooking and bread baking on an open fire. After they ate, Jesus drew Peter out.

"Simon, son of John, do you love me more than these?" He asked.

Peter now spoke with humility, even shame: "Lord, you know that I love you."

Jesus didn't scold Peter. He didn't berate him. He didn't remind him of his betrayal. Instead, He said, simply, "Feed my lambs." Jesus asked the question a second time, then a third, and each time Peter affirmed his love for Jesus. And Jesus reissued His call to Peter; he said, "Follow me."

No matter how bruised or weak I sometimes feel, I can always come to Jesus knowing that He'll receive and restore me. When I've failed, He remains faithful. He never shuts me down, and He never tosses me aside. His tenderness invites my trust, so I can finish each day and rest each night in His loving embrace.

Jesus, You know that I love You.
Thank You for redeeming me and helping
me to follow You day by day. Thank You for so
tenderly receiving and restoring me whenever
I come to You—even when I'm feeling burned
out or weary and weak. Tonight, may I feel
Your tender touch, and please give me energy
tomorrow as I seek to follow You.

Loving Ourselves

JEANETTE LEVELLIE

*But you are God's chosen treasure—priests who are
kings, a spiritual "nation" set apart as God's devoted
ones. He called you out of darkness to experience
his marvelous light, and now he claims you as
his very own. He did this so that you would broadcast
his glorious wonders throughout the world.*

1 PETER 2:9 (TPT)

"Tell me something you like about yourself!" my husband,
Kevin, said last night, like he does every night.

"Well, I was patient with someone who contradicted me
today," I said. "Instead of putting my hands on my hips and
insisting I was right—which, by the way, I was—I just smiled
and changed the subject."

Kevin laughed.

"Oh, and also I exercised, even though I didn't *feel* like it,"
I added. "And I forgave myself for not getting any writing done
this weekend. What about you?"

These questions are part of our nightly routine. Kev and I tell
each other three things we like about ourselves or three things
we are proud that we did that day. It's a way of acknowledging

how Jesus is at work in our lives. It's also a way to love ourselves and each other more.

Kevin's list usually consists of tasks he's accomplished. Getting up early to read his Bible. Visiting a church member who's been under the weather. Balancing the checkbook. My answers focus mostly on what I see as "problem" areas in my life, issues that sometimes make me judge myself harshly. My quick temper. My big mouth. My lack of self-discipline. I could go on, but you get the picture.

I learned this soul-nourishing practice of dwelling on the positive elements of our days or parts of ourselves a couple of years ago from a blog post about mental health. At first, I balked at the idea. *Doesn't the writer of Proverbs tell us not to brag on ourselves, but to let others praise us?* I thought (Proverbs 27:2). But my next thought reminded me of one of Jesus's commandments: Love your neighbor *as you love yourself.* If I didn't have a healthy self-image, how could I obey Jesus's command to love someone else?

> *Keep your thoughts positive because your thoughts become your words. Keep your words positive because your words become your behavior. Keep your behavior positive because your behavior becomes your habits.*
>
> MAHATMA GANDHI

At first, we found this practice awkward, and we had to start with baby steps. I listed things like my spontaneity, my red hair, and my love for cats. Kev was reluctant at first, too, but played along to humor me. Each night we grew a bit bolder in our sharing. Our hearts slowly opened to the wonder of Jesus helping us grow as Christians. We embraced this new habit as a way to recognize God's favor and generosity. We weren't bragging on how great *we* were. We were boasting about the love and grace of Jesus.

In the past, I often lamented that I'd been a Christian for decades and couldn't see any evidence of growth in my life. But now, after ending our days this way, I am encouraged that Jesus's Holy Spirit is maturing me. Our nightly sessions became praise parties in honor of the God who not only redeems us from sin, but also renovates and regenerates our hearts.

Our nightly habit also helps us encourage each other. When Kevin says he's pleased about getting up early to read his Bible, I tell him how proud I am of him. When I mention that I exercised four times this week, Kev says, "Way to go!" We build each other up as we look, with gratitude, at our Savior who is doing good work in us.

Jesus, thank You for maturing me and doing good work in my life. I ask that You help me continue to grow in love for You and others. As I end this day, I give You thanks for all the ways You bless and encourage me.

An Ocean of Love

SUSANNA FOTH AUGHTMON

He is the Maker of heaven and earth, the sea, and
everything in them—he remains faithful forever.

PSALM 116:7 (NIV)

Last week our family took a road trip to Southern California to visit our twenty-year-old son, Jack, for spring break. We love our new home in Idaho, but one of the things we miss most about living in California is the vast beauty of the Pacific Ocean. During our short visit, my seventeen-year-old-son, Will, and I walked down to the beach near the Santa Monica pier. Will and I couldn't resist the pull of the steady waves upon the shore. The crunch of the sun-warmed sand underfoot, the salty tang of the air, the cry of the gulls dipping in the wind—they called to us.

We walked down the winding stairs to the bridge that crossed over the freeway, trudging a quarter of a mile across the beach to the waterline. Plopping down on a small outcropping of sand, we sat with our faces in the sun. Warm. Happy. Relaxed. There is something about the deep rhythm of the ocean and the immensity of its presence that releases all the stress my body holds and lets me breathe.

The ocean has had this relaxing effect on me throughout my life. As a child, I would play in the frigid waters of the Pacific in Santa Cruz with my siblings. We would let our bodies get numb in stages—ankles, knees, waist—and then, taking the full plunge, we would body surf. The surging waves would carry us into shore. After hours in the water, we'd stumble up the beach to the worn cotton blanket my mom had laid out and let our bodies collapse on top of it. We let the sun beat back the cold in our small, ocean-chilled bodies. We revived ourselves with Kool-Aid and peanut butter and jelly sandwiches so we could race back into the water. After a day at the beach, we would tumble into bed at night, thoroughly worn out and happy.

In high school, my friends and I walked along sandstone cliffs to watch the surfers paddle out. They sat on their brightly colored boards, biding their time, waiting for the perfect wave. Finding their moment, they would jump to a crouch and maneuver along the curling crest of the wave as it folded in on itself. We would walk to the lighthouse and press up against its fence to catch a glimpse of the sea lions on Seal Rock. Barking to their friends, the sea lions slid off the rocks and plunged into the deep waters, looking for lunch. Those lazy strolls along the cliffs anchored my love for the ocean.

My college was located ten minutes from the Santa Cruz Beach Boardwalk. Countless spring hours were spent missing my afternoon English class to lay out on that beach, slathered in baby oil. While my tan was amazing, my grades were not. The siren song of the boardwalk was more powerful than the fear of failing an exam or getting a poor grade on my latest essay. When the pressures of college were weighing on me, sifting pebbled sand through my fingers soothed me. Sometimes I would find mini starfish, the size of a thumbnail, bleached white and hardened by the sun. Their intricate, tiny forms fascinated me. Beauty upon beauty. Peace upon peace.

When I took a break from college after my junior year and headed to Hawaii for discipleship training school, the calming rhythms of the ocean met me there. My best friend at the school lived on the island. Each Friday we would leave campus and stay with her parents in their small hillside home. Nestled between the palm trees and luscious foliage, it felt like a secret hideaway. We slept on their screened porch and were lulled to sleep by the crashing of the waves. When we woke up, we would drive to Hapuna Beach and spend our Saturdays knee-deep in the aqua blue water. Those moments in the ocean refreshed my soul. After a weekend at the beach, my spirit was restored.

I will refresh the weary and satisfy the faint.

JEREMIAH 31:25 (NIV)

Three years after my time in Hawaii, I met my husband-to-be, Scott. When we got married, we headed to Maui for our honeymoon. Deep water snorkeling, sun-soaked beaches, Kona coffee, and chocolate-covered macadamia nuts seemed like an ideal way to launch our marriage. We carried our love of the ocean into our family culture. Sandcastles and boogie boarding have shaped our three boys' childhoods.

Fast-forward to three years ago, when I became a middle school teacher in Pacifica, another California coastal town. The shift from freelance writer to full-time teacher stretched my body, mind, and spirit. My stress levels were at an all-time high. On my lunch breaks, I would drive the mile to the beach and sit in the parking lot, watching the surfers ride the waves. Sipping coffee and listening to worship songs, I would let the rhythm of the ocean calm my heart. Those stolen moments gave me a minute to breathe and regroup. Beauty upon beauty. Peace upon peace.

My connection with Jesus is deeply tied into my love of the ocean. I find real rest for my soul in the presence of Jesus's all-encompassing love. The vastness of the ocean, its breadth and width and depth, remind me of that fathomless love. It is too enormous for me to grasp. The endless pounding of waves upon the shore bring to mind His faithfulness. While life's seasons roll on, while stress and happiness, joy and pain, color my life, Jesus remains steadfast. His mercy and forgiveness stretch into all of eternity. His never-ending grace washes over the ups and downs of my days. I can sit in Jesus's presence and feel the stress leave my bones. Because of His great goodness, I am forgiven, loved, and held in a place of hope. His constancy in the trials of life let me breathe. As I meditate on His greatness, I find true rest. Beauty upon beauty. Peace upon Peace.

> Jesus says, *"Come to me, all you who are weary and burdened, and I will give you rest. Take my yoke upon you and learn from me, for I am gentle and humble in heart, and you will find rest for your souls."*
>
> MATTHEW 11:28–29 (NIV)

Jesus, You invite me into Your presence, offering relaxation and restoration. As I fall asleep tonight, remind me that Your faithfulness anchors me in a place of hope and healing. Thank You for Your great enduring love that surrounds me like the ocean itself.

A New Season

BETH GORMONG

There is a time for everything, and a season for every activity under the heavens: a time to be born and a time to die, a time to plant and a time to uproot, a time to kill and a time to heal, a time to tear down and a time to build, a time to weep and a time to laugh, a time to mourn and a time to dance, a time to scatter stones and a time to gather them, a time to embrace and a time to refrain from embracing, a time to search and a time to give up, a time to keep and a time to throw away, a time to tear and a time to mend, a time to be silent and a time to speak, a time to love and a time to hate, a time for war and a time for peace.

ECCLESIASTES 3:1–8 (NIV)

My husband, Jeff, and I sat in a restaurant at the airport in Sioux Falls, South Dakota. We were exhausted and emotionally spent. We had spent the last few days driving a trailer from Indiana to the small college town of Brookings, South Dakota with our oldest daughter, Jaena. Just out of college, she had found the perfect job, except for the location, which was sixteen hours from home.

In a matter of a couple of days, we packed all her possessions in a U-Haul and then drove it through a blizzard to this snow-covered land where we had to dig her car out before we could drive it off the trailer. I had never seen snow piled so high. It was a foreign world out here. Then we watched her sign a yearlong lease on a tiny apartment. We unloaded her furniture and boxes of clothes into the two empty rooms, filling them until there was barely room to walk. I helped her unload dishes into the kitchen, which was more like a hallway between the living room and bedroom than an actual kitchen. We drove to the utility company and watched her put the water and electric in her own name. She drove us past the church where she would work, and on to Walmart, where we filled a cart with groceries to get her started.

Go at life with abandon; give it all you got. And life will give all it has to you.

NORMAN VINCENT PEALE

That night we went to bed exhausted, with sore muscles and aching hearts. Jeff slept on the floor, and Jaena and I shared her bed. As I lay next to Jaena, I thought about Ecclesiastes 3:1, "There is a time for everything, and a season for every activity under the heavens." This night marked an ending. But could I see the beginning that followed?

The next morning Jaena drove us to the airport, where we gave her long, hard hugs, thinking of all the things we should have told her before she grew up and moved away. And now here we sat, trying not to look at each other. Tears threatened. Our baby had grown up, and neither one of us was ready to let her go. We couldn't talk without crying, so we sat in silence.

At the end of our sad meal, Jeff said, "We should be happy. We wanted this day to come. We hoped to raise her to be independent and competent. She's going to be just fine. Remember when the two of you were arguing over the definition of a muffler and she told you she was smarter than you?" he asked, eyes twinkling.

"Yes, at five years old! She insisted there was 'no such thing as a muffler.'" I chuckled at the memory. "Jaena was always ready for a good debate, wasn't she? You're right, she will be just fine."

When the plane took off a little later, I looked down at the white wonderland below me, realizing that the writer of Ecclesiastes was right, there is "a time to weep and a time to laugh, a time to

Evening Evaluation

As the heavens are higher than the earth, so are my ways higher than your ways and my thoughts than your thoughts Isaiah 55:9 (NIV).

Mornings are good for grabbing a singular purpose and striding into your day.

Evenings offer an opportunity to sort through the various purposes of our lives. Raising a family. Making a living. Helping in our churches or communities. Taking time to relax. Cheering on our favorite teams.

As you get ready to go to sleep, talk with Jesus about His purposes for your life. He will likely help you remember those moments during the day when you showed love to others— even in small or simple ways. Remember that no matter what work, responsibilities, or tasks fill our days, our deepest purpose as followers of Christ is to love.

mourn and a time to dance." And sometimes they happen at the same moment. As I mourned leaving my baby behind, I began to see how God was working in Jaena's life. For her it was "a time to plant" and for me, "a time to uproot." I was moving from a mom of three kids to a mom of adult daughters.

Soon I was to find that the fun part of parenting was just starting: requests for recipes, advice on cleaning up muddy dog prints, and calls just to catch up on each other's lives awaited me. The first time I received a Mother's Day card from Jaena after her move, knowing that she was thinking about me from far away, that she'd picked out a card, that she'd bought it with her own money and then mailed it to me, I was brought to tears. It felt like my first "real" Mother's Day card.

No longer do I have to drive anyone to cheerleading practice or choir concerts. There are no forgotten lunches or gym clothes. Much of the stress of constantly thinking about others' needs has lightened. I can sit and read a book without disruption. I'm finding I have room in my life to pursue new interests. I'm learning to: "Forget the former things; do not dwell on the past. See, I am doing a new thing! Now it springs up; do you not perceive it?" Isaiah 43:18–19 (NIV).

Dear Jesus, thank You for those I love.
Show me how to move on to new phases of life
when it's time. Help me to love others well through
the years and in the different stages of life. Give me
comfort, peace, and hope for the future.

Best Self

DURWOOD SMITH

For I can do everything through Christ,
who gives me strength.

PHILIPPIANS 4:13 (NLT)

She told me one day, "You are an unusual child." For a while I wondered if that was a compliment, or a complaint. *Is it because I'm so different from my older brother,* I wondered. I liked going barefoot in the summer. My brother never took off his shoes except to climb into bed. I always removed my shirt to get a tan on sunny days. He did not. His afternoon paper route was all business to him. My paper route was a daily social event, chatting, visiting, a quick game of "horse" with boys on a customer's basketball court. Perfecting my piano recital piece was important to me while he typically gave a "got through it" performance. Actually, my brother went on to do well in his life. He never seemed to cause our mother as much concern as I did.

"Why do you say I'm 'unusual'?" I once asked her.

"Um, well, um, you just are. You scare me sometimes. You please me at times. You fail miserably now and then, and you succeed amazingly from time to time. I just want you to be your best self," she admonished. "Jesus wants you to be your best self. And that is up to you."

The words "fail miserably and succeed amazingly" stuck in my mind.

The idea "I just want you to be your best self" motivated me sometimes and at other times was a burden I didn't want to have placed upon me.

At fourteen, I wanted an "A" on a history test. Cheating, I squeaked out the desired grade. Scores were called for in alphabetical order of students' names and recorded in the teacher's gradebook. When the teacher announced my grade, I felt immediate shame, my worst self. It lingered in my conscience, especially followed by the memory, "I just want you to be your best self." The Biblical words written by James in the New Testament stung. "He who knows to do right and doesn't do it, to him it is sin." I had failed miserably; Mother was right. I had nobody to blame but myself.

> *Whoever is open, loyal, true; of humane and affable demeanor; honorable himself, and in his judgment of others; faithful to his word as to law, and faithful alike to God and man—such a man is a true gentleman.*
>
> RALPH WALDO EMERSON

The high calling of Jesus has an irresistible pull. Feeling it even now, I know I'm safe. I'm more sensitive to His call. I feel safe because of Jesus's forgiveness. The apostle Paul, onetime enemy of the Gospel, keenly felt the call, though weak, to finish strong. The disciple Peter, singled out after his anguishing denial of Jesus during the crucifixion trial, was called to succeed amazingly. "Feed my sheep; I will be with you," Jesus said, directly to him.

Thankfully, I am becoming my best self. Jesus's heart of forgiveness far outweighs my failures and fears. I strive to become

Approach Life with a Forgiving Heart

The New Testament is clear when it comes to how we're supposed to treat those who have offended us. "Be kind and compassionate to one another, forgiving each other, just as in Christ God forgave you," says Ephesians 4:32 (NIV). Christ sets the standard, and we are to be like Him. "Bear with each other and forgive one another if any of you has a grievance against someone. Forgive as the Lord forgave you" (Colossians 3:13, NIV).

Forgive as the Lord forgave you. Becoming a truly forgiving person requires commitment. Fortunately, our days are filled with plenty of opportunities in which to grow stronger. Every little conflict we face gives us another chance to grow into forgiving people.

Did you ever notice that the word *give* is part of *forgive*? Forgiveness is a precious gift we've received—and one we're called to give others. But sometimes people get stuck by thinking that if we forgive, it's as if we're saying that what the other person did didn't matter. Not so! We can only forgive when there's something to forgive.

Praying for people who have hurt or offended us is an important step toward healing. When we pray for someone, it changes us as much as the other person.

the best self He wants me to be. When I'm feeling that the challenge is too tough, my resolve to reach my personal best is a spiritual fortification. At the end of each day, I want to hear Jesus's words, "Well done, good and faithful servant." He whispers,

"Come away a while and rest from the struggle. My yoke is easy." I take a deep breath, close my eyes, knowing a new day lies ahead. I hear Him say, "Tomorrow you will do well, dear one, unusually well."

Dear Lord Jesus, I give my days and my nights to You. Help me honor You. Thank You for Your strength that empowers me and guides me as I seek to please You. Thank You for knowing me, just as I am. And loving me, just as I am.

Thanks for the Little Things

NORM STOLPE

*I have come that they may have life,
and have it to the full.*

JOHN 10:10 (NIV)

My wife, Candy, and I tingled with gratitude when our oldest son, Jon, told us he was planning to visit us in Wisconsin from Pennsylvania. Thanks to the wonders of the internet, he could work remotely from our place after taking a few days off. It would be such a delight, after such a long time, to be with him again. We thanked Jesus for this gift.

But then, just a week before his scheduled visit, Jon's wife, Leanne, was not feeling well. While waiting for the results of a COVID-19 test, our son's travel plans were put on hold. Candy and I waited with apprehension. Fortunately, Leanne's results were negative, and Jon was on his way.

At the end of each day while he was with us, we recounted our thanks for all the little ways Jesus walked with us through Jon's visit. In part because of being separated from him for so long, every detail of our time with him felt like a treat.

We share a duplex with our middle son, David, and his family. David is a high school teacher, and he gave Jon a tour of his school. All through dinner that evening, Jon shared his delight that David has such energy and enthusiasm for his school, colleagues, and students. When they'd stopped at a bakery to pick up a loaf of bread for supper, one of David's students was working there. He went to great lengths to tell Jon how much David meant to him as a teacher, and he threw in a free loaf of sweet bread for them to bring home to us. More blessings!

Candy's dad lives in a senior residence near our home. Because of pandemic restrictions, none of us had been in his apartment for a year. Just before Jon arrived, the rules were loosened, and Jon was his first face-to-face visitor. Candy and I were thrilled to hear about their conversation. For the first time, Grandpa told Jon how he had been drafted into the Army immediately after graduating from high school. He reminisced about his youthful adventures as an ambulance mechanic with the occupation forces at the conclusion of World War II.

Part of the reason for his trip was that Jon was anxious to see for himself how his mother is doing with her Alzheimer's. One afternoon, he and I had a relaxed conversation about his observations and the wonderful support Candy and I have on this journey. Jon offered me substantial affirmation and encouragement. He joined us in our evening Scrabble games, and his mom beat him in our first game, but he eked out a win the second time. (I was a distant third both times!) Jon told Candy, "Mom, I think playing Scrabble keeps your brain working pretty well." We both agreed!

Candy and I also were also grateful to be able to meet one of our son's colleagues, a man named Rick. Chatting in our driveway, Rick asked Candy and me what we had done to raise such a special son. We laughed as he expressed his appreciation not only

Let Gratitude Shine

"Give thanks to the LORD," Psalm 107:1 (NIV) admonishes us, "for He is good; His love endures forever." If you want to feel better physically, if you want a better outlook on life, remember that verse.

Every morning before quickly moving into accomplishment mode or jumping right into worrying and fretting, first go look out the window, take a deep breath, and say, "Give thanks to the LORD, for He is good; His love endures forever."

Doesn't it make you feel better just to think of doing that? Think how much better it will make you feel if you follow that practice every day.

for Jon's competence and the integrity of his character, but also for his personal friendship. More prayers of thanks to Jesus!

All in all, Jon's visit was characterized by gratitude for small, everyday moments and affirmations and for the gift of family.

Thank You, Jesus, for all the ordinary and extraordinary moments and interactions that affirm and sustain us. Thank You for the gift of family and friendship. Tonight I thank You, most of all, for walking with us through this life. Your love is a gift.

Tender Shepherd

RICK HAMLIN

The one who enters by the gate is the shepherd of the sheep. The gatekeeper opens the gate for him, and the sheep hear his voice. He calls his own sheep by name and leads them out. When he has brought out all of his own, he goes ahead of them, and the sheep follow him because they know his voice.

JOHN 10:2–4 (NRSV)

Did you have a favorite bedtime prayer when you were a child? In my family, "Jesus, Tender Shepherd, Hear Me," was the prayer we were taught. It continued: "Bless this little lamb tonight. Through the darkness, be down near me. Keep me safe 'til morning light." We'd close our eyes, say those words, and then get a kiss on the forehead before our parents turned out the lights. Remembering this bedtime ritual from my boyhood, I can still feel the brush of my father's whiskers and the faintest whiff of his cologne. It smelled like lilacs.

When my wife, Carol, and I were raising our two sons, we sang the lullaby from the musical *Peter Pan* to them at bedtime. It's a round, so Carol would lead one of our sons with the opening phrase, and I would sing with the other. We sang: "Tender shepherd, tender shepherd, let me help you count your sheep. One in the meadow, two in the garden, three in the nursery, fast asleep." Our voices blended together in harmony until we came to the final words, "fast asleep, fast asleep." We then kissed our sons on their foreheads and turned out the light.

Of course, there were nights when one boy or both of them couldn't fall asleep or had a bad dream and came into our bedroom. There was always the option, especially when they were very young, of crawling into Mommy and Daddy's bed and lying between us. Sometimes our sons spent the night in our bed; other times, we'd escort them back to their bedroom, praying with them and rubbing their backs until they drifted off to sleep again.

> *The LORD is my shepherd, I lack nothing. He makes me lie down in green pastures, he leads me beside quiet waters, he refreshes my soul.*
>
> PSALM 23: 1–3 (NIV)

I can understand why Jesus used the imagery of shepherds and sheep when He described God's loving relationship with human beings. Jesus lived in ancient Judea in an agricultural society. His followers knew quite well what it was like to lead a flock, overseeing the animals grazing on nearby hills. But these references might make less sense to modern kids. The closest firsthand experience that my own children, for example, have had to shepherds and sheep was when they performed in the Christmas pageant at church. Some years they were cast as shepherds and sometimes they played the role of the sheep, "baaaaa-ing" their way up the church's center aisle. They frolicked in fuzzy wool costumes, making their way to Mary and Joseph and the Baby in the manger.

Despite limited knowledge about real sheep, they did come to know Jesus as the Good Shepherd who knew them and would look after them, day and night. They knew Jesus was with them, just like Carol and I were, and that He was present with us as we sang our nighttime blessing together, our voices echoing off the bedroom walls.

One year on Father's Day, our older son, William, declared that he and his brother would put *us* to bed. He was then about seven or eight. Our boys made sure we brushed our teeth and then they tucked us in. They listened quietly as we said our prayers, and then they turned out the light.

Carol and I whispered in bed for a little while, wondering how they would get to bed on their own that night. We needn't have worried. A few minutes after they'd left us, we heard them down the hall in their room reciting their favorite bedtime prayer. Then, all was quiet. The Good Shepherd was truly with them and at work in our home and in their hearts.

Dear Lord, thank You for being a tender shepherd and a constant protector in my life and the lives of those I love. Thank You for knowing and calling me by name. May I always know Your voice as You know mine. Thank You for being with me, all night long.

More Than Words

LOGAN ELIASEN

*For where two or three are gathered in
my name, there am I among them.*

MATTHEW 18:20 (ESV)

"So good to see you," Oscar said, grinning and waving as I opened the passenger door of his car. Oscar is possibly the most genuine person I knew. He truly loves both people and life. When he had invited me to meet his family, I had been excited to accept. But I was a little nervous as well. Oscar's family is from El Salvador, and he had invited me over to share a traditional meal from his country. As much as I loved to learn about different cultures, the unknown created anxiety in me.

I care deeply for Oscar, and I did not want to hurt my friend.

"We're going to have *pupusas* tonight," Oscar said. "They're corn cakes, stuffed with beans and cheese."

"That sounds delicious," I said. "I'm looking forward to trying them and to meeting your family."

"My mom is excited to have us over," he said. "She only speaks Spanish, but she loves to meet my friends."

I tensed. Oscar hadn't told me that his mom didn't speak English. That added a whole new wrinkle for me. I hadn't taken a Spanish class in over ten years. How could I thank my host when I couldn't even speak her language? I was a writer and a lawyer—I communicated through words. Today, I would be totally out of my element—culturally and linguistically. My stomach churned from both hunger and nerves.

After a short drive, Oscar parked in front of an apartment complex. We walked to a ground-floor apartment, and Oscar knocked on the door. A small woman answered. I was surprised, as Oscar is over six feet tall. Then the woman broke into a familiar smile. This was definitely Oscar's mom. Oscar and his mom began a brisk conversation in Spanish.

"This is my mom, Luz," he said. "She told me she's just finishing the pupusas."

Luz nodded politely to me. I nodded back. She then motioned for us to enter her home. Immediately, I smelled something rich and savory. I was sure I would enjoy the food!

Luz returned to the kitchen, and Oscar led me to the living room. There, he introduced me to his younger sister. We sat down and talked while Luz finished preparing the meal. Oscar and his sister were friendly and easygoing. Still, I felt nervous. Then I remembered how Jesus connected with people who were different from Him. A Roman soldier. A Gentile woman. A Samaritan. He listened to them. He ate with them. Jesus proved that social and cultural barriers could be overcome when we approach one another in love. But I still didn't know how to bridge the language gap with Luz. Soon, Luz called out in Spanish.

"The food is ready," Oscar explained.

> *Love is our true destiny. We do not find the meaning of life by ourselves alone—we find it with another.*
>
> THOMAS MERTON

At the kitchen table was a heaping tray of pupusas. They were thick and golden-brown, and next to them was a bowl of light red sauce. I took a seat at the table. After praying, Oscar passed the tray to me. I placed a pupusa on my plate and, at Oscar's instruction, covered it with sauce. After everybody had been served, I took my first bite. It was delicious—warm and full of flavor.

Then I made eye contact with Luz. I smiled and held up another piece with my fork. She grinned. And in that moment, we understood each other. I couldn't speak Luz's language, and she couldn't speak mine. But we didn't need to have a complex conversation to connect. She had invited me into her home and shared a meal from her country with me. And through simple body language and a smile, I could communicate my gratitude.

I realized that I didn't need to worry about the differences between Oscar's family and me. My anxiety melted away thanks to inspiration from Jesus and the example from Oscar, who so easily conveys joy toward others just by being present and being himself.

The room that night was filled with love.

Jesus, thank You for the good gifts of this life: of friends, family, and gathering together for a meal. Thank You for sustaining us and nourishing us with food and laughter. Thank You for being present with us.

A Heart Like Jesus

LAWRENCE W. WILSON

I am leaving you with a gift—peace of mind and heart. And the peace I give is a gift the world cannot give. So don't be troubled or afraid.

JOHN 14:27 (NLT)

When I was eight years old, one of my great aunts came for a visit. Great Aunt Ethel was a widow. Her husband, my grandfather's older brother, had been a renowned preacher in our denomination. Everyone treated her with great respect. However, my impression as a little boy was that nobody seemed to like her. And I admit, I certainly didn't. She was bossy and demanding and seemed always to be finding fault with others, including my sister and me. Honestly, I couldn't wait for her to leave. I filed that experience away for future reference, telling myself what, of course, I'd later learn to be false: Old people are mean.

By my mid-thirties, I'd entered the pastorate and was leading a congregation through what we look back on as "the worship wars." Many congregations were bitterly divided over the issue of "worship music." I'd encountered my share of parishioners, often older folk with a deep love of traditional hymns, who weren't fond of contemporary music. Nevertheless, I'd begun to introduce new music to my congregation's worship. The reviews were mixed.

One day a parishioner named Doris stopped by the church office. She was a widow, like my aunt Ethel had been, and had reached a similar age. Doris had a lung ailment that afflicted her with a chronic cough. I knew it was quite painful in addition to being a great frustration to her. When I heard Doris in the outer office, asking if the pastor was free, I felt sure the visit concerned worship music. I was right.

"Pastor," Doris began, "I just wanted to tell you about a fabulous church I visited last weekend."

> *Start each day with a positive thought and a grateful heart.*
>
> ROY T. BENNETT

"Here it comes," I thought. Parishioners were fond of bringing back tales and artifacts from other churches—a bulletin listing a traditional liturgy, or a story about a magnificent choir or pipe organ. On a busy workday, it's hard to make time to hear about how other places are doing so much better a job than our own church.

Doris continued. "I visited my nephew in Rochester, and they have the most wonderful church. They're meeting in a movie theater. It was so exciting to see how the younger people are reaching out with the Gospel!"

She went on for several minutes raving about the wonderful new music, the clever use of video, and the relevant sermon.

"I think it's just wonderful to see people trying new things," she said. "I won't keep you, pastor. I'm off to lunch with friends. I just wanted to stop by and tell you to keep up the good work.

You're doing a fantastic job, and I love seeing the way Jesus continues to move in churches today."

I sank back in my chair, delighted and a bit bewildered. I thought right then that I hope to be like Doris when I'm her age if I'm fortunate enough to live such a long life. Doris had peace about herself and her life. No one could give her joy, and no circumstance could take it away, and she remained curious about the changes she saw around her, in church and in the wider world. She was alert to how Jesus continues to move among us. Her heart reflected His.

"I want to be like Doris when I grow up," I said, smiling to myself. And I hope I will be!

Dear Jesus, thank You for all You have done for me. Thank You for putting elders in my life, people whose love for You is contagious. May I ever be curious and full of expectation as I look for the way You meet us, today and always.

before going to bed. Summer, though, is different. Longer daylight means more work can be done outside.

I reluctantly changed my clothes from conference presenter to gardener. I grabbed a bucket and hoe and went to the flowerbed. It looked like a jungle. The spring flowers had died. They needed to be cut down so the next round of flowers could grow. I cut stalks and pulled weeds, section by section. The late afternoon sun was hot. Sweat rolled down my back, but I was surprised that this labor actually energized me. After hours of talking with people, instructing, and giving advice, cleaning the flowerbed was therapeutic. Each area I worked in looked orderly and fresh when I was finished. I put the discarded weeds and foliage in our wheelbarrow and made several trips to and from our pasture, dumping them there for the cows to eat. My energy increased with each jaunt back and forth.

> *Cast your cares on the LORD and he will sustain you; he will never let the righteous be shaken.*
>
> PSALM 55:22 (NIV)

After two hours of gardening, I felt satisfied with the work I had completed. It was like time was being redeemed from being stuck inside on a beautiful day. What I thought was going to be exhausting work turned out to be refreshing both physically and mentally. My mind relaxed and was cleansed, more and more, with every weed I removed from the overgrown mess.

I fell into bed that night, my body tired but my spirit renewed. I felt a sense of contentment I couldn't explain. A full, productive day of both ministering and completing such a big task in the garden brought me joy, peace, and an indescribable type of rest.

Genesis 2:2 says that on the seventh day of Creation, God finished the work that he had done, and He rested. That verse intrigues me. I wonder if the rest God felt was similar to what I experienced that day: a feeling of contentment and peace after a productive day of meaningful labor. I enjoy that feeling when I've completed a project, achieved a goal, or created, cleaned, or organized something. It's a type of satisfaction that provides mental and emotional order. It's a rest that's almost holy.

Since that day, I often pull weeds as a stress reliever. It may be in the cool of the evening or even on a Sunday afternoon. More than once I've heard the clip-clip of an Amish neighbor's horse and buggy go by when I'm bent over in a flower garden. At first, I worried about being judged by others as I toiled in the dirt. I wondered if they thought I don't know how to rest. But, I don't worry about that anymore. Though it's physical labor, I accept that it's relaxing to me. I feel close to Jesus when I'm gardening. I often pray and take in the blessing of being surrounded by the beauty of nature as I find my own sort of rest.

Jesus, thank You for meaningful work and satisfying rest. Thank You for the beauty of Your creation. Tonight, as I prepare for sleep, I thank You for the rhythms of work and rest.

Created for Good Works

LORI HATCHER

We are God's handiwork, created in
Christ Jesus to do good works, which God
prepared in advance for us to do.

EPHESIANS 2:10 (NIV)

It took me most of our lunch hour to admit to my friend Karen what I'd been struggling with for years. After chatting about the weather, our children, and summer vacation, I pulled the plug, and all my secret thoughts gushed out.

"Before we had children, David and I spent most evenings serving the Lord," I said. "We attended classes at the Bible Institute, volunteered in the children's program, served on the bus ministry, and never missed an outreach night."

I took a breath, glanced down at my hands, and admitted what felt to me like an awful truth. "But, after our first was born, we could barely make it to church. She had separation anxiety and screamed the whole time she was in the nursery, so we couldn't leave her. And I couldn't exactly lug her along on door-to-door visitation," I confessed. "About the time our second child was born, we decided to homeschool. I never dreamed it would take so much time and energy."

Karen nodded sympathetically.

"I feel so useless," I whispered, tears filling my eyes. "I'm afraid God is disappointed in me because I'm not serving Him the same way I used to."

My friend reached out and gently touched my arm.

"You're in a different stage of life now," she said. "You can't expect to serve God like you did before you had children. Right now, your primary ministry is to your family—and it might just be your most important one. As you love and care for them, you're loving and serving Jesus."

Then she asked: "Can I pray with you?"

I nodded.

Finding Your Purpose in Life

Through the seasons of life, discerning our purpose can be one of the most challenging tasks we face. But the good news is God has a purpose for each of us. Here are some suggestions:

- Engage in different activities, ones that make a difference in your life and in others' lives, until you discover the one that makes you come alive. This process leads to understanding what truly brings you joy.

- Whatever your circumstances, whether you are in a time of joy or hardship, continue to search for your purpose.

- Listen to your heart. When you feel passionate about something and are willing to work hard, you are capable of anything.

- Pray. Prayer provides insight and clarity on what your heart yearns for and the ways you can help others. Prayer opens the way.

Taking a deep breath, she said, "Jesus, You know that Lori has a heart for you. She loves You and wants to serve You. Right now, though, it's tough. The needs of her family keep her close to home. Help her know that her ministry at home pleases and honors You. Give her creative ways to impact those around her. In Jesus's name I pray, Amen."

> *The two most important days in life are the day you are born and the day you find out why.*
>
> MARK TWAIN

That evening, I remembered her words as I gathered a stack of homeschooling books to take to a neighbor who had asked to borrow them. Night was falling, and lights blinked on in the houses that lined the road. As I passed each home, I thought about the family that lived there, and I tried to imagine how Jesus might be lovingly thinking about them.

My neighbor Cheryl had a new baby and two older children. "Jesus, give her patience, energy, and good rest tonight as she does the work You have given her to do," I prayed.

I passed my widowed next-door neighbor's house. My heart filled with affection as I remembered the last time my kids and I visited her. She played the piano for us and loved telling my kids stories about her knickknacks. "Jesus, please be a loving companion to her," I prayed. "Thank you for the love she shows to us."

Across the street, Mr. Lee tapped on a tin dish with a spoon to call the neighborhood cats.

"Hi Mr. Lee," I called. "How's Mrs. Lee today?" We chatted across the street together for a few minutes. "Jesus, please heal Mrs. Lee from her cancer," I silently prayed as I walked away. "Bless Mr. Lee and thank You for all he does for Mrs. Lee and for the neighborhood."

Down the block from my house, I leaned over the fence to pet Scooby, a golden retriever. Scooby and I have a special relationship, especially after my family and I dog-sat him a while back. That evening, he greeted me with a slobbery kiss and a furiously waving tail.

"Hi sweet boy," I said, grateful for his love.

I glanced back at my own home, now lit up with the others against the backdrop of night.

In the silence, Jesus spoke to my heart. Somehow, in that moment, I knew I was exactly where I needed to be. The ordinary gifts I gave or received, right close to home, were opportunities to see Jesus at work, extending love to His children.

I saw that I wasn't a benched player on Jesus's ministry team. I hadn't been sidelined while other players scored field goals and touchdowns. I'd been ministering in His name all along, and others were ministering to me.

I *wasn't* useless.

God *wasn't* disappointed in me.

It's been twenty years since that epiphany, but the truth Jesus revealed to me that night continues to shape the way I view Christian service and its role in my life. After five years of ministry as a newly married woman with no children, my ministry once I was a mother looked different. I was able to look for ways to serve Jesus at home and in my neighborhood. Now, as an empty nester, Jesus has moved me into more formal ministry again in my writing and speaking careers. In retirement, my ministry will undoubtedly look different too.

Each season will look different, but none is insignificant. Jesus uses us, right where we are, to bring His love and comfort to the world.

Jesus, thank You for creating me for good works and giving me ample opportunities to accomplish them. Help me fulfill my purpose by loving You and loving others in whatever stage of life I find myself. Thank You, too, for the different ways You are at work in my heart and in the world.

Places You'll Go

DURWOOD SMITH

And the Lord will guide you continually, and satisfy you with all good things, and keep you healthy too; and you will be like a well-watered garden, like an ever-flowing spring.

ISAIAH 58:11 (TLB)

Traffic in Seattle, where I live, serves as a useful analogy for all the waiting we do in life. We describe our bad traffic with terms like "rolling parking lot" and "the Nisqually crawl." To avoid it, we use our bus system and light rail. Recently, to escape waiting in traffic, I left my car at home and boarded the bus for downtown. However, a surprise was waiting for me. The bus turned around and took me back through my neighborhood, right past where I'd started. Winding through side streets, it hissed and ground its way into and out of many sectors of the city on its way downtown.

"Wait a minute, I don't want to go to Beacon Hill," I told the driver. "I want to go directly to the city center."

"You're going to need to transfer to bus No. 134 at Georgetown," the driver responded.

A trip that should have taken thirty minutes became a ride lasting one and a half hours as we wove and swerved and stopped and started twenty-five times before arriving at my destination.

The route Jesus has led me down over the course of my life resembles this experience. I know He has been with me through it all, but there have been detours, rough roads, and experiences I didn't want to encounter. And there has been lots of waiting.

My trip through cancer was unexpected, a stop along the way where He allowed me to learn patience and His healing power. The prayers of a multitude of faithful warriors sustained me. A career failure after twelve years of trying was a grim time, but seeing His light ahead calling me to a new vocation encouraged me. An eight-hundred-mile move home with my family to rejoin relatives, brought me only to witness the death of my mother twelve months later. Yet He was there, saying, "My grace is sufficient." Years later, heart disease and a stroke broke down the door, like sudden intruders, demolishing my definition of myself as an invincible male. The lyric from "Amazing Grace" is so true of my life: "Through many dangers, toils, and snares, I have already come / 'Tis grace hath brought me safe thus far and grace will lead me home." Jesus has permitted my circuitous path, and I am grateful for all of it.

> *'Tis grace hath brought me safe thus far and grace will lead me home.*
>
> JOHN NEWTON

In Seattle, we also travel by boat. One foggy October morning, I boarded the *Victoria Clipper*, a high-speed hydrofoil-like passenger boat whisking people to Victoria, a wee bit of old England on Canada's Vancouver Island. Fog, thick as pea soup, slowed our nautical speed to less than half of normal. No speedy voyage that day. The wonder of the ride was greatly curtailed.

"What's to see?" questioned tourists as they peered out seven-foot-high windows viewing nothing but thick, cotton-like sea-level clouds.

"There's snowcapped mountain peaks in the distance. Islands dot the waterway," I said, enthusiastically. "Stunning shoreline views show all along the seventy-mile boat ride. Small settlements hug the edge of hidden inlets. Mount Rainier rises 14,000 feet above sea level just to the south."

"Oh!" A collective moan went up. "We paid good money to experience all this ride has to offer and we're missing half of it."

Such is life, I thought to myself. But even I was disappointed.

But then, a bit later, the *Victoria Clipper* emerged from the clouds and sailed the remainder of the voyage in glorious sunlight. The fog was forgotten. Joy abounded. The day finished with rewards and delight. The beautiful views, there all the time but shrouded in fog, were stunning. Like Jesus, they were with us all along, even though we couldn't see them.

As I come to rest at the end of each day, I am grateful for so much. A taste of heaven, right here and now. Yes, there have been places I didn't want to go in my life, but I know the route is safe and perfect for me. I may not see everything clearly, but I have a faithful guide, Jesus.

Dear Jesus, help me to trust You in the fog and in the waiting. You have led me safely in the past. You will not let my foot slip as I walk closely with You. Help me to remember that You are in all the places I'll go—today, tomorrow, and always.

Library Day

BETH GORMONG

*The only thing that you absolutely have
to know, is the location of the library.*

ALBERT EINSTEIN

I'm a book lover. Each evening, I try to spend the last portion of the day reading until my eyes refuse to stay open. And this bedtime routine means I need a lot of books. Probably not as many books as are currently strewn across my bedside table, but acquiring new books is also a priority for me. So, in addition to being a book lover, I'm also a bookstore lover, and even more, a library lover. After all, both types of buildings are filled from floor to ceiling with my favorite things, books of all kinds. They wait, neatly organized, ready for me to easily find the ones I want, along with thousands of titles on other subjects I never even considered needing to know about. It's the definition of a dream come true.

Every Thursday, I wrangle my bookbag from the floor of my car. It's heavy and jam-packed with items, ready to return. I lug it across the parking lot to the library. Yellow and red tulips line both sides of the long sidewalk. I stop halfway up and sit on a wooden bench for a few moments to take in the beauty of the warm spring day with its blossoming flowers and crisp air. With my eyes closed, I take in a deep breath and slowly let it out. I feel my tense body relax. This is a favorite part of my week. Library day.

My local public library is an odd-shaped building, an architectural piece from the 1980s. The roof juts out at weird angles. Tall, thin windows reach from floor to ceiling. Inside, dark wooden beams crisscross the ceiling. The main lobby is a pergola-like area, connecting two larger rooms. The opening on the left is filled with patrons on computers and lined on one side with small study rooms. The space to the right is filled with rows upon rows of books. This is where I love to go exploring.

But first to unload the back-breaking bag on my shoulder. I head into the lobby, where I slide book after book into the return slot. With an empty bag crying out to be filled again, I scan the "New Additions" section to see what catches my eye and grab the latest novel from Louise Penny, a volume on lace knitting, and Marie Kondo's *The Life-Changing Magic of Tidying Up*, with a hope that the book's presence in my bag will miraculously declutter my home.

> *Live your days on the positive side of life, in tune with your most treasured values. And in each moment you'll have much to live for.*
>
> RALPH MARSTON

By the time I've roamed all the aisles, I've collected at least ten hardbacks on a variety of subjects, including container gardening. I've snatched up a murder mystery paperback too. Checking out all these books is my version of guilt-free impulse shopping. It's also how I feed my mind. It is my place to learn about important people or fall in love with imaginary ones and to be lulled to sleep. I always leave the library excited about what I will learn from the titles in my bag.

The first library I remember visiting was my church's little book area in the back of the sanctuary. It consisted of two walls of handmade walnut bookshelves, loaded down with Christian books for adults, and a small, beloved children's section. After every service, I would run to this area and scour the shelves until my mom told me it was time to head home. She would help me write my name on the little card in the front of the book I chose and put the card in the box where it stayed until I returned the book on the next Sunday. I learned to love reading from that tiny

How to Let Go and Let God

Identify what you can control—and what you can't. Often, the things that stress us and worry us are things we can't control.

Address what you can control. One antidote to worry and stress is action. So, once you have found something you can control, take action.

Surrender what you can't control. Turn what you fear over to God. Fear is keeping things in your own hands; faith is turning them over into the hands of God.

Meditate on the promises of your faithful God. Focus on comforting scriptures, such as "Never will I leave you; never will I forsake you" (Hebrews 13:5, NIV). Resolve not to act on fear but on faith. To quote E. Stanley Jones, "Never act on a fear, for fears are usually false."

Focus your mind and heart on trusting Jesus today. Jesus said, "Do not worry about tomorrow, for tomorrow will worry about itself. Each day has enough trouble of its own" (Matthew 6:34, NIV).

church library. I read biographies about men and women who loved God and served Him all over the world. Those stories gave birth to dreams about my future place in the world. I was motivated by how God used others, and realized that God wanted to use me too. I learned to trust that Jesus loved me and that He was my constant friend through the stories of His faithfulness to others.

Yesterday it struck me that my Bible is a library of sorts too, a library that consists of 66 books that feed my soul. And even though it's so small that I can carry around with me, its collection of stories is the most important bibliotheca in the world. I love to read in the New Testament how Jesus interacted with his friends, followers, and skeptics. Psalms, from the Old Testament, is my favorite book. I find comfort and encouragement in its poetry.

Psalm 119:103–105 (NIV) is right: "How sweet are your words to my taste, sweeter than honey to my mouth! I gain understanding from your precepts; therefore I hate every wrong path. Your word is a lamp for my feet, a light on my path."

Jesus, thank You for the gift of language. Thank You for those who weave words into sentences, and sentences into books. Thank You for those books that inform, inspire, or encourage me. And most of all, thank You for the Bible, the library You wrote to tell us how much You love us.

The Roots of Community

ERYN LYNUM

For where two or three are gathered together in My name, I am there in the midst of them.

MATTHEW 18:20 (NKJV)

The trees have a familiarity about them. Their blanched bark resembles so many woods painted white by paper birch I knew well from growing up in Wisconsin. Yet these are different. My husband and I, along with our four kids, drive slowly along a narrow dirt road—one of many old fire roads inscribed in time across the map of the Rocky Mountains. As summer gives way to our first fall living in Colorado, the leaves of the aspen trees begin to glow. Full groves of them light up hillsides in a brilliant golden yellow.

Not only does their rich color catch my attention, but also a less obvious characteristic: their robust root system. Individual aspen trees do not grow from seeds. Instead, "suckers" are sent out from its interlocking root system. Aspen trees are vitally connected to each other through their roots, and the health of one tree affects the tree standing beside it.

Beneath the soil of an aspen grove, God provides vivid imagery for Ecclesiastes 4:9–12 (NKJV), where I read, "Two *are* better than one, because they have a good reward for their labor. For if they fall, one will lift up his companion . . . a threefold cord is not quickly broken."

During our first year in Colorado, as I became acquainted with the aspen trees, they served as a beautiful reminder of the work Jesus was carrying out in my own life. We'd arrived in the West with a prayer on our lips: *Lord, lead us to a strong faith family.* We were aching for community. Over the course of that first year, He sowed deep relationships with friends who love our family, pray for us regularly, and have seen us through incredibly difficult seasons.

It really boils down to this: that all life is interrelated. We are all caught in an inescapable network of mutuality, tied into a single garment of destiny. Whatever affects one destiny, affects all indirectly.

MARTIN LUTHER KING JR.

As I read the Gospel, this deep level of community is highlighted throughout Jesus's life. Stepping into ministry, one of His first acts was gathering the disciples—a close-knit community of followers. Time and again, we see Him bringing His community together and imparting words of life and wisdom to them. He brought them together for parables and prayer, for breaking bread, and to bear one another's burdens. He gathered them in the garden and around the table, on the seashore and in the synagogue. He was preparing them for the grief and confusion they would endure once He would leave them and return to His Heavenly Father.

Living in the desert of the Rocky Mountains, it's not only the yellow aspen leaves that, at times, cause our hills to glow. We also endure wildfires. These fires have devastating effects on our landscape, yet in the wake of them, we witness new life sprouting across the landscape—including in our aspen groves. Where other types of trees die due to their individual nature, an aspen grove can survive, bearing new trees from the network of roots protected underground.

The community Jesus gathered around us in Colorado has walked beside us through our own fires. They have stuck close as we've moved across town twice, journeyed through a frightening

Connecting to Life through Gardening

Science is proving what people with green thumbs have long known to be true: Gardening is good for you. Gardening occupies our left brain in tasks like planting and fertilizing, while immersing our right brain in the aroma of flowers and the feel of soil. The rhythmic nature of weeding, trimming, and sowing can take you to a state of singlemindedness, which harnesses all emotions into one action and stimulates feel-good endorphins.

Researchers have determined that the plant-person relationship is beneficial because it requires the nurturing dynamic that allows humans to bond without the drama of human emotions.

Gardening allows us to experience the transformative power of caring for something. Plants teach us that things never stay the same, and that although growth may be invisible to us, it is still happening all the time. Gardening teaches us patience and the hopeful anticipation of new life.

high-risk pregnancy, suffered prolonged illness, endured financial strains, and raised our four children. They have left meals on our doorstep, cared for our kids, held us up in prayer, and, countless times, directed our gaze back to Jesus. Jesus brought us into community with His people—their roots are interlocked with our own, and our lives directly affect and support one another's.

Dear Jesus, during Your life on earth, You counted it of utmost importance to show us what a faithful community looks like. Gather believers around me who will spur me on to good works and remind me of Your great promises. Thank You for Your beautiful design of community and the ways You are establishing it in my life.

Audio Overload

LORI ROELEVELD

*He said to them, "Come with me by yourselves
to a quiet place and get some rest."*

MARK 6:31 (NIV)

My world was full of noise.

They were mostly necessary, even joyful noises. A household full of children and their playmates. Needed construction on the road outside our home. Books on tape playing for my dyslexic son. Our yapping dog and chirping parakeet. My father visiting to see the children with his fire radio clipped to his belt, tones, static, and intermittent announcements adding to the fray. And the phone always ringing.

Wonderful, loving, happy sounds but, still, noise.

Some moms daydreamed about bigger homes or jewelry. My fantasies were about long uninterrupted naps in quiet places. My doctor confirmed that my nerves were a bit jangled, and I would benefit from reducing stress. The problem was that the source of stress in my life wasn't apparent to me. I adored being a mom. I enjoyed homeschooling. I loved having my dad drop by or friends call.

One day, reading Mark, I noticed chapter 6, verse 31. Jesus and His disciples had been thronged by people seeking healing, deliverance, and teaching. Mark says they hadn't even had time to eat. Jesus's ministry was in full swing and the disciples were beside him engaging in vital work to demonstrate the coming of the kingdom.

What interested me was that Jesus didn't tell them a parable about life balance. He didn't chide them for overpacking their schedule. He didn't scold them for being weary or reduce the scope of their ministry. Instead, He invited them to come away to a quiet place to rest.

Quietness. What was that? The disciples lived in a day before gas-powered engines, electronic devices, and phones. If they needed to get away to a quiet place, I certainly recognized I must be on audio overload! Right then, it occurred to me that Jesus was offering a real solution. I began to consider His Words and asked Him to lead me, too, into quiet places.

Not long after, I was engaged in weight loss research through our local fitness center. The researcher had a list of ways people could replace food as a daily reward with other simple rewards. One suggestion was to "schedule regular moments for a time of silence." The researcher explained that we often overeat to quiet our emotions, but we could actually do that by just, well, getting quiet.

Now, Jesus really had my attention and I read another verse that resonated with the theme. Psalm 23:2–3 (NIV) says this about the Lord who is our shepherd, "He makes me lie down in green pastures, he leads me beside quiet waters, he refreshes my soul." At the time, we lived near the ocean and took frequent walks on the shore. Others told me it would be calming but I didn't find it so. Now I began to wonder if the reason was that my soul yearned for silence, for a breather even from lapping waves.

Jesus's yoke is truly light. These biblical messages didn't feel like demands but more like gifts God wanted me just to receive. Jesus—who lived a life of full-time ministry, investing in people, serving, teaching, caring, healing, and interacting—was inviting me into quiet.

So, I tried it. Silence. At first, it wasn't easy to locate but then I started finding it everywhere. In my car, the bath, an empty conference room, walking in the cemetery, sitting in the church sanctuary, and in my own room with noise-cancelling headphones. I called it "silence bathing." I didn't coin the term, I discovered, but that didn't matter because Jesus had led me into a place of calm.

> *Silence is more musical than any song.*
>
> CHRISTINA ROSSETTI

I went with Jesus to quiet places and just sat. I didn't try to worship, gain insight, or think spiritual thoughts. It was like rocking on my front porch with Him rocking beside me. Us, just being quiet together, as I aligned my heartbeat, my breathing, my pace with His. It's similar to the times I hold my baby grandson on my shoulder so that he calms and falls asleep. But Jesus is holding me.

Now my children are grown with children of their own, but my world can still be full of noise. My phone rings constantly for my job, the dog barks, notifications beep with emails and news alerts, and my carpenter husband is always banging on something. It's become my habit to escape into silence at least once in the middle of the day and always at the end.

Recently, I even dared to attend a weekend silent retreat in the mountains. No electronics. No conversation with others. Just silent walks in the woods, prayer beside the still lake,

Pray Yourself to Sleep

Incorporating prayer into your existing pre-sleep routine could lead to better sleep patterns as well as a closer walk with God. Here are suggested evening prayers for your bedtime routine:

PRAY AS YOU ENTER THE BEDROOM.

May the Lord Almighty grant me and those I love a peaceful night and a perfect end.

PRAY AS YOU UNDRESS FOR THE NIGHT.

Almighty God, my heavenly Father, I confess that I have sinned against you in thought, word, and deed, in what I have done, and in what I have left undone. For the sake of your Son, our Lord Jesus Christ, forgive all my offenses and grant that I may walk before you in newness of life, to the glory of your Name.

PRAY AS YOU WASH YOUR FACE
AND BRUSH YOUR TEETH.

Praise the Father, the Son, and the Holy Spirit, the God who is, who was, and is to come, at the end of the ages.

PRAY AS YOU CLIMB INTO BED
AND TURN OFF THE LIGHT.

Into your hands, O Lord, I commend my spirit, for you have redeemed me, O Lord, O God of truth. Keep me as the apple of your eye and hide me under the shadow of your wings.

and contemplation of His Word before the evening fire. It was remarkably restorative to my soul.

Silence is an incredible gift from Jesus. It's free. It can be found or created with a little creativity. And it is a healing balm in a world of audio overload. Especially at the end of each day, I come into the quiet and He is there.

Jesus, You've created many beautiful sounds in this world but like a rest in a score of music, You've accented these sounds with silence. Thank You for silencing the noise in my spirit and providing the refuge of silence.

Keeping Watch

CRYSTAL STORMS

*Ask, and it will be given to you; seek, and
you will find; knock, and it will be opened to you.*

MATTHEW 7:7 (NKJV)

I was the first one to see them. My husband, Tim, and I were walking along the Fred Howard Park causeway in Florida, past oak trees draped in Spanish moss and sandy pines, when dolphins swam by, just beyond the shore. I moved to the edge of the water for a better look and saw that there were three dolphins—one large, one medium, and one small. They reminded me of the family of bears in the story of Goldilocks: Papa, Mama, and Baby.

I pointed out the dolphins to Tim, and he joined me at the shoreline. Other people overheard me sharing the news, and a small crowd gathered on the north side of the causeway. Two of the dolphins circled and then disappeared below the surface of the water. It looked like Papa was teaching Baby how to dive for food. After a while, the dolphins stopped searching for prey and swam farther out. The crowd dispersed, and we continued our walk toward the beach on the Gulf of Mexico.

A little later, on our way back to the car, Tim said, "You were the first one to spot the dolphins."

"I never stop looking," I responded, my gaze still directed toward the water. I didn't want to miss them if they returned. "I still have my dolphin eyes on!"

At the ocean, I have my "dolphin eyes" on. Elsewhere, when I think there's a chance I might see a rabbit, I have my "bunny eyes" on. Sometimes I'm on the lookout for rainbows, other times wildflowers or sunsets. And so it goes. I've learned to look for simple delights in nature; they remind me of Jesus's constant presence, creativity, and care.

James 1:17 says that "Whatever is good and perfect comes to us from God" (NLV). That verse reminds me that every good gift is from God above, sweet delights from His heart. I've experienced Jesus's presence in a multitude of ways. But I've learned that in order to see the good things around me, I have to seek them out and keep my "eyes on."

The Psychology of Optimism

The psychology of optimism is striking. Researchers suggest that positive thinkers tend to be effective problem solvers and that they tend to pursue strategies that make a rosy future a reality.

Some skills associated with optimism are the ability to positively re-frame a challenge as an opportunity; awareness of thoughts, emotions, and mental patterns; flexible thinking; and cultivating feelings of gratitude.

The researchers note that optimism is only effective when it's authentic, though. Pursuing positivity at all costs can actually backfire, tempting us to ignore warning signs of serious situations or deny the full reality of our emotional lives.

My continued scanning of the water that day was not in vain. Tim and I were crossing a small bridge when I saw them again. The family of dolphins had returned, and I moved toward the water for a better view. A fisherman stood on the ledge with his line in the water. I sat down on the cool cement in the shade of the bridge, and Tim sat beside me. The fisherman turned to us, and I pointed toward the water.

"Dolphins," I said.

He nodded.

The three swam in a big circle, popping up above the water's surface time after time. We watched the pod play, without saying a word. My sense was that all three of us—Tim, the fisherman, and myself—felt the same quiet reverence and delight in witnessing the dolphins play. We were experiencing something good and perfect, the gift of beauty and God's creation.

When they swam away again, Tim and I rose, said goodbye to the fisherman, and headed back to the car. I reached for his hand.

"What was your favorite part of our walk?" I asked. "My favorite was spotting the dolphins."

Tim stopped walking and looked me in the eyes.

"My favorite part was seeing your delight," he said. "I know that, at times like that, you are thanking Jesus for His grace."

And he was right.

Lord, thank You for the gift of Your creation and, Jesus, thank You for Your grace and presence. I fall asleep tonight grateful for the beauty You bring into the world.

Sunny with a Chance of Grace

RICK HAMLIN

*Our steps are made firm by the LORD, when he
delights in our way; though we stumble, we shall
not fall headlong, for the LORD has us by the hand.
I have been young, and now am old, yet
I have not seen the righteous forsaken.*

PSALM 37:23–25 (NRSV)

It has become my nightly habit to check the weather on my phone at bedtime. Then, before I fall asleep, I start to think about what I'm going to do based on what I've read. Will I go running in the morning? Will I need my parka and waterproof pants? Which shoes should I wear? Often, my last thoughts of the day are spent on these things.

One recent evening, the weather app predicted that it was going to be thirty-four degrees the next morning. Sunny, yes, but with a fierce wind from the northwest blowing at seventeen miles per hour, making the "feel-like" temperature twenty-one degrees. I was planning on going for my usual morning run, but would I do it in temperatures like that? What would I wear?

The next morning, it was still dark when I got up, and I sat, as usual, on the sofa for some quiet contemplative prayer time. At the end of my prayer time, I prayed for some friends whose names popped into my head, people who were suffering from health setbacks, one in the hospital with a mysterious infection. "Jesus be with them," I asked.

I opened my eyes and looked out the window. As predicted, the sun was shining. Grateful for the app's warning, I wasn't deceived by the appearance of the sunny day. I put on my warmest gloves and hat and scarf and sweatpants and socks and headed out for a run. It was windy and cold, but stunningly beautiful. The sunlight illuminated the last of the autumn leaves on the hills, and

Start and end every day, and in between times, too, by thanking God for everything.

NORMAN VINCENT PEALE

the air was invigorating. Even as I was huffing and puffing up my least favorite hill in the park, I knew I had much to be grateful for.

Once back inside, I fixed myself some warm oatmeal and a hot cup of tea and sat down to read a few psalms and a chapter from one of the Gospels that spoke about being thankful. My heart was filled with gratitude to Jesus for a beautiful day and His presence with me.

Dear Jesus, thank You for being with me as I go to sleep every night and awaken every morning. Your presence fills my days and nights with grace. Thank You for Your love.

Late Bloomer

SUSANNA FOTH AUGHTMON

But I have raised you up for this very purpose,
that I might show you my power and that
my name might be proclaimed in all the earth.

EXODUS 9:16 (NIV)

This is our second spring in Idaho. Last summer, we planted a snowflake crabapple and two javelin pear trees in our backyard. They've made it through their first fall and a very cold winter, and now a miracle is taking place. They are flowering! Every limb on both javelin pear trees is covered with white delicate blossoms. The crabapple's white blossoms will have a sunrise pink center, but most of them are still closed, waiting for the sun to penetrate their petals. I know it's going to be a show when they open and reveal their full glory.

I am just as excited about the day lilies poking up around the dwarf magnolia tree. And don't get me started on the dwarf magnolia! We planted that sapling the year we moved in. Its maroon blossoms are still closed, and I can't wait to see it burst into color too.

I also bought some potted bulbs for our front porch. Then the greenery started pushing up from the soil, but I wasn't sure what flowers were going to show up. The daffodils were first, then the golden tulips. Yesterday, I called my mom. "Mom, I have hyacinths. Pink hyacinths." She was excited with me. She has had her hands in the soil for years and knows the peace and joys that gardening yields.

I shared concerns with her about the two plum trees and the pear tree that she and I planted in the backyard when she visited us this March. There are buds on a plum tree, but nothing on the others. She encouraged me, saying, "Some trees are late bloomers." I agreed but noted that there are no guarantees in gardening.

> *Let us not become weary in doing good, for at the proper time we will reap a harvest if we do not give up.*
>
> GALATIANS 6:9 (NIV)

The joy of seeing a flower flourish is worth the risk and uncertainty. We planted a "knockout" rose in the front yard last summer. There were so many fuchsia-colored blooms it really did knock us out.

Getting to help these flowers and trees flourish has unleashed a new passion in me. Have you ever noticed how detailed and amazing a flower petal is? Or how perfect the one next to it is? Such amazing delicate creativity. As I see it, plants are living out their purpose, taking each season seemingly in stride. There are setbacks, yes, and uncertainty. And—perish the thought—rot could set in. But with pruning, water, and sun, most plants seem to come back even stronger than they were before.

It seems harder for me to find my purpose at times. Flowers bloom. Trees bear fruit. What am I supposed to do? In the past few years, I have transitioned from writer to teacher and back to writer again. I have sent one son off to college and am getting ready to send off another. An empty nest is looming in the next three years. I moved out of state and am finding my footing in new relationships. I have gone from lead pastor's wife to church member. I have been transplanted, pruned, and trimmed back. Rot has set in on occasion. But I have found that my purpose has less to do with my titles (gardener, writer, teacher, mom, pastor's wife) and more to do with *how* I live. Whether I am crafting a pretty paragraph or making my son's lunch, am I rooted in and nourished by the One who gives me life?

I am learning that my identity has to do with *Whose* I am, not who I am. Am I growing in the rich soil of Jesus's truth? Am I allowing Him to move in my heart? Am I open to the power of His Spirit? Am I honoring Him with my words and actions? I've been known to be a late bloomer, but I want my life to be a knockout because of the greatness of His love at work in my life. I want to reflect Jesus's goodness and faithfulness to those around me. I want His hope and beauty to work itself out through the ins and outs of my days. My purpose is to reveal His hope and peace in any way I can. How can I not? Jesus is truly glorious.

Jesus, I am rooted in You. You are with me through changing seasons. You help my roots grow deeper. You help me bloom. As I fall asleep tonight, I praise Your Holy Name for Your faithfulness and the beauty You bring into my life.

Just as I Am

BOB HOSTETLER

Just as I am—of that free love
The breadth, length, depth, and height to prove,
Here for a season, then above,
O Lamb of God, I come!

FROM THE POEM, "JUST AS I AM" BY CHARLOTTE ELLIOTT (1835)

One day when my daughter Aubrey was eleven or twelve years old, she and I went together to the grocery store. I was wearing my usual Saturday attire: an old Cincinnati Reds T-shirt, a pair of red cotton shorts, white socks, and white tennis shoes. As we walked side by side, approaching the store, I made a mistake: I asked for fashion advice.

"What do you say, Aubrey, should I tuck in my shirttail or leave it out?" I asked, tugging on my shirt.

She cocked her head to one side and looked me up and down. Her nose wrinkled. "*I* say you never wear that outfit again."

Ouch.

Fashion-conscious young girls can have strong opinions, especially when it comes to their fathers' clothing choices. But, embarrassingly, this exchange came after my wife—Aubrey's mother—had diligently worked on my personal appearance and style for nearly twenty years. I'd thought I'd made at least *some* progress and had even attained something approaching present-ability. But, clearly, my firstborn child thought otherwise.

I wish I could report that my sartorial instincts sharpened after that experience, but I don't think that's the case. I still seem to require careful attention from my wife and children—and even grandchildren—before venturing out in public. I'm still very much a work in progress—and not just in terms of my personal style.

Despite and perhaps even because of this, I take great comfort in the fact that Jesus accepts me, every day and in every moment. Ever since that long-ago day when I responded to the invitational hymn "Just as I Am" and received forgiveness of sins and newness of life, I am confident in His love, even when I don't feel

Don't Give Up on Doing Good

Most people want to do good in the world, whether it's helping an elderly neighbor get the mail, volunteering at a soup kitchen for the homeless, or raising money for an organization.

These are all great ways to give back, but sometimes we let our busy lives or negative thoughts prevent us from doing good.

When challenged by these negative thoughts, remember what the prophet Isaiah said, "Learn to do good. Seek justice. Help the oppressed. Defend the cause of orphans. Fight for the rights of widows."

We have the ability to lift up the banner of righteousness and justice. We can stand up for those who are in need. When we give back to the world, we not only help others, but we also feel good about ourselves.

"presentable." The Gospels are full of stories of Jesus's unconditional love for those others found unacceptable or unfit.

Bartimaeus comes to my mind. He was a blind man who spent his days at the side of the road begging from passersby. When he heard Jesus approaching, Bartimaeus called out, "Jesus, Son of David, have mercy on me!" Some of the people around him tried to silence him. After all, Bartimaeus was a beggar. He was unkempt. *Hardly* presentable. But Jesus heard the man's pleas, stopped, and called for him to come near.

"What do you want me to do for you?" Jesus asked him.

Bartimaeus said, "Rabbi, I want to see" (Mark 10:51, NIV).

Jesus could have asked, "Are you a Jew?" or "Do you believe in me?" He might have said, "Get someone to clean you up and then come back later," or even, "Are you sufficiently sorry for your sins?" But He didn't say any of those things or anything like them. He said, "Go, your faith has healed you" (Mark 10:52, NIV).

> *Hide yourself in God, so when a man wants to find you he will have to go there first.*
>
> SHANNON L. ALDER

I think also of the moment when Jesus entered the pool of Bethesda in Jerusalem where he met a friendless and dejected paralyzed man. This man, weak and alone, must have sometimes wondered, *How did I get here? How did I become* this?

John, the Gospel writer, says, "Jesus saw him lying there." He was surrounded, John writes, by "a great number of disabled people . . . the blind, the lame, the paralyzed." Yet Jesus saw *him*, and simply asked, "Do you want to get well?"

He didn't ask if the man had been "good" or if he was willing to give up his vices. Jesus didn't demand that he make himself more presentable. No, He just asked: "Do you want to get well?"

The man answered, "I have no one to help me into the pool when the water is stirred. While I am trying to get in, someone else goes down ahead of me," to which Jesus answered, "Get up! Pick up your mat and walk." And the man was healed (John 5:2–9, NIV).

So, when I come to Jesus in prayer each evening, I approach Him just as I am. I come, sometimes feeling blind and beggarly. At other times, I come feeling friendless and dejected. I come, weary and weathered. I come with all of the mistakes that I've made throughout the day.

And Jesus doesn't wrinkle His nose at me. He doesn't frown or shake His head. He doesn't tell me to quiet down or dust myself off or make myself a little more presentable. He sees me, welcomes me, holds me, forgives me, heals me, and restores my soul. Just as I am.

I can't express how much I need this acceptance and how highly I value it. How grateful I am, not only that Jesus accepted me years ago when I called out to Him for my soul's deliverance, but also that He invites and accepts me now. I rely on His acceptance, morning and evening. I need no other argument, no other plea, but that His blood was shed for me, and that always He bids me to come to find rest and renewal for my soul.

Jesus, I come to You in prayer tonight, my heart full of gratitude and wonder that You will receive, welcome, pardon, cleanse, and relieve me. I believe in Your promises to me.

Give Yourself Grace

JEANETTE LEVELLIE

But he answered me, "My grace is always more than enough for you, and my power finds its full expression through your weakness." So I will celebrate my weaknesses, for when I'm weak I sense more deeply the mighty power of Christ living in me.

2 CORINTHIANS 12:9 (TPT)

After speaking at a writer's conference, I mentally beat myself up for a silly remark I'd made during a panel discussion. On the stage. In front of 100 people. And I kept ruminating over this moment for *years*.

Each time this scene replayed in my mind, I relived my embarrassment. After years of listening to me berate myself, Jesus's gentle voice resonated in my heart. "Jeanette, those people that heard you a decade ago aren't lying awake thinking about you and wondering when you'll grow up." I sensed a smile in His voice.

"Besides," my Savior continued, "When you make a mistake, you're the only one who obsesses over it. All the others in the room feel relieved that they aren't the only ones who mess up."

I laughed. How ridiculous was it to think I had a monopoly on mistakes. That when I stumbled, the world stopped spinning and everyone who witnessed my lack of judgment stared in astonishment. Instead, the Lord seemed to imply, I was doing them a favor by proving that no one is exempt from making a faux pas.

My friend Cecil often ends his emails to me with the words, "Be kind to Jeanette." I love that. Cec knows that I'm often hard on myself. His encouragement helps me give the same amount

Forgiving When It's Not Easy

One of the hardest commandments of Jesus can be the order to forgive. Anything. Anyone. Seventy times seven. But how do we do this when whatever wrong we've suffered is raw—and our hurt feelings are still fresh? Worse yet is when the other person isn't sorry.

Corrie ten Boom wrote, "Forgiveness is an act of the will, and the will can function regardless of the temperature of the heart." The idea here is that we can separate our feelings from our wills—and sometimes we must. We tend to want to feel whatever we're doing. To feel love when we're supposed to be loving. To feel compassion when we're supposed to be kind. To feel bold when we need to be brave.

It's nice when our feelings match up with our will, but it's not always going to be that way. Forgiveness can be like this—only harder. We feel like we cannot forgive someone who has broken our hearts. Even if they are sorry, but especially when they're not. But Jesus is greater than our feelings. He provides us the power for any commandment He gives. And often, it's the power of the will. Do what's right in your will, and eventually your feelings will follow.

of grace to myself that I extend to others when they don't act perfectly.

If my husband, Kevin, spills coffee on the kitchen floor, I run to grab paper towels to help him clean it up. I never shout, "Oh, you clumsy fool," like I might if I spilled my own coffee. If my granddaughter, Grace, forgets to thank me when I give her a snack, I don't holler at her. I have an abundance of grace for the ones I love—and even strangers—because I want to pass along the immeasurable kindness Jesus has extended to me.

One of my favorite Bible verses is found in 2 Corinthians. The Apostle Paul, a former persecutor of Christians, had every reason to cringe at all the painful memories and missteps of his past life. Yet he chose to focus on Jesus's grace by rejoicing in his own weaknesses. He kept his eyes on Jesus, not his own shortcomings. He realized that you can't earn God's love by perfect behavior. You simply receive it by God's grace.

These days, I'm learning how to be kind to Jeanette. To quiet my heart, take some grace from Jesus's outstretched hand, and give it to myself. Sometimes I even look in the mirror and say, "I love you just as you are, and so does Jesus."

Jesus, thank You for showing me
Your heart of kindness and grace. Tonight,
as I leave the day behind and ready myself for
sleep, may I embrace a measure of that grace
and rest in Your love for me.

Blessed Intersections

BRENDA YODER

I was a stranger and you invited me in.

MATTHEW 25:35 (NIV)

When each of my kids was in middle school, usually the summer before their eighth-grade year, I took him or her on a summer road trip. I looked forward to these excursions as much as my kids did. I've always loved traveling and meeting new people. I've been known to strike up conversations with random strangers. My kids, as teenagers, would often corner me when I finished talking to someone and usher me out to our car so I wouldn't begin chatting with yet another person.

Road trips, though, are made for impromptu conversations. I love talking to storekeepers, waitresses, and other neighborly people. I'm fascinated by commonalities and shared interests that connect me to strangers. One of the most meaningful such interactions happened when I met a woman from Indiana on my last road trip, with my youngest son, Kent.

We'd gone from our home in Indiana to Virginia, and then on to Charleston, North Carolina. It was a lot of driving for one person, and I felt especially weary on our return. On the stretch home from Charleston to northern Indiana, I had driven several hours and night was falling. In the darkness, I had a hard time staying awake. I knew, for our safety, we needed to call it a night and find a hotel. I drove off the interstate and stopped at the first hotel I found. Kent stayed in the car while I went inside to check on room availability.

I walked past a van with Indiana license plates that was parked in front of the hotel lobby. I stood in line with one other woman as we waited for the desk clerk to come out from her office. I asked the woman if she was from Indiana. She said yes, and we made mutual Hoosier connections. We talked as if we had known each other for years. After we got our room keys, we took our conversation outside. We chatted for what seemed like hours under a lamppost that shone right on us. We laughed, cried, and finally knew it was time to end the conversation so we could go to bed. It felt awkward parting ways with someone who felt like a long-lost friend. As we began our goodbyes, I asked her if I could pray with her. She said yes. So, under the lamplight in the dark of night, we held hands and prayed for one another before heading to our respective rooms.

> *I've learned that people will forget what you said, people will forget what you did, but people will never forget how you made them feel.*
>
> MAYA ANGELOU

I was embarrassed by how long I had been away from Kent. How would I explain such a lengthy absence just to check in? I opened the door to the car, and he said, "Only you, Mom, would pray with a stranger in the parking lot of a hotel." He'd witnessed the whole scene that had played out under the lamplight.

I laughed, but I didn't apologize for not returning sooner. The midnight prayer meeting was a moment I'll never forget. More

The True Meaning of Love

For couples, praying together and enjoying each other's company can help keep your souls connected.

Of course, you will have ups and downs, but love is like faith, and without highs and lows, it will not grow. Relationships and marriages that last prove that it takes great effort, forgiveness, and patience.

Love gives us the strength to work through the difficult and messy realities we all face. Love also teaches us the value of prayer, especially to get us through financial setbacks, family issues, and personal disappointments. Fun, laughter, and silliness are important as well.

than that, I felt satisfaction knowing my son saw Jesus at work in ways no one could orchestrate. Curiosity, conversation, and prayer connected two people who were far from home. I saw how Jesus connects us with other people, but also gives us an opportunity to interact with Himself in the form of a stranger.

Jesus, thank You for the human interactions You plan for me. Equip me to embrace moments where I can be an encouragement to another person, and thank You for all the times a stranger has encouraged me. I end this day in gratitude for all the people whose lives intersect with mine and ask that You bless them tonight.

Freedom through Boundaries

LOGAN ELIASEN

*The L*ORD *is my shepherd; I shall not want.*
He makes me lie down in green pastures. He leads
me beside still waters. He restores my soul.

PSALM 23:1–3 (ESV)

The September sun was low as I drove home from work. It had been a long day. Getting out of the office by five in the afternoon was no longer the norm, but the exception. I parked my car and reached for the briefcase in my back seat. It was Thursday night, but I still had a lot of work to do before the weekend.

The weekend wouldn't be much of a break, either. I needed to clean out my car before the weather got cold. I wanted to put the finishing touches on a writing project. And I had loose ends to tie up from the week's work.

My phone buzzed. *Please don't be work*, I thought.

I looked down at the screen to see that my friend Kendall was calling. I picked up, and he cut right to the chase.

"You. Me. Camping in Minnesota this weekend," he said. "Are you in?"

Kendall and I had gone to law school together. After we graduated, I had remained in Iowa, while Kendall and his wife,

Kayleen, moved out of state. Although I rarely saw Kendall, he was still one of my best friends. I would love to spend a weekend with him. But it was at least a three-hour drive to Minnesota, and I felt that I just didn't have the time.

"I really want to," I said. "But I'm so busy right now."

"Logan," he said. "When was the last time you took a break?"

He had a point. I couldn't remember when I last got away and relaxed. Also, I'd wanted to go camping all year and, with winter coming, soon it would be too late.

"OK!" I said. "I'm in! What do I need to bring?"

I woke up early the next morning to pack, then I worked a full day in the office and left town that evening. Soon, I was driving down a quiet Minnesota road. Businesses became sparse as the foliage became thick. Slowly, my phone lost reception. Three bars. Then two. Then one. Freedom!

The problem was, I didn't feel entirely free. I knew text messages and emails would stack up while I was off the grid. Still, it felt good to roll the windows down and listen to the radio. When I pulled into the state park, Kendall was waiting for me at his campsite. He waved at me as I parked. Together we unloaded my Jeep, and then I strung my hammock between two trees and hung a rain fly overhead. Kendall had already started a fire.

"It's so good to see you," Kendall said, prodding the fire with a stick. "It's been too long."

Kendall and I caught up on each other's lives as the fire blazed. We shared stories and reminisced about law school. When flames became embers, we headed to our hammocks.

"I've got some fun planned for tomorrow," Kendall said.

"Can't wait," I said, drifting off to sleep.

I woke to the sound of birds instead of my usual buzzing alarm. The sun filtered through the rain fly above me. I felt peaceful. Then, I thought of all the work I could have already finished this morning had I been home. Guilt burned in my chest. I looked over the edge of the hammock. Kendall stood over the fire pit, scrambling eggs on a skillet. I stretched my arms and legs then joined him.

"So, what's the plan for today," I asked.

Kendall passed me a plate of eggs. Then he pointed to a kayak lying alongside his car. I hadn't noticed it the previous night.

"There's a stream nearby," he said. "I thought we could spend the day exploring it."

Together, we cleaned the dishes and then carried the kayak to the stream, which was wide and lazy. Kendall took the front seat, and I took the back. As we paddled on

> *Of one thing I am certain, the body is not the measure of healing—peace is the measure.*
>
> GEORGE MELTON

the water, I started to feel at ease. Suddenly my phone buzzed in my pocket, startling me. We must have crossed an invisible line into an area of phone reception. I wondered if I could check my messages without breaking the cadence of our rowing.

"How has work been?" Kendall asked, cutting through my thoughts.

For a moment, the only sounds were trickling water and the dip of our paddles.

"It's a lot to handle," I said. "I want to be the best lawyer I can be. But I also want to enjoy life. Most days, it feels like there isn't enough time to do both."

The two of us fell quiet again, and we just paddled.

"How do you and Kayleen manage it all?" I asked, breaking the silence. "You're both lawyers."

"Boundaries," Kendall said. "Kayleen and I have always established boundaries. We work hard at our jobs. But once we get home, the computers go away. We can talk about work before dinner, but not at the table. If we didn't keep those boundaries, I don't think our marriage would work."

My hand tightened on the paddle. *Boundaries*. There wasn't much separating my home life from my work life. They bled together. Most of the time, work overpowered the rest. I had been under the impression that, in order to do my best at work, I needed to work most of the time. But what if that wasn't the case? Kendall's method of drawing boundaries seemed to make him a good husband and a good lawyer. Everything had a time. Everything had a place.

> *A well-spent day brings happy sleep.*
>
> LEONARDO DA VINCI

I then thought about Jesus's ministry. He spent much of his time with crowds of people, teaching and healing them. But He also made it a point to share moments with only His close disciples. And, at times, Jesus retreated to spend time alone with His Father.

Kendall stopped paddling, and I followed suit. We drifted down the stream, and he pointed to a hawk flying above the tree line. Kendall was focused on the here and now. He wasn't thinking about briefs he needed to file or deadlines he needed to meet. He was truly enjoying this trip.

I slipped my phone out of my pocket. But, instead of checking my messages, I shut it off. This would be my first boundary. And, in setting that boundary, I began to feel free.

Jesus, thank You for restoring my soul. Thank You for times with dear friends and out in nature, times that help me to slow down and recalibrate my mind and spirit. Thank You for the example You set of getting away on Your own to rest and to pray.

Unexpected Gifts

LORI HATCHER

Whatever is true, whatever is noble, whatever is right, whatever is pure, whatever is lovely, whatever is admirable—if anything is excellent or praiseworthy—think about such things.

PHILIPPIANS 4:8 (NIV)

My family attended our town's Fourth of July parade every year when I was a child. One year, a kind-faced man in a striped hat marched beside the bands, fire engines, and Revolutionary War reenactors. As he walked in step with the beat of the drum, he drew near to the curb where my sisters and I sat. Reaching into his vest pocket, he extracted three shiny half dollar coins and pressed them into our hands. We shouted our thanks and quickly pocketed our treasures; his kindness made a special day even happier!

It's been a long time since I received that unexpected gift, but the memory lingers. Although I never saw that man again, God has brought many other kind and generous people into my life. Like him, they leave unexpected treasures behind and make me smile. My friend Lisa is one such person.

I met Lisa when I was a young mother, struggling to figure out how to parent and homeschool my two daughters. Although she was spiritually mature and wise, she never made me feel like she was judging me or looking down on me. Every time we hung out together, she'd say something that lifted my spirits and built me up.

I remember, for example, her response after I shared feelings of frustration with her one gloomy winter day.

"Some days I spend so much time breaking up squabbles and making sure my kids do what they're supposed to do that I barely have time to teach math and reading. They complain about doing their chores and wait till the last minute to finish their assignments," I said. "Yesterday I sent the youngest to clean her room. She finished in ten minutes and ran out the door. When I checked her work, she'd stuffed everything under the bed and into the closet. Sometimes I get so angry I yell." I looked down, afraid to meet Lisa's gaze.

> *Life is a web of intersections and choices. Your first choice is to recognize an intersection. Your second choice is to be grateful for it.*
>
> RYAN LILLY

"Lori, you're doing a great job," she said, "You're building good habits into your children. It takes time to see results. Remember what Deuteronomy 6 says about training our children 'when you sit at home and when you walk along the road, when you lie down and when you get up'? One day your efforts will bear fruit."

I let out a deep sigh, grateful for her words.

Lisa has the gift of encouragement as well as a God-given ability to see the good side of everything—even disobedient children and difficult days—and discern something redemptive in it all. But more than just saying something to help me feel better, Lisa points me to the hope and encouragement of God's Word and Jesus's example. This makes all the difference.

When I lose perspective, Lisa helps bring me back on track, spiritually and otherwise. She often cites a verse from the Bible or an example that Jesus has set for us. She exemplifies what the apostle Paul spoke of when he instructed the Philippian believers to reflect on whatever is lovely and admirable. She calls attention to what's noble. She praises what is true.

The coins that the kind man dropped into my sisters' and my hands that Fourth of July had little material value, but they brought us great delight. They made us feel appreciated, valued, and seen. The same is true of carefully chosen words of affirmation. And encouraging words that are based on the truth of

Positive Thinking Quotes from Norman Vincent Peale

Author, minister, and founder of Guideposts, Norman Vincent Peale is best known as the father of positive thinking. Here are a few of his favorite sayings on how changing your thoughts can change your life.

- Love life and it will love you right back.
- How you think about a problem is more important than the problem itself, so always think positively.
- Do your best and leave the results to God.
- Life is either a great experience, or a small one, dependent on the quality and character of the thoughts we think.
- Sing at least one song every day.

Scripture or the example of Jesus are all the more powerful and life-giving. Unlike a gift of money, the twin treasures of affirmation and biblical encouragement never run out but are like seeds that take root and blossom in our lives.

Lord, thank You for the friends who encourage and sustain my spirit. Thank You, Jesus, for modeling true friendship by Your example of loving Your friends well. Thank You for noticing me and gifting me with Your grace.

Shining a Light

NORM STOLPE

*Let your light shine before others, that they may
see your good deeds and glorify your Father in heaven.*

MATTHEW 5:16 (NIV)

Before the COVID-19 pandemic, I joined a support group, sponsored by the Alzheimer's Association, for caregivers. We met every month at the Lutheran Home in Milwaukee. Listening to the experiences and wisdom of others who had been on this journey longer than I have was both helpful and encouraging. Instead of awkwardly explaining issues I'm confronting to someone with limited familiarity, these folks understood the challenges I currently face as my wife's caregiver. Though our group was diverse, people shared both their spiritual needs and sources of spiritual strength freely, whatever their religious backgrounds or convictions. I was not the most vocal participant, but people quickly figured out that I was a retired pastor.

A woman named Pat and I typically sat on opposite sides at the same end of the table. We got acquainted during the informal chatting before and after the meetings. When I first started attending, she reported that her husband was coming near the end of his life. On their journey, she'd learned the importance of self-care and she regularly reminded us that practicing self-care was essential as we looked after our loved ones. At one meeting, when prompted by the leader, she told us that her husband had died shortly after our last meeting, and she was navigating the emotions of grief and relief. On the way out that morning, she handed me a tightly folded note as she walked to her car. It read, "I think you can help me" and included her phone number.

I called her that afternoon. During the course of our call, she told me that she was raised in a Roman Catholic home, attended Catholic school, and still identified as Catholic, though the prolonged caring for her husband precluded church participation. After such a long time away from church, she was asking new religious questions and thought I could help her on her search for answers. Although I am generally familiar with Catholic theology, I didn't feel I should be the one helping her sort out her questions. She responded that, from my participation in the support group, she knew I was a person of faith who loved Jesus and had spiritual insight. I was amazed that she concluded all of that from my limited contributions to the support group conversations. But I also told myself that though I was officially retired, I still was called to point people to Jesus and nurture them spiritually.

I have a friend who teaches theology at Marquette University who was able to put me in touch with a Catholic priest willing to talk with Pat. At the next support group meeting, Pat thanked me for the referral and with relief said, "He was exactly who I needed to speak with. He assured me that my questions were normal and in line with trusting God and consistent with the teaching of the Roman Catholic Church." Satisfied that the priest and I were actually on the same page, Pat then asked if we could get together to talk again.

My wife participated in a weekly program called Mind Effects for people with early memory loss, also at the Lutheran Home. So Pat and I set a time to meet in the café there while Candy attended Mind Effects. By then, Pat had met with the priest, and I mostly listened to her account of how assuring that conversation was for her. She also told me how much she appreciated my insights along the way and asked if we could get together again. Over time, Pat, Candy, and I got to know each other better at the Lutheran Home. Pat got to know more of our family too.

> *The purpose of life is a life of purpose.*
>
> ROBERT BYRNE

When COVID-19 changed our world, Candy and I could no longer meet with Pat in person, but our relationship with her continues via email. With no real schedule, we probably exchange emails about once a week. Pat says I have helped her find her way as a new widow who wants to continue to grow in faith. I know she is a healthy reminder for me to keep up with my self-care: sleep, eating, exercise, pace of life. Her emails always remind me to breathe. We have become prayer partners, bringing each other's burdens, hopes, and fears to Jesus.

I know that nourishing other people spiritually is not the obvious purpose of everyone's life. Out of her journey with her husband's Alzheimer's, Pat's consistent acknowledgment of the importance of self-care became a fruitful purpose for her. She also helped me accept that Jesus shines His purpose through me, even though my official pastoral career is over. I thank Him for shining His love through His people.

Scripture that Reinforces Our Purpose

He has saved us and called us to a holy life—not because of anything we have done but because of his own purpose and grace. This grace was given us in Christ Jesus before the beginning of time.
   —2 Timothy 1:9 (NIV)

For it is God who is at work in you to will and to act in order to fulfill his good purpose.
   —Philippians 2:13 (NIV)

Then make my joy complete by being like-minded, having the same love, being one in spirit and of one mind.
   —Philippians 2:2 (NIV)

Each of you should give what you have decided in your heart to give, not reluctantly or under compulsion, for God loves a cheerful giver.
   —2 Corinthians 9:7 (NIV)

Jesus, thank You for friends who affirm my gifts and Your hand in my life. Thank You for putting people in my path who teach, support, and encourage me. I thank You for the love You shine on me.

Hard Training, Rich Harvest

LORI ROELEVELD

*No discipline seems pleasant at the time,
but painful.*

HEBREWS 12:11 (NIV)

The men at the track believed I was a terrible mother. I could see it on their faces. Their whispers hinted at judgment. Momentarily, I doubted myself, but then I remembered my daughter Hannah's goal.

By age ten, she'd been studying karate for four years. It was her passion. Hannah was a joy to watch. Her katas, or karate moves, were crisp, strong, and precise. Her weapons practice fierce. Her sparring was powerful and controlled. Watching from the parent chairs, I was in awe. Karate had helped Hannah when, at six, she'd struggled with social anxiety. My girl was "all in" the moment she stepped onto the mat. It was worth every hour and every penny we invested in her martial arts training to see her confidence grow.

Now she was in training to test for her black belt. This was her goal, and she was committed to it, but there was a Goliath in her path. Every black belt candidate had to pass a physical test that included a timed three-mile run. Hannah was ready with all her forms. She'd passed a written test. She'd conditioned herself to achieve the push-ups, crunches, and army crawls. But running was her kryptonite.

To make things worse, her test would be on a Saturday afternoon in mid-July, and we were experiencing unprecedented heat that summer. I'd talked with her pediatrician, her karate teacher, and several friends who were also runners, so we knew the best way to prepare was to train in the same conditions.

I learned about proper hydration, the right pre-running foods, and the best shoes. Now she had to do the work. Hannah and her fellow candidates were expected to run three miles, three times a week. We scheduled one of her weekly practice runs for the same time as her test—2 p.m. Smack dab in the heat of the day.

> *Character cannot be developed in ease and quiet. Only through experience of trial and suffering can the soul be strengthened, ambition inspired, and success achieved.*
>
> HELEN KELLER

This is where the men found us on a stifling Saturday afternoon. They were out for a walk, and my unhappy child drew their attention. It was hard not to notice us out under the unforgiving sun or not to see her jogging around the school track, tears streaming down her cheeks, and me on the sidelines urging her on whenever she slowed or indicated a desire to quit.

"Does your daughter want to be out there running? She doesn't look very happy," one of the men said. Their eyes narrowed, studying me as if I were a monster.

I felt a little like a monster. Neither Hannah nor I have great tolerance for the heat. I was miserable just standing on the sidelines. There were many moments that I wanted to choose a different course. Other parents had allowed their children to give up. They were sitting in air-conditioned rooms right now, enjoying movies and cold drinks. No one was questioning those parents. But at the end of every practice run, we'd tick another day off the calendar, and she'd renew her determination to pass the test and reach her goal.

Now all that misery is a distant memory. Looking back, I remember feeling like every single run would last for an eternity, but it didn't. The training did its work, and my daughter reached her goal not once, but twice.

She's a young woman now, a wife and a mother with a small farm. There are moments when, in the stifling heat, it might be easier not to clean out a goat pen or set up a water trough for the pigs, but she has developed the strength to endure temporary discomfort in order to achieve a greater purpose. Her heart for Jesus is strong and she is not afraid of hard work. The hardship of that training had lasting impact on her health, character, and ability to work toward her goals.

Similarly, the struggles Jesus has allowed into my life have, by His grace, produced in me a greater harvest. He loves me and He is good, even when I am shedding tears and straining with the effort of life. He is with me, cheering me on as I round every curve. I know for certain He waits for me at every finish line.

Jesus, help me trust that there is a greater purpose in the struggles You allow in my life every day. Use them to develop in me a harvest of righteousness and peace.

A Regular

BETH GORMONG

*I long, as every other human being, to be
at home wherever I find myself.*

MAYA ANGELOU

I swung open the door to my local pizza joint, Wise Pies, and was greeted with a huge smile by Kory, the twentysomething man behind the counter. The blackboard wall behind him listed the variety of pizzas available. As I approached the counter, Kory slid a wooden pizza spatula under a slice of my favorite type of pizza, the WOW. This New York–style pizza was topped with sun-dried tomatoes, spinach, fresh tomatoes, pesto, garlic, and feta and mozzarella cheeses—a deliciously strange combination. I imagined folding it in half like a sandwich and taking a huge bite. I'd been craving a hot slice of WOW since last week. I meet my girlfriends here every Thursday for lunch, and rarely order anything else.

"Side salad with ranch dressing and water, right?" Kory asked. I smiled, nodded yes and he called my order through the back window. I love being a "regular." But it wasn't always that way.

I resisted calling this town my home for several years; I thought my move here was only temporary. My husband had left his career in the ministry to help out on the family farm and then fell in love with the work. So the days here turned into months, and the months became twenty-six years. And through most of those years I denied the obvious fact that we were here to stay. I didn't put down any roots. I complained about the smelly sewage plant next to the mall, the multitude of trains slowing down trips to work, and the small town feel where everyone grew up together—a fact that reinforced my sense that I didn't belong.

Part of Something Bigger

The connections we have with those in our lives remind us that we are a part of something bigger than ourselves.

Consider your dearest friends, those for whom you feel a connection without judgment, strain, or competition—a connection filled with unconditional love, respect, and appreciation, where you can be yourself completely.

Although you likely treasure these deep connections, there are other relationships that might not be so deep, yet they give you energy, direction, focus, strength, or simply a good feeling. For example, think about the connections you have with the mail carrier, the UPS driver, an acquaintance at the gym, a new friend from work. These connections matter too. They remind us that we are a part of something bigger than ourselves. Without both kinds of connections, we can feel less rooted in our daily lives, less a part of our world around us.

May we be mindful and grateful for the connections in our lives and how each and every one contributes to us feeling a part of something greater. We all need this. We all deserve this. These connections are gifts from Jesus.

My heart grew bitter. Life hadn't turned out the way I planned. I now lived on a Midwest farm, outside a town full of people I didn't grow up with, and where I didn't feel I belonged. It wasn't what I had planned for my life.

When my husband joked that we'd live in our house until we died, I'd laugh and respond, "Only if I die first. Because if you go first, I'm moving into an RV and hitting the road." The laughter only slightly hid the honesty of my response. This attitude lasted years, until one day I realized I had lived here longer than anywhere else. When people asked where I was from, I had to answer, "Outside of Terre Haute." I grew tired of being unhappy. The only option was to start liking my "hometown." I prayed to see this place through different eyes. I asked Jesus to soften my hardened heart.

Slowly He began to open my eyes to the beauty of this place and its people. I found a lovely park just a few miles from home where my daughters and I went for picnics and took walks by the pioneer village, exploring the log cabins and watching the ducks and geese floating on the pond. Our family started a tradition of going out to eat at a local Mexican restaurant after church on Sundays. One day, our favorite waiter brought my husband's burrito

> *The wise woman builds her house, but with her own hands the foolish one tears hers down.*
>
> PROVERBS 14:1 (NIV)

before he even ordered it. I found a group of kindhearted women to knit with on Tuesday afternoons. Over time, my Bible study group morphed into my weekly Thursday lunch date. We friends grew closer to Jesus and to each other through deep, honest conversations and light, silly moments of shared laughter. One day Kory, from Wise Pies, asked how long we had been meeting. I looked around the table as my friend Jody answered, "A long, long time. Way back when Bella Rosa's was still open."

His answer? "That was *years* ago."

These women are now some of my oldest friends. Today I have friends in every corner of this town and the surrounding communities. I've learned where the hidden gems here are, like a coffeeshop where a friend paints murals across the walls regularly and the service staff writes sweet notes of encouragement on the top of every cup of coffee. Or the Chinese restaurant whose owner knows and asks about my daughters. And the farmers market where my neighbor sells a vast variety of heirloom tomatoes. My evening walks with the dog often lead to stops on the road, bent over a neighbor's car window catching up the latest news. Now I usually see at least one person I know at every outing.

I'm a regular.

What started out as a temporary situation became my place to belong, but only because I gave up what I had planned and allowed Jesus to give me new vision and a tender heart.

Lord, thank You for opening my eyes and heart to the goodness of the place where I am. Thank You for softening my heart into a shape that fits right where it is. May I always stay pliable to Your will for my life.

What Brings Peace

BOB HOSTETLER

I wish you knew today what would bring you peace.

LUKE 19:42 (NCV)

Years ago, I found myself—for the first time in my life—in a battle with low mood and mild depression. That's the bad news. The good news is that, a few years earlier, I had the wisdom and foresight to seek out a professional counselor.

When he asked me, in our first session, "Why are you here?" I gave a great deal of thought to my answer.

"I think I'm doing pretty well right now," I said. "But I know there'll come a time when I'll need a counselor. I'm just giving myself a head start and preparing for that day."

He tilted his head to one side and said, "Well, that's new!"

This decision paid off because when my stress levels rocketed and I was struggling, I already had a relationship with a trusted professional. Once, early on, he'd asked me to make a list of the things that nourish me. It was what some people refer to as a "gratitude list." In my case, books; time with my wife, kids, and grandkids; and hikes and time spent outside fill me up. At that point, he also asked me to make a list of the things that sap my strength. These include criticism, hurry, overwork, and unnecessary meetings.

The Gospel writer Luke relates an incident in his account of our Lord's life when Jesus wept over Jerusalem. You might remember it. But do you remember the "wish" Jesus made? We don't usually think of Jesus suffering from a low mood or making wishes, but in that case, I think he expressed a combination of both a wish he had and a lament. He said, "I wish you knew today what would bring you peace."

Some things bring you peace, and some things sap your peace.

Some things restore and energize you; some things deplete you and depress you.

Some things nourish you, and some things leave you malnourished.

As I learned more about the things that nourish me and bring me peace, I added something important to my list: journaling. My counselor suggested that I end each day by listing at least three things for which I was grateful. My journal's pages soon

Bible Verses that Inspire Gratitude

The LORD has done it this very day; let us rejoice today and be glad.
—Psalm 118:24 (NIV)

Let the peace of Christ rule in your hearts, since as members of one body you were called to peace. And be thankful.
—Colossians 3:15 (NIV)

Give thanks to the LORD, for he is good; his love endures forever.
—Psalm 107:1 (NIV)

filled with nightly prayers of thanksgiving to Jesus for all of the positive, life-giving, peace-bringing things in my life. My journal catalogued new blessings: a call from a friend, a scrumptious meal, a sunny day, and a fond memory among them. Because I also like variety, my nightly list eventually came to include even the tiniest or most overlooked blessings including puppies, oranges, and the beauty of the changing seasons.

After doing this for some time, I devoted a separate journal to prayers of gratitude. Over time, I realized that nurturing a grateful heart was one of the things that brings me peace and lifts my mood. It restores and energizes me. I discovered that even after the hardest and most discouraging day, giving "thanks to the Lord for his faithful love and his wondrous works for all humanity" (Psalm 107:8, CSB) gives me hope, strength, and peace.

Dear Jesus, thank You for being here with me tonight. As I move toward sleep, I am grateful for all You have given me.

Message on the Mountain

DURWOOD SMITH

*At sunset, the people brought to Jesus all who
had various kinds of sickness, and laying
his hands on each one, he healed them.*

LUKE 4:40 (NIV)

It was preposterous that I would even try. Minutes before we
reached the trailhead, we had driven past Fallen Leaf Lake
in the California Sierras. I wondered whether the lake's name
subtly mocked me. At age twenty-nine, I felt like my body was an
autumn leaf, fallen onto rocky ground. Withered. Useless. Spent.
Two cancer surgeries and chemotherapy had ravaged my body
that summer. For months an army of Christian warriors prayed
for my healing.

Shouldering my forty-pound backpack would test my stamina. Was I well enough to attempt this eight-mile hike from 5,000
feet to 9,000 feet above sea level on the very first day? *I can do
this; I have to do this.* This four-day hiking trip carried secret questions, ones I was keeping to myself. They made me feel restless,
unsure. *Was I cured? Am I well? Had God healed me? How can I
know?*

Bob and Ralph, my hiking buddies, shot out ahead of me up
the trail and around the bend, the steep incline melting away

beneath their strong legs. A former Olympic decathlon trainee, Bob was tall and robust. To him a sixty-pound pack was nothing more than a flea on the back of a bull. Ralph, seasoned by outdoor work as an employee of the California Highway Department, thrived in the sun.

"Hey, guys, wait up!" I called, and my friends shouted back encouragement and slowed their pace.

Trail switchbacks crisscrossed the gravel mountainside as the path gained elevation. The air grew thinner. Above the tree line now, the heat intensified. We would hike higher still, where, surprisingly, we would find ourselves with a new problem: cold.

Having voluntarily stopped chemotherapy treatments because of complications, I now had questions. Actually, one question: *Was I going to be all right?* On the trail, perspiration trickled down my

> *The more you lose yourself in something bigger than yourself, the more energy you will have.*
>
> NORMAN VINCENT PEALE

forehead and stung my eyes. Far away from any possible emergency rescue, I told God and myself, *If anything's still wrong with me, this is where it will show up.* It was a comfort knowing Jesus endured testing in the wilderness. *He "made it." Maybe I can too.* I didn't fear death, but my secret question lingered. *Am I well? If only I could be sure, I would be in a kind of paradise. My soul would find rest.*

We reached 9,000 feet and set up camp just down slope from a snowbank.

"Where's Bob?" I asked Ralph.

"Oh, behind those bushes," Ralph said. "He's not feeling so great. Thin air, stress of the hike, all that."

"With that snowbank just up slope, temperatures are dropping fast," I noted. "I'll make a fire." I didn't feel the least bit sick, maybe even a little energized.

Returning to camp with firewood I asked, "Where's Ralph?"

"Oh, his stomach wasn't feeling too good. He's over there behind some bushes."

Could I be the one with plenty of stamina?

A sound stomach?

Am I well? A feeling of hope fluttered in my chest.

"You know, guys," I announced, "when this hike is over I'm going straight to Burger King to order a Double Whopper with cheese and a huge Pepsi."

A Recipe for Peace

Try this recipe of just three ingredients—prayer, supplication, and thanksgiving—to enter into nightly rest and peace.

First, begin just talking to God and laying out all the things you have going on. You'll find this gives you a calm sense of being able to sort through the tasks. There is no need to use fancy words or to disguise what you are feeling, because after all, you are talking to God, and what would be the point of not being honest?

The word *supplication*, from a biblical perspective, is associated with bending of the knees. Kneeling is a sign of humility. Tonight, if possible, talk to God while kneeling before getting into bed.

The final ingredient is thanksgiving. Thank God that He is faithful, has heard your prayer, and through Jesus Christ, has set a guard of peace over your heart.

"I don't want to hear about food," growled Ralph.

Wait a minute, I thought to myself, *people with cancer usually don't have a good appetite.*

Each of us bedded down, but I was up at 3 a.m. Waiting for morning light, I shivered and prayed for an early sunrise, still wondering: *Am I well? Dear Jesus, am I well?*

The next day we trudged two hours over the snowcap and descended into a valley. Crossing the swampy river, we stopped, built a small fire, and stood in the smoke to escape the mosquitos while we ate lunch. Just like before I had cancer, the mosquitoes still chose to bite me. *A good sign?* In wet hiking boots we slogged up the next slope to 9,000 feet again, crossing through a narrow pass. A thousand feet below us lay the glimmering blue waters of a lake so beautiful it defied description. Although I hadn't slept long the night before, I felt strong, rested somehow.

"Wait a minute, what lake is that?" I asked.

"Check the trail map, let's see where we are," Bob said.

"Here we are," said Ralph. "It's called Lake Aloha, right here on the map. Let's camp there for the night. Looks too beautiful to pass up. I think we have stumbled into paradise."

Paradise.

We set up camp lakeside. Carrying boulders for two hours from the shoreline, I constructed a windbreak on the ground at the head of my sleeping bag. I began to add it up; physical stamina, strong stomach, great appetite, mosquito bites, two hours of steady work. *Is there a message here?* In my heart, I heard Jesus say, "Go in peace. Your faith has made you well." Unseen angels had taken care of me, and Jesus had healed me and given me comfort.

That first night home after the hike, I rested, no chill breeze from mountains of fear could wake me from my peaceful sleep. I was well!

Thank You, Lord for seeing me through the hard journeys I have gone on. You are always with me, in unexpected ways. Thank You for making weakness into strength, fear into confidence, and doubt into certainty. Thank You for the adventure of following You.

Much to Learn

LOGAN ELIASEN

*A cheerful heart is good medicine,
but a crushed spirit dries up the bones.*

PROVERBS 17:22 (NIV)

Sport, my five-month-old Labrador puppy, barreled between my legs and across the living room floor. He circled around the room in a rush of fur then raced down the hallway.

"Sport!" I shouted. "Here!"

This chase had begun when I had heard Sport chewing on something. I still wasn't sure what was in his mouth, but Sport knew he was in trouble. Now I could hear him scampering around in my bedroom. When I entered, I could see his tail sticking out from under my bed. I crouched down and felt around under the bed until I made contact with a paw. I held tight and pulled out the wriggling puppy. Clamped in his jaws was an ink pen.

"This is not for dogs," I said, shaking the pen at him. I pocketed the pen, then picked him up. "This is why you can't be free in the house," I said, as I deposited him in the playpen that took up the bulk of my dining room.

Sport stared at me and then lowered his head.

I felt bad keeping Sport captive in the pen, but every time I gave him freedom, he would knock over furniture or chew up a book or something else. I wanted good things for Sport. I loved him. But he constantly seemed to be testing that love and exhausting my patience.

Several weeks later, Sport and I visited my parents' home. I talked with my mom while Sport sniffed around, exploring his new environment. My parents' older dog, Rugby, lay quietly in the middle of the room. Rugby watched Sport with apprehension.

"How is training Sport going?" my mom asked.

Sport attempted to snag a throw pillow from the sofa.

"No," I told him, removing the pillow from his reach. I turned back toward my mom.

"Training isn't going well. Sport doesn't sit. He doesn't stay," I said. "He's wild and adventurous and constantly getting into trouble."

"He's just being a puppy," my mom said.

"I know," I said. "But I'm tired of him being a puppy."

I looked around the room to find Sport. He was crouched, hiding just outside of Rugby's field of vision.

Sport sprang at Rugby. Rugby howled.

"No!" I shouted. "Bad dog." I grabbed Sport and returned to the sofa while holding him tightly.

"I just don't know what to do with him," I said.

Sport whined.

"Have you thought about enrolling him in a puppy class?" my mom asked.

I held Sport out at arm's length, facing me.

"Should I take you to dog school?" I asked him.

Sport twisted, then let out a yowl.

"You should take that as a yes," my mom said.

On the first day of puppy class, I was nervous. I wanted Sport to become the best dog he could be. But I was concerned he would be out of control. Sport strained against his leash as we entered the classroom. The room was filled with pairs of dogs and owners. Most of the dogs were barking. Sport joined in.

"Quiet, boy," I said.

He responded with a howl.

A woman at the front of the room whistled over the barks. The noise grew quieter.

"We are going to start class by letting your puppies acclimate to each other," the woman said. "Go ahead and let your dogs explore."

Sport paraded around, exploring the owners and their dogs. Soon, an older man with a large husky approached. Sport's ears perked up, and his body became rigid. The husky leaned forward, and Sport gave a low growl. The growl deepened as the husky came closer. Suddenly, Sport lunged and snapped at the husky.

"No, Sport!" I shouted. I reeled Sport in, pulling him back.

Having heard the outburst, the instructor came alongside me.

"Everything OK?" she asked.

Sport strained against the leash. The husky remained several feet away.

"We had a standoff," I said.

Sport began growling at the husky again.

"Sport," I said. "No!"

The instructor looked at Sport, then at me.

"Do you use positive reinforcement with Sport?" she asked.

"What do you mean?" I asked.

"There are two ways to train dogs," she said. "You can either negatively respond to bad behavior or positively encourage good behavior. I recommend positive reinforcement—let me show you."

She took Sport's leash and led him closer to the husky. Sport growled. The instructor reached into her pocket and pulled out a handful of treats.

"Are you meeting a new friend, Sport?" she asked. She crouched and slipped Sport treats, one at a time. He wagged his tail as he gobbled them down.

Meanwhile, the husky begun sniffing Sport, but now Sport didn't even seem to notice.

> *We can complain because rose bushes have thorns, or rejoice because thorns have roses.*
>
> ALPHONSE KARR

"That's a good boy, Sport," the instructor said.

Distracted by praise and treats, Sport had forgotten about the standoff.

"Dogs thrive from positivity," the instructor said. "Sometimes, negative reactions are necessary. But too much negativity will frustrate your dog."

By now the husky had moved on, and Sport was waiting patiently for another treat.

"Most of the time, we can turn bad interactions or behaviors into good ones," the instructor said. "It's all about what we choose to focus on."

I thought back over the last several months. For the most part, I had focused on Sport's bad behaviors. When he had chewed on things, I scolded him instead of providing appropriate toys.

When Sport was wild, I had penned him up instead of giving him room to run.

I considered the mistakes I made in my own life. How bleak would life be if I focused on my flaws and mistakes rather than Christ's forgiveness? No wonder focusing on the negative would be frustrating for Sport. If I wanted Sport to be a good dog, I needed to start treating him like one.

The instructor gave Sport a final treat, then stood. I thanked her. Then I reached down and patted Sport on the head.

"You're a good boy, Sport," I said. Sport tilted his head. "You have a lot to learn, but then again, so do I."

Jesus, thank You for seeing me with Your eyes of love. Help me, too, to look with love and acceptance at the people around me, seeing them as Your children.

Service Leadership

LAWRENCE W. WILSON

For even the Son of Man did not come to be served, but to serve, and to give his life as a ransom for many.

MARK 10:45 (NIV)

"Close your eyes and imagine yourself twenty years in the future. When you look back over these years, what do you see?"

Honestly, I thought that was the dumbest question I'd ever heard. I hadn't known exactly what to expect when I engaged a leadership coach, but this certainly wasn't it. A leader. That's what I fancied myself when I was younger. I wanted to make a mark on the world, to succeed in some grand way. I wanted to be a success. In his first political speech, Abraham Lincoln said, "I can say for one that I have no other [ambition] so great as that of being truly esteemed of my fellow men, by rendering myself worthy of their esteem." That's exactly how I felt. He entered politics, and I entered Christian ministry, but we both had the same objective: to do great things in the world.

Now this well-meaning coach was asking me to play a game that felt like a total waste of time. Yet I went along with it. After all, we hadn't yet finished our lunch.

"Well," I said, "I see a shelf filled with books I've written. Important books that have gained a lot of attention. I see a new church building, larger than the one we meet in now, probably seating about two thousand on a Sunday. Maybe a radio broadcast—"

He cut me off there. "Where are the *people*?" he asked.

"The what?"

"The people. Where are the people you have served? When you look back on a lifetime of leadership, you should see people."

Hmm. I hadn't thought of that. I sat quietly, taking bites of my Caesar salad.

"You've given me something to think about," I said. "Good talk."

I left the session unconvinced. The point of a leader is to accomplish great things, I thought. If I'd wanted to "see people," I could have become a therapist.

> *I am seeking, I am striving, I am in it with all my heart.*
>
> VINCENT VAN GOGH

Sometime later, I tackled a household repair that had languished for too long. Having small children, which my wife and I did, meant that my first task was to gather the tools that always seemed to disappear between Saturdays.

"Have you seen the hammer?" I called out.

"It's in the backyard," my wife answered.

"Really? What's it doing there?" I asked.

"Your son was digging a hole."

"Kids," I muttered. *Who would use a hammer to dig?* I trudged out to search for the missing tool, which, sure enough, was lying beside a mound of dirt, caked in mud.

A month passed before my subconscious mind connected the threads of these two incidents. My son dug a hole with our

A Prayer for Purpose

Sometimes if you don't accomplish the goals you set out for your day, you feel behind, as if life has gotten away from you. Don't worry! You have a purpose for being here, and the best part is that Jesus will help you fulfill it. As you turn your day over to Jesus and let Him bring you to rest, pray for His guidance: Heavenly Father, Author of Purpose, I am ready to serve. Guide me on the path You've set for me.

hammer, but, as an adult, I knew that the purpose of a hammer is to drive nails. I'd been harboring a wrong and even childish understanding of leadership. The purpose of leadership is to serve others, not to accomplish something for oneself.

You should see people, my coach had directed. And he was right.

Those words have come back to me, again and again, over the years. I try to make sure to stay focused and ask myself why I'm doing something, whether it's volunteering, donating money, or any good thing. If I'm doing it, following Jesus's example, in order to serve others, I know I'm on the right track.

Lord Jesus, enable me to feel more joy
in serving others than in serving myself.
Bring me back to my true reason for being and
help me, following Your example, to look
on others with love.

Precious Time

RICK HAMLIN

I define joy as a sustained sense of well being and internal peace—a connection to what matters.

OPRAH WINFREY

We established the half-hour rule early in our marriage. My wife, Carol, and I were busy twentysomethings, writing, editing, working during the day, rushing home, making dinner, and watching TV before collapsing into bed. OK, not a bed actually, but a futon on the floor in a tiny one-bedroom apartment.

We set aside one half-hour each day to talk with one another. We talked about the important stuff. Or so it seemed. "Did you balance the checkbook?" "Got anything to add to the marketing list?" "Did you call your mom?" "What time do we need to be there for choir on Sunday?" But sometimes there was other stuff that came up only when we sat down and talked for a while. How we felt about something that was discussed earlier. A reaction one of us had, hurt feelings or a sense of closeness with each other. An insight into our spiritual lives. A frustration we were struggling with.

We couldn't attend to any one of those things by just going through a quick check list. Topics and feelings bubbled up when we sat together at the end of the day, usually at dinner. We discovered things we didn't know about ourselves or about each other. If this time didn't happen at dinner because we had a meeting to go to or some other commitment, we'd try to observe it later. Just lying on that futon and talking before we went to sleep. The half-hour rule.

Of course, we haven't always succeeded at keeping it consistently. Life interrupts, the kids would interrupt, school might interrupt. But as I remember the author Richard Bolles saying to me years ago, "The Holy Spirit is the Lord of our time." We might make plans. Things can and will change. But I know that Jesus's love for us will never change.

After thirty-some years of a good marriage, the half-hour rule still abides. Once again, most often at dinner. We bow our heads and say grace, taking turns over who says it. If the now-grown kids are joining us, they take turns praying, too, as they did when they were younger. Then we talk for at least half an hour. It's surprising how some open-ended question as simple as "How was your day?" or "Anything on your mind?" provides the opportunity for a touching realization or epiphany.

A Foundation of Connection

Connection is important to our well being. By committing to connecting with Jesus, you will build a foundation for all relationships in your life.

Connect with Jesus first by committing to a Jesus-centered life, asking Him to guide you in all your decisions, behaviors, and treatment of others. Trusting in Jesus will help you to learn to trust others as well.

Be sure to keep Jesus by your side as you seek to build deep, authentic relationships with those you love.

Just the other night, for instance, our half-hour talk occurred when Carol and I had returned home after a long cross-country flight. After unpacking our bags, putting away clothes, sorting through the mail that piled up in our absence, and responding to texts and emails, we sat down for takeout from our favorite restaurant. Instead of going back to the mail or the emails, we talked. For over a half hour.

"You know one of the most meaningful things that happened to me in the last few weeks," Carol began, "was when I gave blood at the church."

My ears perked up. Our church's annual blood drive. You sign up for a slot, show up, get hooked up, and are given a glass of juice and some cookies to recharge the blood sugar before you leave.

"It was in the sanctuary this year, and I was at the front of the aisle looking to the back of the church," Carol said. "There was Jesus, that big picture of Jesus, on the cross. And I thought, 'Yes! This is what I'm doing for Jesus.'"

What a moment—and memory—for both of us to share.

I wouldn't have ever heard about this powerful moment in her life if it weren't for the half-hour rule. I'm forever grateful for it.

Dear Jesus, help me honor the commitments that I make to those I hold most dear. Let me cherish the mundane and the profound in our conversations and moments together. And, through these, help me grow in my love for and connection with You.

His Love

SUSANNA FOTH AUGHTMON

He has saved us and called us to a holy life—not because of anything we have done but because of his own purpose and grace. This grace was given us in Christ Jesus before the beginning of time, but it has now been revealed through the appearing of our Savior, Christ Jesus, who has destroyed death and has brought life and immortality to light through the gospel.

2 TIMOTHY 1:9–10 (NIV)

At the ripe old age of twenty-one, I found myself lost and alone in a beautiful place. I had arrived on the big island of Hawaii for a six-month discipleship training program and outreach. It was to be my fresh start after a tumultuous year and a half in and out of college. I had started my junior year of college with high hopes. I was hoping to find the love of my life at school because, deep down, I believed that having a boyfriend would make me feel like I was enough. Pretty enough. Smart enough. Interesting enough. I set out to make it happen. I would get what I wanted no matter what. But in fact, just the opposite happened.

The end of the school year found me lacking health physically and in my relationships. I was struggling just to pass most of my classes. My longing for love and getting what I wanted no matter what had led me down a path of self-destruction. Away from friends and family. Away from the truth and hope of Jesus. I needed help.

How had I gotten it so wrong? As a pastor's daughter, I knew better. I had walked away from Jesus, choosing to do my own thing when I knew He called to me to be holy. I was anything but holy. I was afraid that I had missed my chance at the life He had for me.

I arrived in Hawaii looking for a new way to live. Negative self-talk troubled me. *You messed up. You aren't good enough.*

As I drove up Kuakini Highway toward King's Mansion, where I would be living, I felt upset. I hardly noticed the lush green landscape or the frothy waves crashing on the white sand beaches along the road. I was anxious about what was in store for me. I had a deep fear that while living in this close-knit community, someone would realize how unworthy I was. I knew that I really didn't deserve a new beginning. I had a sense that here amid the coconut palms and hibiscus, the heavy hand of the Lord was going to break my stubborn spirit. And I knew that was exactly what I deserved.

But just the opposite happened. At the most challenging moment of my life, Jesus met me with the brightness of His love. He didn't give me what I deserved. Instead of punishment, anger, and judgment, I was overwhelmed by a tidal wave of grace. Each speaker that came to teach us re-affirmed Jesus's overwhelming love and His unstoppable forgiveness. Each morning that I sat in the hammock under a huge banyan tree with my Bible and my journal, His words sprang to life, bringing hope and comfort to my anxious mind. His mercy poured out on my bruised spirit. The truth was dawning on me: I was wholly known and deeply loved. I was forgiven. I was being made new. The lies that I had been listening to were canceled by His truth. I penned these revelations in my journal with brightly colored pens.

I can live free from guilt and condemnation. Because of Him and Him alone, I can live the holy life that He has called me to. He loves me. He loves me. Jesus loves me!

Swept off my feet by the depths of His love, I began seeing life through a lens of grace. For the first time in long time, my mind wasn't filled with worry. Instead, it was filled with gratitude. I was grateful for a new beginning. For a Savior that saw beyond my sin. For Jesus's faithfulness even when I was far from Him. For His constant presence and abundant generosity.

> *Feel God's presence within you, lifting you up, and filling your heart with the deep abiding assurance that all is well.*
>
> NORMAN VINCENT PEALE

My gratitude spilled over from my quiet time into my daily routine. I was thankful for guava juice and macadamia nuts. For visits to Hapuna Beach. For the salt in my hair. For my amazing tan. For the love of my family. And for every beat of my heart thumping in my chest. Jesus had given me life! How could I not be thankful? Every moment and experience became an opportunity for gratitude.

All these years later, this pattern has been woven through my life. It is a journey of walking in His grace and responding with gratitude. Jesus continually shows me His undeserved favor, saving me from myself, blessing my life, and guiding my steps. And I thank Him for it every day. I don't always get it right, but He does. Caught up in His grace, I can focus on what He has done for me, instead of what I have done to Him. I am still imperfect. I still

Pause for Gratitude

There's nothing like being present in the moment, appreciating the company of those we enjoy and love and allowing ourselves to be spontaneous with our time. Moments and experiences that take us out of our scheduled and programmed thinking and doing can give us the chance to pause in gratitude, to be more present, to allow us to be more open to the kind gestures of others, and even to be kinder to ourselves.

sin and have selfish moments. But that early anchoring in grace has anchored me for life in a place of thankfulness.

I find when I am tired or anxious or fearful about what the days ahead may hold, gratitude can shift the way I see things. The truth is, as I realized so long ago in Hawaii, I am wholly known and deeply loved. When I focus on Him, thankfulness abounds. He loves me. He loves me. He loves me. Thank You, Jesus!

Dear Jesus, thank You for Your love.
Thank You for forgiving my sins. Thank You
for Your grace that fills every corner of my life.
I am grateful with every beat of my heart.
I love You. I love You. I love You.

Soul Rest

ERYN LYNUM

There remains, then, a Sabbath-rest for the people of God;
for anyone who enters God's rest also rests from their
works, just as God did from His. Let us, therefore, make
every effort to enter that rest.

HEBREWS 4:9–11 (NIV)

"Mama, why does the crab have salt on it?" My four-year-old son holds a half clamshell in his tiny hand, his fingers hardly long enough to grasp it. A baby crab scurries left then right, back and forth within the shell.

"I think that's sand," I say, smiling at him. "Not salt."

Beneath each of our steps, the sand shifts. The tide draws near, water gathering up, time kept by gravity's pulse. My three boys chase the sunset until they run out of land. The Ben Ure spit, a half-mile of sand shooting out from Whidbey Island in Washington, dead-ends at Puget Sound, and that is where the boys stop, toes planted at the water's edge.

In the wake of our sons' footprints, my husband and I follow down the shore, with no rush in our steps. As the sun quickens its pace, trickles of water begin to swell in the spaces around our feet. The tide works to fill in each crack and crevice of the spit.

Just like the web of sand crevices becoming tiny rivers before our eyes, empty space is always quickly filled. It is this reality that brought us to Puget Sound. We are on a nine-week excursion across the Pacific Northwest. Twenty-three days ago, we packed a twenty-foot travel trailer full of our belongings. With our three children and our black Labrador, we headed west over the Rocky Mountains. We are creating space. Just like those crevices beneath our feet filling with ocean water, we know empty time always gets filled up, and we want to be the ones choosing how to spend the hours in our days. Specifically, as we move toward the birth of our fourth child, we are searching for rest.

My husband and I had found ourselves packing our days full of activity, events, responsibilities, and plain old busyness, and we set aside this trip as a reset. We want to practice filling our days with intention. We want to sort work and rest into their rightful places, to no longer allow them to seep into one another, diluting the impact of both.

It's in Jesus's life that I observe this sacred rhythm of rest. Time and again, He broke away from the crowds, seeking solitude with His Heavenly Father. He knew this was where He would find the strength and endurance to persevere in the work God called Him to. Without careful attention, I miss these important notes of Jesus's life. After He fed and ministered to a crowd of over five thousand, "He went up on a mountainside by Himself to pray." Not only did Jesus make quiet time a priority in His life, but He also encouraged His followers to do the same. In Mark 6 (NIV), after His disciples tell Jesus of the work they've been doing, He instructs them, "Come with me by yourselves to a quiet place and get some rest."

I want to heed Jesus's invitation to draw near to Him, to find quiet and solitude in His presence. Hebrews 4 offers similar encouragement, "Let us, therefore, make every effort to enter that rest," or in the KJV translation, "Let us labour therefore to enter into that rest." In a society that praises activity and worships a packed calendar, I must make a conscious effort to pursue God's promise of rest.

Jesus invites us to rest in Matthew 11:28 (NIV), "Come to me, all you who are weary and burdened, and I will give you rest." Before I can come and enjoy His rest, I must first heed the instruction of Hebrews 12:1 (KJV), "Let us lay aside every weight." Often, the burden keeping me from Jesus's rest is my affection for busyness.

Our road trip is an attempt to jolt my husband and me out of the orbit of activity we've plunged ourselves into. What I've come to discover is that our unfortunate trajectory is the result of mixing up two crucial steps of the Christian life. We've chosen work before rest instead of the other way around. In doing so, we've forgotten what rest looks like. We can lose sight that we already have everything we need in Christ.

> *A life built upon Sabbath is contented because in rhythms of rest we discover our time is full of the holiness of God.*
>
> SHELLY MILLER

I admit that I have fallen prey to the allure of endeavoring to attain more—more material resources as well as more spiritual ones. Yet Christ has already accomplished the work of my redemption, and I am liberated to rest in Him. I see it in Ephesians 1:3 (NKJV), "Blessed be the God and Father of our Lord Jesus Christ, who has blessed us with every spiritual blessing in the heavenly places in Christ." I don't have to languish in my efforts or exhaust myself to get ahead. Instead, I get to begin with rest and allow God to work from there.

The heart behind our two-month road trip and—I pray—for our lives moving forward is to do just this and enter into God's rest, letting my work spring from there. During the first weeks on the road, I came face-to-face with the overbearing tension between work and rest. The first week found me sidestepping three feet left, three feet right, back and forth, all in attempts to grab an internet signal from our campground in the middle of the woods, in the name of getting work done. After an hour of fruitless efforts, it's as if I heard a small whisper saying, "Set it down." At first, setting the work aside took considerable effort. Over time, it became easier. I began seeing it as an invitation to restore my spirit. As I allowed chunks of our days to remain available, laying aside every encumbrance of constant activity, time began filling with the most profound rest of Christ. We are coming to Him with vacant days and available hours, ready for Him to fill them with the richest of blessings.

Dear Jesus, Your rest runs deeper than anything this world offers. It's more than peaceful sleep or a lazy afternoon—it is soul rest. Lord, teach me to leave space empty. Help me to recognize when I'm "chasing after the wind" in my busyness. As I leave margin in my days, please fill it with Your rest and blessings.

A Moment of Clarity

RANDY PETERSEN

A new command I give you: Love one another.
As I have loved you, so you must love one another.

JOHN 13:34 (NIV)

For eleven years, I was hired by my high school alma mater to direct its spring musicals. *The Music Man* was my first. And I moved on through *Carousel, Camelot, Fiddler on the Roof, The Secret Garden, Into the Woods,* and others.

My teammate in this endeavor was the school's choir director. While I was a freelancer, brought in for a few months every year, she taught at the school full-time. And she was very good at her job: The sounds she got from those young voices were exquisite. She also managed publicity, scheduling, interacting with administrators, and many other details related to producing the musical. With each show, her reputation was on the line. I was just a freelancer who could easily move on to another gig. This was her *life.*

Not long after we started working together, it became apparent to me that we had very different styles. My theater training was what you might call "organic." I coached the students to seek the inner workings of their characters and externalize them. We often warmed up before rehearsal by "walking into character," making decisions about how each character's personality would affect his or her pace, stride, and posture.

In contrast to my style, my colleague had a more "presentational" style, one that affected some of the choices I'd made as director. Some of this had to do with the physics of singing. "He can't hit that high note while sitting," she might say. "He needs his full column of breath." And so, we'd rework the scene, and I'd change the blocking.

Our greatest difference showed up in how we interacted with the students. She was a taskmaster—challenging the performers and insisting they do their best work. She was a master musician and pushed them to take their performances to the next level. I'm an encourager and believed that the students would be most creative when they felt safe to explore. Although we were effective partners in our work, internally I sometimes fumed about our differences, that is, until I gained a new perspective one year.

I vividly recall the afternoon when something changed in me. My colleague and I were working on a scene with a young actress named Juliet. The choir director was insisting that Juliet repeat the scene until she got it right. I kept trying to offer encouragement. "You've almost got it," I'd say. "Think about what your character *wants*." The girl was, understandably, getting more and more frustrated. Finally, the choir director was called out of the room on some business, and we took a break. Nearly in tears, Juliet turned to me and said, "Thank you for being so encouraging, Mr. P. You make me feel better."

Just then I had a moment of clarity, and I replied, "Juliet, I may make you feel better, but she makes you better." I realized that the students were fortunate to have us both working to help them connect with the material *and* give the best performances they could. Of course, my colleague and I knew we weren't going to win any Tony Awards. These were high school productions—after all—featuring kids who were still learning to sing, act, and dance. But we both recognized and shared another purpose: education. We both wanted our students to learn and grow.

Upon deeper consideration, I recognized that my approach to teaching acting could be called "inside out." I tried to help the students to believe in themselves, to embody a character, and then to perform the best they could. My colleague's approach, I came to see, was "outside in." She pushed kids to do their best work, so they would realize how good they could be. We both had the same goals but different ways to work toward them. After that experience with Juliet, I better appreciated and respected my colleague's style.

> *By this everyone will know that you are my disciples, if you love one another.*
>
> JOHN 13:35 (NIV)

I began to change how I dealt with my colleague and with the students: I rooted myself in a deeper purpose—as a follower of Jesus. In doing so, I was better able to show God's love to others. When I found that I was veering off track, I reminded myself that when Jesus was asked to name the most important commandment, He named two: loving God and loving "your neighbor as yourself" (Matthew 22:34–40). He said this would be the identifying trait of His followers.

How could I show love to my colleague, with whom I privately disagreed so often? I realized I could love her by showing respect, appreciation, and loyalty. Although our teaching styles were different, I needed to humbly see and accept the value of her approach and support her. But I also needed to show love to

Turn Your Past into Purpose

Therefore, there is now no condemnation for those who are in Christ Jesus, because through Christ Jesus the law of the Spirit who gives life has set you free from the law of sin and death.

—Romans 8:1–2 (NIV)

Jesus gives us the power to be free of pain and burden of past mistakes. Pray for Him to help you let go of the past and stop obsessing over things you should have said or done. Ask Him to help you walk forward with purpose. Pray for the wisdom to learn from the past and look ahead with faith.

the many students like Juliet when they were struggling. Could I comfort them without undermining their teacher? I certainly could. I didn't always get it right, but the task became easier when I resolutely refocused my purpose on Christ's love.

Dear Lord, thank You for loving me and serving as a powerful example of love. Thank You for reminding me that when I live my life "on purpose," I love. Give me the wisdom to show love even when I'm in challenging circumstances, even when I feel I'm at cross purposes with someone else. Thank You for guiding me each day and giving me rest this night.

My Beliefs, My Choices

LAWRENCE W. WILSON

*Do your best to present yourself to God as one approved,
a worker who has no need to be ashamed, rightly
handling the word of truth.*

2 TIMOTHY 2:15 (ESV)

Most of my core values were not my own for much of my life. They were borrowed. Or given to me. Or imposed by the cultural expectations of my family, the church, teachers, or others. I didn't realize that, of course. I grew up hearing that certain things—including dancing and playing cards—didn't belong in a Christian's life. I was curious, though and wondered what was so wrong with these things. Instead of making waves with my family or church community, I simply learned to keep my questions and doubts to myself. I developed a set of public values and a set of private ones. All in all, this duplicity seemed harmless. So what if I didn't fully accept or understand the values of my church? I chose to live by them, and why rock the boat?

Many years into my life as a minister, I attended a gathering of the pastors in our district. One of the items under discussion had something to do with the time off allotted to pastors. In those days, most pastors took only a single day off each week, if that, and were granted two weeks' vacation every year. Some younger ministers were growing weary of the weekly grind. Someone had proposed a liberalization in the rules: Could they have more time off for rest and relaxation?

One of the older pastors, Pastor Madison (not his real name), rose to address the conference. He had been in the district for over thirty years, faithfully serving a string of smaller churches. Most had been unable to support a full-time minister, and he'd also worked as a schoolteacher to make ends meet. He began by speaking about the sacrifice of great heroes of the Bible, a quasi-recitation of Hebrews 11. Did these great saints whine about "burnout"? "Certainly not," he said. He was clearly against giving pastors more time off and continued to make his case. As Pastor Madison went on, I noted a rising tension in his voice. It occurred to me that this man, for all his dedication to Jesus, had privately harbored resentment over the labor that had been required of him. It must have seemed unfair to him that the younger pastors were unwilling to take on the burden he'd carried his entire life.

> *It's not hard to make decisions when you know what your values are.*
>
> ROY DISNEY

More than feeling a bit frustrated by Pastor Madison's words, I felt a warning in my own spirit. Living up to borrowed standards was not a benign patch over the mild tensions we all feel in our own system of values. The only way to resolve it would be to live according to my values, not those of my parents or my congregation. I must fully voice and be clear about whatever values guide my own life, humbly looking to Jesus for guidance.

That summer, I took an inventory of the things that were important to me. Then I lined them up against the things that were expected of me. Fortunately, the list was nearly an exact match. Truth, integrity, family, service, faithfulness. All these I gladly owned. They were not imposed by others. These values were *mine*.

Yes, there were one or two points at which I disagreed with my church. In those cases, I determined at least to be forthright about my differences, to deceive no one, especially myself.

I also decided, for the sake of my relationship to Jesus and others, to take two days off each week. It was the right choice for my soul.

Lord Jesus, thank You for the way You guide me, deepening my understanding of living for You with authenticity. Thank You for the way You patiently wait for Your children to mature in wisdom and love.

Changing My Attitude

BETH GORMONG

Do not be anxious about anything, but in every situation, by prayer and petition, with thanksgiving, present your requests to God.

PHILIPPIANS 4:6 (NIV)

I sat down at my kitchen table, earbud stuck in one ear, computer open, ready to get to work. But no words came. My mind felt foggy with anxiety on this sunny Saturday morning.

"Beth, can you help me with Max?" my husband, Jeff, yelled from the bathroom.

"What do you need?" I muttered. Even I could hear the grumpiness in my voice as I got up to see what he wanted.

A freshly washed puppy raced past me and jumped onto the couch I had worked hard to keep free from pet hair. He started rolling around.

"Ugh, Max, stop!" I led him off the couch and back to Jeff. "Sorry, I'm grumpy."

A deep sigh followed my words of apology. I safely transferred the wriggling, slippery pet to the towel in Jeff's hands.

"Why are you grumpy?" Jeff asked.

After all it was morning, my favorite time of the day, and he and Max were leaving for a vet checkup, giving me a few precious hours alone to work. I should have been excited.

"I'm worried about this article. I can't seem to find the right words. I've been stressed about it since I woke up." I didn't see how I was going to finish it by the time it was due.

"We'll be gone in just a few minutes." Jeff wrapped the puppy in a towel and began drying him. I couldn't help but smile at the adorable dog, now wrapped up like a puppy

Cultivating Positive Friendships

"There is nothing on this earth to be prized more than true friendship," said the medieval theologian Thomas Aquinas. Friendship is indeed a prize, and research has shown that positive behaviors and emotions may even be "contagious" among social groups.

What does a positive friendship look like? It typically starts with common interests. This might seem intuitive, or counter to the idea that "opposites attract," but even if you love spicy food and your best friend craves comfort food, a shared love of cooking and eating together is a bonding experience that forms a solid base for an authentic, deeply meaningful friendship.

While social media allows us to stay connected with friends, it's the "real" connections of conversation, time in the same place, and even phone calls that cement friend-ships and bring out their most positive aspects. Researcher Dan Buettner told The New York Times, "In general you want friends with whom you can have a meaningful conversation. You can call them on a bad day, and they will care."

Cultivating just a few positive relationships can be a source of joy, support, and satisfaction throughout your life.

burrito, his tail flapping back and forth from out of the end of the towel.

"I'd be happy to help if you need me again," I said. I giggled as Jeff struggled to keep a hold of Max. My mood a little lighter, I returned to the computer.

This time I stopped, closed my eyes, and prayed for inspiration and a right attitude. *"Jesus, change my attitude. I trust You to give me the help I need,"* I prayed.

I turned on some music, lit a candle, and began to type. A few minutes later I heard the back door shut as Jeff and Max left for the vet's office. With the house suddenly quiet, I was able to spend the rest of the morning working uninterrupted.

> *The unthankful heart discovers no mercies; but the thankful heart will find, in every hour, some heavenly blessings.*
>
> HENRY WARD BEECHER

When the dog and his best friend returned home, it was later than expected. My computer was shut. The burden of unfinished work, gone. Jeff updated me on the extra errands he ran, taking Max with him to give me additional time to work in peace.

I was reminded of the verse in Proverbs 12:25 (NIV), "Anxiety weighs down the heart, but a kind word cheers it up." So does a kind deed and some time in prayer.

❧

Jesus, You understand our needs, our worries, and how our emotions affect our actions. Thank You for being a God who provides peace in the midst of anxiety. When I am troubled, remind me to turn to You for help.

What's in a Name?

LORI ROELEVELD

James son of Zebedee and his brother John
(to them he gave the name Boanerges, which means
"sons of thunder").

MARK 3:17 (NIV)

I've never liked my name: Lori Ann.

It's plain and there's no story behind it. There were many, many Lori's in my classes in school. Sometimes it was spelled differently, but still, toss a rock in my school and you'd likely hit a Lori Ann—or a Laurie Anne or a Lorianne.

My brother was given a name imbued with meaning. His first name was after the pastor who married my parents, and his middle name is a family name. I was named after a character on a soap opera my mother fancied during her pregnancy. Seriously. It was *As the World Turns*.

I always longed for a tight circle of friends who would one day give me a cool nickname. It didn't happen for years. In fact, it wasn't until I was in my thirties that I even had a tight circle of friends. In the nineties, my husband and I socialized frequently with a small group of other church friends raising children. We enjoyed watching the Super Bowl together every year, worshiped together on Sundays, and planned summer outings as a group.

Our children were friends too. We encouraged one another's marriages and were close enough to confront one another when we were wrong. Our friendships endure to this day.

During a trying time for our church, I spoke so frequently of the need to "battle in prayer" that my friends began jokingly calling me "Xena." At the time, *Xena: Warrior Princess* was a popular TV show featuring a bold and mighty main character. It was our inside joke and would cause a few eyerolls whenever anyone used it because as self-assured as I was in prayer, I was usually afraid of my own shadow. Still, it was a long-awaited answer to prayer for me that I had a group of friends close enough to feel they could "rename" me. Finally, I'd earned a cool nickname from people who knew me well and still loved me.

Scripture records that Jesus renamed Simon, calling him Peter, or "Rock," at one point announcing that on that rock He would build His church. He nicknamed two other disciples that we know about, brothers James and John, calling them "Boanerges" which means "Sons of Thunder." There's no real explanation for this in the Gospels, so that means even more to me because it speaks of an "inside joke" or a private understanding between Jesus and His close followers. The intimacy of a relationship grants us the authority to nickname someone. We don't rename strangers or acquaintances. We nickname dear friends. This is the closeness Jesus desires with us.

I will also give that person a white stone with a new name written on it, known only to the one who receives it.

REVELATION 2:17 (NIV)

Sometimes we receive names where the meaning isn't made clear to us and that can feel as if our names were given to us carelessly. Like Lori Ann. Other times, the world gives us names that don't quite fit. Some are labels or unkind nicknames. But the truth is that we belong to God, and He knows our real names.

In fact, He knows our true name because we originated with Him. He knows our true purpose. Jesus promises in Revelation 2:17 (NIV), that to the ones who are victorious or to those who overcome, "I will also give that person a white stone with a new name written on it, known only to the one who receives it." As we overcome in Christ, we will experience connection, with Him and with one another, just as His first followers did. And we can look forward to receiving a new name, a name untarnished by this world, a name that testifies to our redemption.

No matter what we're called here, at the end of the day, He is waiting for us with a new name, one that speaks to our connection with Him, our value, our true worth.

Jesus, thank You for knowing us so well and loving us. Thanks to You, we are called by Your name as Your daughters and sons. Thank You for knowing our names.

Trusting in Jesus

CRYSTAL STORMS

When I am afraid, I put my trust in you.

PSALM 56:3 (NIV)

My husband, Tim, pulled into a parking space at the far end of Anclote Gulf Park on the Florida coast. He chose a spot next to a vacant space so he could pump up our tandem kayak with air. A car pulled in, and a couple backed into a spot across from us. I smiled at the man as he walked by, but he kept his head down and seemed to avoid my gaze. After a few minutes, he returned to the woman who still sat in their car.

Tim completed the final preparations for our adventure on the water. I took our Yorkie, Minnie, for a short walk, and then I hopped back in the car to put her life preserver on. As I got Minnie ready, I felt an uneasiness stirring in my chest. Something about the grim mood of the man and his failure to greet me made me worry that this couple might be staking out the lot to steal from people's cars.

"I'm going to move the car," I said, inspired to park in a more central and traveled area of the park.

In the new spot, I hid my purse behind the seat under a sweater and moved my wallet from my purse to the glove compartment. I locked the car and joined Tim.

Going down to the water, I held the front end of the kayak, and he grabbed the back. We navigated the steep dirt path to the launch spot. I got in front with Minnie on my lap, Tim pushed us out, and then he climbed in.

We paddled around the pier, heading north along the Gulf of Mexico toward Key Vista Nature Park. Although the view was stunning, I found myself struggling to appreciate it. My thoughts remained back at the car, remembering the couple I'd found suspicious and thinking about the valuables in the car. I had no real reason to be anxious, and I knew I was missing out on the delights of the day. So after a while, I stopped paddling and turned back to look at Tim. "Will you pray with me?" I asked. "I can't stop thinking about that couple and the way they stared at us."

"Of course," Tim said.

The Art of Thanksgiving

The art of thanksgiving is one of the most important skills a human being can develop. Very closely related to the art of thanksgiving is the art of appreciation. If we develop the ability to appreciate, we also develop our capacity to be thankful.

When we are thankful for our blessings, gratitude activates the flow of even more blessings. And by the same token, ingratitude, fear, or doubt has the opposite effect. If you hold a thought—positive or negative—you create a soil that is hospitable to the germination of the fact for which the thought is the symbol. And the seed you plant, whether good or bad, "produces a crop yielding a hundred...times what was sown" (Matthew 13:23, NIV).

So don't entertain negative thoughts. Fight them—with Jesus's help.

Praying with my husband and giving my worries over to Jesus lightened my burden. I was reminded of His faithfulness and provision and how He would be with me whatever happened. I began to look up at the sky, listen to the water splashing on the side of the kayak, and feeling a sense of awe in God's creation. We navigated around the boulders that lined the inlet and headed up Rocky Creek. A canopy of trees sheltered us from the morning sun. We slowed our paddling and heard the rustling of leaves and the chirping of birds. Fish swam around us. We waved at a mother and daughter who cheerfully greeted us from the dirt trail. My shoulders relaxed; I felt serene. In that sweet place, I knew I'd released my fears to Jesus and felt His peace.

We had just rounded the pier when I spotted two dolphins up ahead. Two more appeared a few minutes later. My heart filled with delight as I watched them disappear to the waters below and pop back up. We paused to enjoy their antics before paddling back to shore.

After we carried the kayak up the hill with little Minnie trailing behind, I headed straight for the car. I peeked in the window to see if anything looked disturbed. All was well. No smashed windows. No missing purse or wallet. All safe.

"Thank You, Jesus," I whispered.

Jesus, You ask us to cast our cares and worries on You. Thank You for the peace and rest You provide to us. Thank You for surrounding us like a shield. As we settle in tonight, we express our heartfelt thanks to You.

Jesus Is My Refuge

JEANETTE LEVELLIE

Those who live in the shelter of the Most High will find rest in the shadow of the Almighty. This I declare about the LORD: He alone is my refuge, my place of safety; he is my God, and I trust him.

PSALM 91: 1–2 (NLT)

Psalm 91, one of my favorite psalms, has been called a "911" call to God. In North America, when we have an emergency and need immediate help, we grab a phone and dial those three life-saving digits, 911. We know that, shortly, help will be on the way. For me, as I know has been true for Christians throughout the ages, Psalm 91 is where I run when I need immediate assistance, protection, and love from God.

It's no surprise, then, that Psalm 91 was part of my husband Kevin's and my strategy when our children needed comfort when they were young. Like all kids, sometimes they would wake in the night after having a bad dream. When they did, through Psalm 91, God came to the rescue.

In addition to his gifts of teaching and preaching, Kevin also composes music. He's written more than 2,000 songs, some of which are simply stunning. But his composition "The Stillness of the Night" is a once-in-a-lifetime song, anointed with Jesus's heart of care for His lambs. And it's based on Psalm 91.

Here are the lyrics:

The stillness of the night, a message from Him brings,
for He who keeps His own will not be found asleep.
The fear that flies by day, the terror sped by night,
will find an even stronger One holds me within His might.
My pillow's in His hand, I'm covered with His love,
Our house is made secure; He calms me with His touch.
The beating of His heart lies close upon my ear,
The presence of His comfort stays; I know to Him I'm dear.

Kev and I recorded this lullaby and played it for our children when they had trouble sleeping or just before they went to bed. On the recording, between its two verses of lyrics, I recite Psalm 91 in its entirety. More times than I can count, Jesus used Kevin's sweet lyrics, God's powerful Word, and the tranquil melody to calm and reassure our children.

> *I love the silent hour of night, for blissful dreams may then arise, revealing to my charmed sight, what may not bless my waking eyes.*
>
> ANNE BRONTË

"The Stillness of the Night" has comforted children other than our own too. Kev took the recording to a Christian camp one summer when he served on staff as a counselor. Late one night when he was attempting to quiet down his ten squirrely campers, a counselor from the girls' camp knocked on the door requesting help. One of the girls in her cabin was feeling upset. Nothing seemed to comfort her. The counselor asked if Kevin would come with her and try to help?

Leaving another counselor in charge of his cabin, Kevin headed across the campgrounds with the young lady, his recording of "The Stillness of the Night" in hand. When the two arrived at the cabin, Kevin prayed for the girls and then played the recording. The campers in the cabin listened, their attention focused, their breathing calmer by the second. In the middle of the second time hearing the lullaby, the girl who'd had such a tough night fell fast asleep. Jesus had done it again.

God created music to serve as a conduit of His power. The combination of music and God's Word infuses truth into our minds and hearts. Our fears or anxiety are no match for Jesus's strength and love. When I'm tempted to worry, listening to music based on Scripture helps replace my fears with faith. It reminds me that Jesus will never leave me and that I can rest underneath His protective wings.

Thank You for Your powerful Word, dear Jesus. You are my refuge. I breathe in Your soothing promise to be my place of safety, tonight and always. I relax under Your wings.

Still Good, Still Beautiful

BOB HOSTETLER

*Then He said to them, "Follow Me, and
I will make you fishers of men."*

MATTHEW 4:19 (NKJV)

My wife's maternal grandparents once owned a farm in south central Ohio. The farm was situated between Routes 159 and 180, near a stream bearing the Indigenous name "Kinnikinnick." While we were dating and in the early years of our marriage, Robin and I delighted in visiting the farm together. Though cows and pigs were no longer raised on the farm, chickens still clucked and capered through the yard. Freshly washed laundry waved from the clothesline. Tomatoes, cucumbers, and carrots sprouted in the garden, and hummingbirds dashed to and from several birdfeeders. It was an idyllic place, to say the least.

On arriving, Robin and I always ignored the front door but entered through the back into the kitchen where Grandma would have something cooking or baking. It was always five or ten degrees warmer in there than the rest of the house, and the smells—oh, the smells! Freshly baked cookies and pies. Homemade noodles simmering in gurgling broth. And, always, coffee percolating on the counter.

The farm was the gathering place for Robin's sizable, extended family. Those in the area came for Sunday dinner almost every week after church, and those who lived farther away returned for the holidays. Hugs and laughter were liberally dispensed, and after meals the adults gravitated to the living room or kitchen to talk while the children ran outside to play. Sometimes, if Grandpa felt up to it, he would take kids for rides on the tractor or in the wagon, and some of the older cousins might hike up the hill to look out over the farm from "Jake's Knob," named for Grandpa—and probably, now that I think of it, *by* Grandpa.

As the years rolled by, however, the farm changed. Grandma and Grandpa, always hardworking and fastidious, apologized that they couldn't "keep it up" as well as they had in the past. The chickens were gone, and the garden was overgrown. On one of our last visits during their lifetimes, I walked the fence line, plodded along the farm's foot-worn paths, and ventured in and out of its aging buildings. A rusty pump cast a long shadow over warped floor boards in an out building, and fenceposts leaned down low, close to the ground, carrying twisting wire with them. A small woodpile blocked the closed doorway of a shed.

It saddened me to see a place which had once churned with industry and energy no longer function as a farm. No crops were cultivated. There were no animals to feed and water. We still had our memories, of course, but we missed the old farm in the days when it gave life, love, and laughter to a large family.

The very last time Robin and I visited, the farm had been parceled into residential lots. Where there had once been fields and pastures, there were now several brand-new houses and garages with bikes and tricycles in the yards and scattered on the sidewalks, the sounds of hammering and of children shouting and laughing. It was quite a change. Obviously, it was different, but

I thought to myself then that this place was still good and still beautiful but just in a new way.

When Jesus called His first disciples, He walked beside the Sea of Galilee until He saw two brothers He knew: Simon and Andrew. They were in their fishing boat, within shouting distance from the shore, casting a large net into the water.

"Come, follow me," Jesus said, "and I will send you out to fish for *people*" (Matthew 4:19, NIV).

They immediately left their nets and came along with Him. It must've been a drastic change for them, but still good and beautiful in a new way. Maybe they sometimes missed the Galilean sunsets over Mount Arbel and the ebb and flow of the fishing life. They may have struggled to make ends meet. Of course, their fishing business never made them rich, but life in an itinerant band, following a country rabbi around offered no regular income or financial security. When they followed Jesus, however, they found a new purpose, a shared purpose with Him: proclaiming "good news to the poor ... freedom for the prisoners and recovery of sight for the blind, to set the oppressed free, to proclaim the year of the Lord's favor" (Luke 4:18–19, NIV). They "went from village to village, proclaiming the good news and healing people everywhere" (Luke 9:6, NIV). They even witnessed the dead coming back to life!

Much has changed for Robin and me since we last saw the old farm. We moved out of Ohio to relocate in a new city and state

> *To live a fulfilled life, we need to keep creating the "what is next" of our lives. Without dreams and goals there is no living, only merely existing, and that is not why we are here.*
>
> MARK TWAIN

Living a Life of Intent and Purpose

Every day we live out our story through our words, actions, and decisions. We must remember to live with intent, to focus on what matters most in life, and to regain that focus when we get sidetracked. Without intent, we can become distracted in matters that don't add to a life of significance and difference in our world.

2,000 miles away. We sold our home of twenty-four years and downsized. We're adjusting to a new community and church family. And we are blessed to live closer to our children and grandchildren, whom we see much more frequently now. We still keep busy work schedules and social calendars, but spending as much time as possible with our family has become one of our highest priorities. It's quite a change, but our purpose and priorities are different now. They're still good, still beautiful, but just feel new as we walk through life's changes with Jesus at our side.

*Lord Jesus, I've learned throughout life
that the only constant is change, and that change
can bring about much beauty. Thank You for being
present with me when changes come. As I prepare
for sleep tonight, I turn toward You with love
and gratitude for all the blessings
You've given me.*

Treasures in Heaven

BRENDA YODER

But Mary treasured up all these things
and pondered them in her heart.

LUKE 2:19 (NIV)

I walked downstairs to bed, knowing that my 5 a.m. alarm would sound soon enough. I wasn't sure what time it was, but I knew it was very late. I had been upstairs for several hours saying goodnight to my kids. Bedtime normally didn't take this long, but it was one of those nights when they opened up with me and had important matters to discuss. On that ordinary enough night, I made memories with my children that I'll always treasure.

My husband and I did our best as parents. We spent most of our non-working hours chauffeuring the children to sporting events and making sure they had what they needed for the next school day. We talked them through their highs and lows and helped them with schoolwork, but most days, to be honest, I just hoped they'd make it to adulthood in one piece. By 8:00 every night, I often just wanted to go to bed. But there was homework to help with, laundry to do, and my own agenda to consult before the next day. As busy and chaotic as life sometimes felt, however, we always kept their bedtime routines consistent.

A predictable nightly rhythm felt like the right ending to each day. It was often one of the only times I really talked to my kids individually. Beginning with the youngest child, my husband and I went from room to room saying goodnight and praying with the children. Most of our visits were fairly quick because I was tired too and had a lot yet to do before the day ended. But there were random evenings when I'd slow down because one or more of the kids invited me into their world.

That particular night, I hit the jackpot in terms of connecting with my children. When I asked my elementary schooler if there was anything specific he wanted us to pray for, he shared his insecurities and worries about peer relationships. I prayed with him, using Scripture to let him know that Jesus would always be with him. I went to the next bedroom where my son, then in middle school, opened up about some pretty sensitive issues. He was worried that a few of his friends were getting involved in risky behavior. I listened to his concerns and was able to share a biblical perspective on the matter. As I walked out the door, he said, "Thanks, Mom." I knew our time together had been as important to him as it was to me.

Though I was tired, I popped my head into my high-schooler's room, asking her if she was awake. She said yes. I sat on her bed, asking if I could pray with her. She shared several things that were troubling her. We talked for a long time, and I struggled to stay awake. Finally, I told her we needed to get some sleep. I prayed with her, and I told her how grateful I was that she trusted me enough to share her feelings with me.

I left her room and stood on the stairway. I knew the time I just spent could never have been planned. It felt holy and sacred.

I wondered if my feelings were like Mary's when Scripture says she treasured "all these things" in her heart.

I also thought of the verse from Matthew 6:20 (NIV): "But store up for yourselves treasures in heaven, where moths and vermin do not destroy, and where thieves do not break in and steal." I knew I had just invested in something that no one could touch or take away, and that no money could buy. I had stored up eternal treasures that I may not see the fruit of until I get to heaven. My tiredness was something I'll never regret.

I also felt rich in a different way. My kids made me a wealthy woman because they gave me a rare opportunity to see into their worlds. I may have missed it had I not taken the time to do a simple evening routine. Most big moments happen when we least expect it. When I worry that I've failed as parent or friend, God reminds me of times like these, when I've simply shown up and been available. He does the rest. It might be saying a prayer for a friend, answering a phone call, or asking a loved one about his or her day.

> *The first principle of value that we need to rediscover is this: that all reality hinges on moral foundations. In other words, that this is a moral universe, and that there are moral laws of the universe just as abiding as the physical laws.*
>
> MARTIN LUTHER KING JR.

I've learned that Jesus can use me to love others, even when I don't have much energy and even in the most ordinary moments, like when I'd say goodnight to my children. Jesus takes my efforts when I'm open to Him, and stretches my time and energy at just the right moment. And, in those times, I feel wealthy beyond measure and grateful to my loving God.

Praying with Compassion for Others

The Gospel compels us to carry out what many consider to be Jesus's impractical principles: Love our enemies and pray for those who persecute us, forgive others as God forgives us, do not judge, love your neighbor as yourself, and so forth. These Christian principles provide a roadmap for how we ought to live, love, and pray for others.

By reading the Gospel stories, we discover a compassionate Jesus who took great interest and concern in the needs of others. He extended justice, kindness, and love to all He encountered.

How do these acts teach us to pray compassionately for others? They remind us that people and their needs matter to Jesus. It means that we, too, need to embody that spirit in our prayers.

When we pray with compassion for others, we empathize with those whom we lift up to God, connecting ourselves with them. They are part of us, and we are part of them.

Lord Jesus, thank You for stretching my time and energy when I obey Your promptings. Remind me that the biggest moments in life are the result of being available and relying on You.

The Test

DURWOOD SMITH

When he had finished speaking, he said to Simon, "Put out into deep water, and let down the nets for a catch." Simon answered, "Master, we've worked hard all night and haven't caught anything. But because You say so, I will let down the nets." When they had done so, they caught such a large number of fish that their nets began to break.

LUKE 5:4–6 (NIV)

College finals were timed too close together. Accustomed to getting good grades, I always "crammed" the night before. Study would be dealt with in order of the day before they were scheduled, Monday, math; Tuesday, history; Wednesday, electronics and biology; Thursday was free, and Friday was end of quarter. My electronics and biology tests were one hour apart.

Wednesday night found me jamming nine weeks of electronics class sessions and research into six hours of review. Biology would have to wait or be ignored.

"Arrgh!" I complained to my roommate. "I might blow the biology test; no time to cram for both."

I had felt something special about going away to college that year; turning twenty-one was special in its own way. However, I sensed a uniqueness in God's call to find His will. This became a year of searching, testing, asking Jesus to point me in the right direction and to help me succeed. My history class, with its emphasis on Israel during the time of Christ, was exciting. As a historical figure, Jesus seemed to be alive, so vital, so right in the middle of everything. Could I call on Him for help like Peter did, or James and John after fishing all night and catching nothing? Timing seemed to matter to Jesus. Would my night of cramming for the electronics final leave me empty when it came to biology?

Concentrated study the night before paid off during the two-hour electronics test. It seemed easy. However, dread overcame me regarding the biology test in one hour. I was resigned to performing poorly, and how my grade point average would suffer.

> *Instruct the wise and they will be wiser still; teach the righteous and they will add to their learning.*
>
> PROVERBS 9:9 (NIV)

Stopping in the student and faculty post office after the electronics final, I happened to see my biology professor opening her mail. She was a short, thinly built European woman with an obvious German accent.

"Hello, Dr. Schwartz," I said.

"Oh, hello, and how are you today?" she asked me.

"Not good."

"What's the problem?" she asked. "You're not sick, are you? Will I see you in class? Finals today, you know."

"Yes, I know. That's what's bothering me. You see, I had to concentrate last night on my electronics test that was held earlier this morning. So, I didn't have time for biology review. I'm afraid I may get a bad score and hurt my grade."

I expected "Old World" sternness from her, but looking into my eyes, she said, "I like you; I want you to do well. I have another identical biology class that's taking their exam tomorrow. You come then."

"What time?" I asked.

"Test begins at two in the afternoon, OK?"

"Yes, yes, I'll be there! Thank you, so much!"

Relief, sweet relief! I studied the remainder of the day and into the night. Just as the disciples obeyed Jesus's command to throw their nets on the other side of the boat, I was casting my dilemma into His hands. Surprised student faces greeted me in the Thursday afternoon class. But I knew something they didn't; a personal answer to prayer was working itself out before my eyes. I felt Jesus, echoing my professor's words, saying, "I love you; I want you to do well."

Late that afternoon, the biology exam completed, I returned to my dorm room and flopped on my bed, exhausted. Jesus had performed a miracle of peace in my quest to know His will;

Connected to the Source

Freshly cut flowers can have a spiritual implication. When connected to the source (stem, ground, and roots), the flowers were vibrant and alive. When cut from their source of nourishment where they grew and blossomed, they begin to wilt.

When we are cut from our source—Jesus—by not spending time with Him, we too start to "wilt." We need His strength and nourishment to help us in our daily walk with Him.

trusting Him was the best path for my future. I rested that night. Drifting off to sleep, I heard His spirit voice whisper, "You did well. You passed My test. I love you."

Our lives are a classroom, Lord. There are lessons to learn, tasks to master, feats to perform. Thank You for being at the center of it all. I trust You for all of it, for tomorrow, for next week, for always.

Mom's Nighttime Advice

BETH GORMONG

Come to me, all you who are weary and burdened,
and I will give you rest. Take my yoke upon you
and learn from me, for I am gentle and humble
in heart, and you will find rest for your souls.

MATTHEW 11:28–29 (NIV)

I lay in bed watching the minutes go by. First, my body felt like it was on fire, so I threw the blankets off. Then just as quickly, I shivered, and pulled them back over me. Covering my eyes with my arm, I hoped blocking out the light would help. It didn't. I rolled from side to side, then onto my back and lay as still as possible and closed my eyes, but I couldn't go to sleep. Thoughts raced like a ticker-tape parade across the inside of my eyelids. All the work to be done tomorrow. The meeting in the evening. A meal to prepare for a friend later in the week. On and on it went. I couldn't shut off my brain. I huffed and rolled onto my side again and looked at the clock; it was 1:05 a.m. *Would I ever get to sleep? Why couldn't I turn off my mind?*

My mom's words came to me. "When I can't sleep, I read the Bible. It calms me and puts me right to sleep."

When Mom originally gave me this strange piece of advice back when I was a teenager, I laughed it off. *Of course it put you to sleep. It bored you to sleep*, I thought, promptly disregarding her words as a sneaky Mom way of getting me to read my Bible.

But I needed to get some rest. Work wouldn't stop just because I was tired the next day. *Should I try it? What would it hurt? I was awake either way*, I thought. But I didn't want to turn on the light and wake my husband. How could I read in the dark?

The thought came to me, *Listen to your Bible app*. I grabbed my phone, opened the app, turned the volume so low I could barely hear it next to my ear and hit the play button. A deep soothing bass voice began to read the Psalms to me. I closed my eyes and listened.

A Prayer Routine

Health experts, such as the National Sleep Foundation, say that consistent bedtime routines can make a big difference in promoting a good night's sleep. For that reason, among many, incorporating a nightly devotional and prayer practice into your evening may be beneficial for you.

When time is short and fatigue is high, you may find that saying one of these simple prayers from *The Book of Common Prayer* as you settle in to sleep will bring you comfort and peace:

May the Lord Almighty grant me and those I love a peaceful night and a restorative rest.

Watch, dear Lord, with those who wake, or watch, or weep tonight, and give Your angels charge over those who sleep. Tend to Your sick ones, Lord Christ. Rest Your weary ones, bless Your dying ones, soothe Your suffering ones, shield Your joyous ones, and all for Your love's sake.

"Blessed is the one who does not walk in step with the wicked or stand in the way that sinners take or sit in the company of mockers, but whose delight is in the law of the Lord, and who meditates on his law day and night" Psalm 1:1–2 (NIV).

The next thing I knew, my alarm clock was waking me. Psalms still played on my phone.

"I love the Lord, for he heard my voice; he heard my cry for mercy. Because he turned his ear to me, I will call on him as long as I live .... Return to your rest, my soul, for the Lord has been good to you" (Psalm 116:1–7, NIV).

> *Thou hast made us for thyself, O Lord, and our heart is restless until it finds its rest in thee.*
>
> SAINT AUGUSTINE

I had fallen into a deep sleep, and I woke feeling refreshed.

Now anytime I find sleep eluding me, I listen to the Bible. It works every time.

When any friend tells me about their rough night of sleep, I tell them about my miraculous discovery, making sure to add, "It relaxes me, soothes my racing mind and calms my jittery nerves. Let God's Word calm your mind. It's always helped me. I promise."

Dear Jesus, Thank You for the Bible, for the promises and guidance I find in its pages, and for the peace I receive when I listen to it. Your Word never fails to answer my questions and calm my soul.

Embracing Joy

SUSANNA FOTH AUGHTMON

You make known to me the path of life;
you will fill me with joy in your presence,
with eternal pleasures at your right hand.

PSALM 16:11 (NIV)

I love making people laugh; it's one of the things that brings me true joy. If I can write something or say something that makes people laugh from their gut, I feel like my work is done. I think that laughter is a form of encouragement: It breaks down barriers and builds up our souls. It crosses cultures, and it binds us to one another. It also releases endorphins, the brain's "feel good" hormones, relieves stress, and is contagious in a group setting.

As a child I had moments in church when something struck me funny, and I almost burst an internal organ trying not to laugh. My "trying not to laugh" energy seemed to move down the pew to my friends. Within moments, we were holding our sides, biting our lips, and putting our heads down on the pew in front of us, pretending to pray. Church laughter seems to spread like wildfire. You can't contain it. Maybe it's the joy of the Lord.

When I met my husband, Scott, for the first time, he was playfully teasing a friend of mine. He was quick, witty, and cute, a stunning combination in my book. I was attracted to all that joy inside him. The funny gene has been passed along to our kids. There is hardly a moment with our three sons when they are not trying to make us laugh or shocking us by saying something silly or clever. It is their birthright.

When my sister was visiting, she came with me to pick up my sons from school. They started teasing me from the moment they got in the car. Laughing, my sister Erica said, "Wow! They are relentless." This gave me pause. I asked, "Wait a second. Your kids don't tease you like this?" She laughed and said, "Maybe every once in a while." I was floored. I recalled the incident to our oldest son later on the phone. I said, "Jack, your cousins are nice to their mom. They don't mess with her all the time." Jack said, "Mom, Aunt Erica raised her kids to be nice. You raised us to be funny." I thought I raised my boys to be both! But there is nothing that our family loves to do more together than laugh. It connects us. It invites in joy. It breathes hope into the room.

But the fruit of the Spirit is love, joy, peace, forbearance, kindness, goodness, faithfulness, gentleness and self-control. Against such things there is no law.

GALATIANS 5:22–23 (NIV)

Laughter ushers in positivity. Even in my bleakest moments, laughing gives me room to breathe. When I am lonely, laughing with my husband reminds me of our bond and our love for each other. Laughter reinforces the truth that hope and joy are there to be found even in the unpredictability of life.

Every year, the week after Christmas, my side of the family meets in Colorado at my parents' house. One year, due to COVID-19, we weren't able to do that. My sisters, sister-in-law, and I usually exchange sister gifts. That year, I mailed them each a packet of twelve paper spa facial masks for their sister gift. The masks looked like disinfecting wipes with holes cut out for eyes, nose, and mouth. Each mask had a different purpose—brightening, cleansing, or exfoliating. And then there was the real purpose—making us laugh until we couldn't breathe.

We had a monthly sister Zoom call to check up on each other. Before we got on the call, we donned the mask of our choice. My sister Jenny's mask never seemed to adhere correctly. She looked a little like a wrinkly mummy. The others always had varying degrees of gaps in their masks. I had to put my glasses on over mine to keep it from falling off. Each time a new person joined the call, laughter erupted. We looked so silly in those masks; it was sheer joy to laugh together.

It is Jesus's joy that gives me strength. His hope fills my heart with positivity and peace—because of who He is. In spite of life's stressful circumstances, I can dial into the truth that Jesus is Savior, Redeemer, Deliverer, Healer, and Restorer of my soul. Being in His presence ushers in the fullness of joy—joy unspeakable and full of glory. I want in on all of it.

Jesus, You bring true joy as You remain, despite life's changes and challenges, a hopeful presence in my life. As I lay down to rest tonight, I thank You for holding me in a place of peace.

A Circadian Rhythm of Grace

ERYN LYNUM

*It is good to give thanks to the LORD, to sing praises
to your name, O Most High; to declare your steadfast
love in the morning, and your faithfulness by night.*

PSALM 92:1–2 (ESV)

Immediately on walking in, I second-guessed our decision. I expected the place to look rough, but what I saw around me pushed the bounds of what I'd envisioned. Nagging doubts crowded the crevices of my mind, as plentiful as the cobwebs that claimed each room. This was my childhood home. I hadn't stepped foot in it for over a decade, and now we owned it. My husband, Grayson, and I purchased the house as our first investment property. It had been vacant for some time and needed a great deal of love and repairs. Pulling on work gloves and reaching for a broom, I fought to remain grateful for the opportunity before us. *Could we pull this off?*

Our four young children stayed an hour away with family as we set to work filling the first of two thirty-foot dumpsters. We scrubbed and scraped and prepared a somewhat livable space, then picked up our children and brought them to the house where they joined us for renovations. Our youngest was two, and our oldest was nine. The boys would help us in the coming weeks to clean, paint, and prepare this home for tenants. *Was it a mistake to take this on with our kids underfoot?* I thought of our lovely, clean home in Colorado and questioned if we should have brought them here to this tired home in small-town Wisconsin for a month of intense work.

Each morning, my husband and I poured cups of coffee while the kids sat on stepstools and five-gallon paint buckets to eat their breakfasts from paper plates. We used a dry-erase board and wrote lists and goals for the day. Grayson would tear out the kitchen cabinets. He and the kids would rip down a dividing wall upstairs to create a more "open concept" feel. I would prime the master bedroom, tape off windows in the living room, and sand drywall patches in the office. Every evening, after we settled the kids to sleep on mattresses sprawling across the floor, my husband and I would set back to work.

To make matters stranger, it was Christmas week. Christmas dinner found us handing out sandwiches to the kids as we painted the newly remodeled bathroom. I considered Jesus as a child, working alongside His earthly father, Joseph, as my boys worked next to their Daddy. In Scripture, we're allotted only a few glimpses into His childhood; the rest remains a mystery. Perhaps He was tasked with keeping an eye on younger siblings, as my oldest was. During renovations, my son helped to look after his little sister.

I considered the unrecorded days of Jesus's life as a carpenter, making precise cuts in wood as my husband did now. I wondered if He, volunteering to take on a human body, suffered from the same physical exhaustion that overtook us every night. As my arms throbbed and my hands ached from the work, I considered His words in Matthew 11:28 (NIV), "Come to me, all who are weary and burdened, and I will give you rest." What breadth this invitation took on as I considered it from the lips of One who knows the depth of my exhaustion.

During this season, sleep was hard to come by. We began work before the sun crested the horizon and were not finished until after it set in the evening. However, punctuating the days were sweet moments of respite. I found Jesus's invitation in Matthew 11 echoing sentiments recorded by King David hundreds of years before in Psalm 68:19 (NASB), "Blessed be the Lord, who daily bears our burden." It was as if, as we wrote out the work on the whiteboard each morning, Jesus looked at our list, along with the unwritten burdens on our hearts and minds, and said, "Here, let me carry that for you." As each day lapsed into the next, we steadily checked off the tasks on our board. I even developed deep gratitude for the work. Right

> *I will extol the Lord at all times; his praise will always be on my lips.*
>
> PSALM 34:1 (NIV)

there, in the pressing circumstances, is where Jesus was teaching me to depend on Him. He was proving to me in the sweetest of ways that His strength truly makes up for my every weakness. He is enough.

My exhaustion created an acute sensitivity to the moments of grace Jesus was extending to us. I read in Lamentations 3:22–23 (NASB), "The LORD's acts of mercy indeed do not end, for His compassions do not fail. They are new every morning; great is Your faithfulness." In these words, accentuated by my need, a rhythm emerged. These new morning mercies seemed to take on a cadence. His grace has this way about it, a circadian rhythm of sorts. As surely as the sun would rise, His mercy arrived in regular intervals—never allowing enough of a gap for me to despair. "Come to Me, all who are weary and burdened," I recited aloud while applying yet another coat of "agreeable gray" to the walls, "and I will give you rest." His new morning mercies are not constrained to the hours preceding noon. Each dawn, He doled out mercy sufficient for the needs of that day. These mercies stretched all day long. They were adequate to capture and tame any worry or stretch of discontent I experienced.

Each evening, when at last we would wrap up the paint pans, hang up the hammers, pull shoes off aching feet, and climb into bed, His mercy remained. Just as King David proclaimed in Psalm 92:1–2 (ESV), "It is good to give thanks to the LORD, to sing praises

A Gratitude Journal Can Improve Your Outlook

There are many sayings that express gratitude or that tell or remind us to be grateful for what we have. Yet at times it can be easy to complain, whine, or be discouraged about what we don't have or wish could change rather than being grateful.

Writing in a gratitude journal and thanking Jesus for the blessings in your life could help shift your thinking. Try this to get started. Open your journal or a notebook and inscribe the date and three things you are grateful for. As an example, friends who encourage you, a caring partner, and God's provision.

Continue with this practice daily. Although life won't suddenly become trouble-free, you will discover a new spiritual awareness of the blessings around you that make you see how present Jesus is in your life, handing out gift after gift.

to your name, O Most High; to declare your steadfast love in the morning, and your faithfulness by night." King David recorded this distinct shift: from steadfast love by morning to faithfulness by night. Somewhere between mornings spent gutting the kitchen and evenings passed painting each inch of the house, a pivot carried us from steadfast love to faithfulness. And He gave us rest.

I found Jesus extending love and faithfulness to me at every hour. Yet each seemed uniquely heightened and highlighted by the hands of the clock. Steadfast love was easier to grasp with the sun's rising. Yet as a day's challenges set in, we shifted our weight toward His promise of faithfulness. This is the reliable rhythm of His new morning mercies. Each rotation of the earth proclaims His steadfast love in the morning and His faithfulness by night. His mercy does not wane, thin, dilute, or expire. There is no minute of a day void of His care. For His steadfast love and faithfulness, it is good to give thanks to the Lord.

Dear Jesus, tonight I thank You for your steadfast love and faithfulness. Grow me right where I am. When I wake, please extend sufficient energy and clarity and strength to me, for whatever the day holds. I give thanks to You, Lord.

Barriers Moved Aside

CRYSTAL STORMS

*For he himself is our peace, who has made the
two groups one and has destroyed the barrier.*

EPHESIANS 2:14 (NIV)

I slipped out of the auditorium through a side door the moment
the final "Amen" was spoken. On a break during a conference, I wanted to make a quick stop to a women's room down an
empty hall and then find my friends to visit and debrief. I knew
the building well, and I knew just where to turn, but found that a
wrought iron gate stood between me and the door to the wom-
en's room. My shoulders drooped at the sight of the obstacle,
and I let out a sigh. With the session ended, a long line would
be forming—comprising everyone who went out the main
entrance—at the other restroom. My detour meant I'd be bringing up the rear and would spend the entire break standing in line.

Then, on looking closer, I noticed something: The gate was
only partly closed. I easily slid it open and walked through. A few
minutes later, I joined my friends in the front of the building. We
munched on almonds while sharing our hearts. We even had
time to get a picture with the three of us before heading back
in for the late morning session. Privately, I felt thankful that I
hadn't turned around at the sight of that iron gate.

Looking back on that experience now, I reflect on the many times I allow *perceived* obstacles to keep me from moving forward. Too often, seeing a hurdle or other obstruction up ahead, I lose heart. I hesitate and almost turn back, searching for an easier way. I forget, for a time at least, that Jesus has promised to make my way clear. He arms me with strength to overcome the challenges, either real or perceived, that I face. He has a plan for my life.

Sometimes a closed door is His answer. Sometimes a "not yet" in response to my request. These are invitations to trust Him as well as opportunities to go a different way than the one I planned. Remembering that nothing I face is a surprise to Jesus, and that He sees the end from the beginning, brings me peace. Delays and detours may attempt to distract me, but I don't want them to divert me from following His plan for me. So I cling to the truth that God arms me with strength. It is He who makes a way when I see no way.

> *Obstacles don't have to stop you. If you run into a wall, don't turn around and give up. Figure out how to climb it, go through it, or work around it.*
>
> MICHAEL JORDAN

When I lose sight of Jesus, barriers can overshadow my faith and cause me to forget that He has a purpose for my life. But, my eyes on Him, I can work toward finishing what He started in me. I can trust He will lead me where I need to go. I only need to follow Him, one small, obedient step at a time.

Some days it takes all that is in me to put one foot in front of the other. To trust that the road I'm on still leads to a place worth landing. Taking that next step is all that's needed. One step toward His best. Trusting He will bring about what He said He will do and complete the work He started in me.

How a Divine Calling Brings Life Purpose

Have you ever felt called to a purpose? Examples abound in the Bible and our history books.

Time and again, God called upon people to act. These callings were profound moments in which God showed people what they were put on this earth to do. But divine callings aren't reserved for biblical figures, historical movers and shakers, and visionaries. They are accessible to all of us.

A divine calling can come in the form of a sign, a dream, a vision, a message, a feeling, or a combination of these things. It is insistent, the way only God can be insistent, and will keep coming up if you ignore it. A calling often "feels right" and is felt on a deep and intrinsic level, but that doesn't mean that heeding it comes without struggle. In fact, true callings often pull us out of our comfort zones and demand sacrifices. In those uncomfortable times, taking time to pray and meditate helps.

When we answer a divine calling, we are brought closer to our life's purpose and shown that we are all a part of God's plan.

*Jesus, thank You for breaking down barriers
and removing obstacles in my path. Thank You
for continuing to work in my life. Tonight,
let me relax and trust in You.*

Thank You, Thank You, Thank You

LAWRENCE W. WILSON

Therefore encourage one another and build
one another up, just as in fact you are doing.

1 THESSALONIANS 5:11 (NIV)

I've always thought of myself as a strong person. It's not that I'm a great achiever. I simply prefer to do things alone and complete them by myself. I bike alone. I work mostly alone. I like it that way.

Partly that's because I'm an introvert, I'm sure. But there's more to it. All the great heroes in our culture seem to be loners. Think of comic-book superheroes—Batman, Superman, Captain America. Lone operators all. And we idolize the dreamer, the entrepreneur who builds a successful company with nothing but pluck, defying the odds, the critics, and the competition. Our war heroes almost always act alone. I think of Desmond Ross, the conscientious objector whose story is told in the biographical movie *Hacksaw Ridge*; Ross was awarded the Medal of Honor for rescuing seventy-five men in World War II, unarmed and all by himself. I'm drawn to loner heroes. Real men who go it alone.

Even when presented with problems in life—divorce, chronic illness, career change—I took pride in being self-reliant. So when my son died at the age of twenty-nine, I did what I always had done: gritted my teeth, fought back the pain, and kept moving. So far as I knew, I had entered a highly exclusive club with exactly one member, me. Even if I'd wanted help, there was no one to turn to.

As our family worked through that awful week of grief, preparing for the funeral, our pastor asked if we would accept some help. Meals and such. With a number of relatives that were to visit, I knew we would need help. Then he asked if we would allow some of the "church ladies" to clean our house. Having raised a blended family of six teenagers, our home wasn't exactly pristine. This would mean exposing a bit more of ourselves than I'm usually comfortable with. But again, thinking of the guests we'd be hosting, I reluctantly agreed.

> *God has given us two hands, one to receive with and the other to give with.*
>
> BILLY GRAHAM

The women who arrived the next day were armed with brooms and buckets, mops and rags. But they were not exactly what we'd imagined. They were young, most of them our age or younger. And they came in a horde, perhaps fifteen or twenty in all. They were all people we recognized from church, but some were more than acquaintances. Some were dear friends whom I'd known for more than twenty years. Others we knew less well, but they had children too. And a shared faith. And something else.

"I know there are a lot of us here," my pastor told me. "But they all wanted to come. You'd never have known it, but many of these women have lost children of their own. I just couldn't say no."

Those who knew us the best embraced us with tears.

"I love you."

"I'm so sorry."

Jesus Is Your Lifeline

Have you noticed that seemingly impossible situations often work themselves out after you pray? When life seems like a ship out of control on a perilous ocean, and the deck shifts beneath your feet, grab hold of your lifeline: Jesus.

In these times, Jesus comes alongside to aid you. Have you seen Jesus's work in your spirit, when you, despite stressful circumstances, remain cool under pressure? That's your lifeline—Jesus—holding you fast.

"We loved your boy."

"We're here."

I hadn't intended to cry, not then. Yet, with each hug, my heart melted a little more. In the end, I was bawling.

"Thank you. Thank you. Thank you," was all I could manage to say. I didn't know that I needed a community until that day. And I thank Jesus they were there. These are ties I will never forget, and never neglect. I'm so grateful to Jesus and His followers who showed up for us so that I didn't have to go it alone.

Jesus, thank You for the fellowship of people You have placed around me. As I name each one before You, I pray that I may bless them as they have blessed me.

In Step with Jesus

RANDY PETERSEN

And whatever you do, in word or deed, do
everything in the name of the Lord Jesus,
giving thanks to God the Father through him.

COLOSSIANS 3:17 (ESV)

Anticipating the trip, I could almost smell the sea breezes and feel the sand under my feet. After a long winter in the Northeast that wasn't going away any time soon, I was about to jet to Clearwater, Florida, for a week of relaxation—beach-walking, sun-basking, and watching spring training baseball.

Did I ever need this! The day-to-day anxieties of freelance writing had worn me down. Being in a constant cycle of finding work, doing work, and meeting deadlines had me sorely needing a break. I'd often spend my off hours, in the evening, worrying over what was coming the next day or what would be my next project. But my brother had rented a beach cottage where we could stay, and I had bought my plane ticket. It was all working out, and I was counting the days.

One day before the trip, a publisher's representative called. She needed a short book written in three weeks. Normally I would want three *months* to complete a project like the one she described. But she offered to pay extra for the rush, and I needed the money. *What about my trip and desperate need for time off?* But I really enjoy writing about the Bible, and I loved the subject of the proposed book. I especially like exploring what the Bible says about real-life issues as this book would do. *What was Jesus trying to tell me?* Was this an answer to prayer that only *felt* like terrible timing?

I said yes and accepted the project. I still planned to travel to Florida, but instead of lazing around on the beach with my brother, I'd be working. The change of venue would be nice, the sea breezes pleasant, and it would be great to spend time with my brother. *But would I find rest for my soul?*

To my surprise, it was a great vacation. The mental activity of brainstorming, planning, and organizing the book turned out to be enlivening rather than draining. Instead of doing my usual vacation pursuits like crossword puzzles or reading mystery novels, I mapped out chapters for the new book on my legal pad. My brother and I still enjoyed lounging on the deck overlooking the gulf, often talking about the subject of my book. He also gave me some excellent ideas.

> *God never asked us to meet life's pressures and demands on our own terms or by relying upon our own strength. Nor did He demand that we win His favor by assembling an impressive portfolio of good deeds. Instead, He invites us to enter His rest.*
>
> CHARLES R. SWINDOLL

We took afternoons off to watch baseball games, and we enjoyed some good dinners out. In between these idle times, I completed valuable construction on the book. When I got back home the next week, I was able to write the book in the time allotted. And I felt refreshed.

5 Bible Verses that Encourage Rest

God promises to give us rest, as He tells us in these scriptures from the NIV:

HE PROMISES TO GIVE REST FOR OUR SOULS.

"Come to me, all you who are weary and burdened, and I will give you rest. Take my yoke upon you and learn from me, for I am gentle and humble in heart, and you will find rest for your souls. For my yoke is easy and my burden is light."
—Matthew 11:28–30

HE PROMISES TO BE WITH US.

The LORD replied, "My Presence will go with you, and I will give you rest."
—Exodus 33:14

HE HAS REST WAITING FOR US.

There remains, then, a Sabbath-rest for the people of God.
—Hebrews 4:9

WE CAN COUNT ON REST AND STRENGTH— BUT THE SECRET IS WAITING ON HIM.

He gives strength to the weary and increases the power of the weak. Even youths grow tired and weary, and young men stumble and fall; but those who hope in the LORD will renew their strength. They will soar on wings like eagles; they will run and not grow weary.
—Isaiah 40:29–31

That experience made me think about the need to get rest for my soul on a daily basis. I realized I could use my evenings as a time to remind myself to trust that Jesus will provide, to shut down my worries about tomorrow. I know Jesus will get me through the next day. By going to sleep in Jesus-given relaxation, dreaming of how He will keep in step with me in the dance of life, would I find the rest I need? The answer is yes!

Lord, give me rest—not only a good night's sleep but also the assurance that You and I are in step. Thank You for helping me find balance between my work and my off hours. As I live and work, day by day, I want to relax in You.

Old Heart/New Heart

LORI HATCHER

*I will put my law within them, and I will
write it on their hearts. And I will be their God,
and they shall be my people.*

JEREMIAH 31:33 (ESV)

I began my life of crime at age ten.

My premeditated and carefully executed plan to steal bubblegum from the pharmacy hatched over time. One day I visited the drugstore as an honest patron and noticed that the bin holding Bazooka bubblegum sat at the bottom of the candy display. To reach it, I had to squat out of sight of the clerk who stood on the other side of the counter.

I could easily scoop a handful of bubblegum into my bookbag. If I also grabbed a candy bar while I was down there and paid for it, he'd never suspect a thing, I thought.

I made my purchase that day and headed home to think through my plan. Three days later, I returned to execute it. I waited for my turn at the counter, then knelt before the candy display. I grabbed a handful of gum, shoved it into my bookbag, and rose to face the clerk. With my heart beating wildly, I slid a Mars bar across the counter and reached into my pocket for my money.

"That will be thirty-six cents," the clerk said, taking the coins from my hand.

I left the store, sweaty but triumphant.

I don't know why I stole that bubblegum. I had money. I could have easily paid for it. My parents had trained me to do what was right and taught me never to steal. It felt daring and rebellious and even a little bit exciting to do something so blatantly wrong.

Praying "Forgive Us Our Sins"

When Jesus showed His followers how to pray the Lord's Prayer, He included a plea for forgiveness: "Forgive us our sins, for we also forgive everyone who sins against us" (Luke 11:4, NIV). But what are we really saying when we say this?

First, we're saying, "I've sinned. I've done wrong." It's a confession. That's key, because the Bible says, "If we confess our sins, [God] is faithful and just and will forgive us our sins and purify us from all unrighteousness" (1 John 1:9, NIV).

We're also saying that we want and need forgiveness. When Jesus modeled this for His followers, He linked the petition for daily bread with the petition for forgiveness. "Forgive us" comes after "Give us this day our daily bread." It's a hint that we need both, every day—food and forgiveness.

Jesus also linked our forgiveness from God with our forgiveness of others. "Forgive us," He told us to pray, "as we forgive." When we say, "Forgive us...as we forgive," we're acknowledging the truth that Jesus taught—that being forgiven is tied to our forgiveness of others.

I didn't think about my transgression again until the year I committed my life to Christ. My decision to follow Jesus at age twenty led me to do some spiritual housecleaning. I broke off a relationship that I felt didn't honor God and got rid of a few books that I knew weren't good for my mind and spirit. I began reading my Bible regularly, letting God's word seep into my soul.

One day I read Jesus's conversation with Zacchaeus, the tax collector, in Luke 19. When Zacchaeus placed his faith in Christ, he demonstrated his conversion by making restitution to the people from whom he had stolen.

The memory of my petty theft rushed back to mind, bringing with it a profound sense of shame and regret. I confessed my sin to God and received His forgiveness, but I knew I had to make it right with the store owner.

But how? By then I lived a thousand miles away from my hometown.

One night an idea popped into my head: *Write a letter. Confess what you did, ask for forgiveness, and include money to pay for the gum you stole a decade ago.*

My heart leapt with excitement as I wrote. I chose my words carefully and ended the letter with, "I know you may think I'm making a big deal out of a small act, but I've become a Christian. As much as possible, I want to live in a way that honors God." I tucked two dollars into the envelope, stamped it, and prayed for God to use my apology for His glory.

Looking back, I realize that, as a ten-year-old girl, I had the "head knowledge" to do what was right, but I did not have the heart's desire. I needed something more than values, training, or the fear of punishment to enable me to live in a way that honored God. I needed the transformation that comes through

Jesus's saving faith. After I surrendered my life to Christ, you see, a strange and wonderful thing happened. Instead of being governed by my own impulses or standards, I felt drawn to read God's Word and apply its principles. I didn't obey because I was afraid God would punish me, but because I knew His standards were for my good. The truths of Scripture resonated with His Spirit inside my heart, leading me to act in ways I never had before.

Many years have passed since I came clean and forsook my life of crime. I wish I could say I've never been tempted to steal, cheat, or lie, but I can't. Like all people—including those who love Jesus—I make mistakes and fall short of the mark. I wrestle with my old heart every single day. What I can say is that when I come to Jesus in prayer, He lovingly prompts me to obey His Word, and when I sin, He forgives me.

Jesus, I pray along with the psalmist,
"Create in me a pure heart, O God, and renew
a steadfast spirit within me" (Psalm 51:10, NIV).
Cause me to hunger and thirst for righteousness.
Help me value what You value. Inspire me to
live in tune with Your Word.

Gratitude for the Win

LORI ROELEVELD

To give thanks to Your holy name,
to triumph in Your praise.

1 CHRONICLES 16:35 (NKJV)

The young woman I supervise sat before me, distraught and prepared to quit. We work with families in crisis, and it can be challenging. I wasn't sure what to expect, but I was honestly surprised at what I heard, though I shouldn't have been.

"The mom I helped yesterday was the last straw! I've gone above and beyond helping her with applications, bringing food and clothing donations to her door, and giving her rides," she said.

I nodded because she had been giving it her all.

"Well, yesterday while I was driving her home after taking her into the city for a bus pass, she complained the whole way. She said no one ever really helped her in a way that made any difference. I don't know if I can do this work any longer."

What fascinated me about her outburst was that we work with severe and traumatic situations. We see sadness, rage, child abuse, neglect, and domestic violence every day. But what pushed this woman to the edge of quitting was ingratitude.

I get it; ingratitude is powerfully offensive. I don't know a single reader of Scripture who isn't sadden by the ingratitude of the nine men in Luke 17:11–19. Jesus healed ten men of leprosy but only one returned to thank Him! Jesus also found this remarkable because ingratitude is such an offense.

Moses becomes exasperated with the Israelites' ingratitude during their wilderness wanderings. God delivered them from slavery and provided manna to nourish them in the desert, but the people missed the meat and other food they had in Egypt. They complained as they reminisced, leaving out the memory that they'd suffered bitter enslavement at the time. Moses expressed his frustration to God, wanted to quit, and asked why God had given him the burden of these people.

A Grateful Person Is a Happy Person

Psychologists have found that a grateful perspective impacts our mood and stops us from allowing negative thoughts, such as resentment, envy, and regret, to take over.

When we take a moment to appreciate the good things in life, such as a job, home, friends, and family, we feel good about the present and hopeful for the future. The list of what makes an individual appreciative varies, but the key is to prevent the bad things from getting in the way of the good things. Even in tough times, if we look hard enough, we can find the good.

Research has proven that jotting down positive events can cultivate gratitude in our lives. There are many ways to cultivate gratitude: writing, praying, singing, drawing, and more. In Psalm 103:2 (NLT) it says, "Let all that I am praise the Lord; may I never forget the good things he does for me." What good things has the Lord done for you?

I've stood in Moses' sandals, but I've also been like the Israelites or the nine lepers, failing to express gratitude to Jesus for His provision and His healing. Jesus won't ever quit on us, but ingratitude can cause us to lose heart.

Still, true gratitude can revive a fainting heart.

Later that day in the office, a woman knocked on the door; with her was a three-year-old with whom I'd worked. His mom struggled to care for him, and I'd had to make a hard call to get him to safety. I'd waited with him on the back steps of his home, his belongings in a grocery bag, until the state car arrived.

My supervisee and I greeted them. The woman introduced herself as the boy's aunt. As she asked which one of us was Lori, the little guy provided the answer by climbing into my lap and snuggling into my arms.

As he patted my upper arm, he looked into my eyes and said, "Thank you, Miss Lori."

His aunt explained that for the last few nights when she tucked him in, he insisted that he had to "thank my safety lady."

When they left, my young colleague looked at me and said, "Well, I won't quit today." And we smiled.

Jesus, thank You for your patience with us.
Thank You for bearing with us and forgiving
our moments of ingratitude and complaint.
We thank You for being our safety, our
protection, and our Lord.

Come On In!

NORM STOLPE

They urged him strongly, "Stay with us,
for it is nearly evening; the day is almost over."
So he went in to stay with them.

LUKE 24:29 (NIV)

After my wife, Candy, was diagnosed with Alzheimer's, we moved across the country, from Dallas, Texas, to Milwaukee, Wisconsin. We now share a duplex with our son David, his wife, Rachel, and their children. We were thankful that our house in Dallas sold quickly and easily, but we couldn't move into the duplex in Wisconsin for six months afterward. Our household goods, then, stayed in storage, and Rachel and David explored which of their friends would have space and be willing to take us in for an extended visit.

Candy and I took a leisurely trip from Texas to Wisconsin, with a rental trailer to visit family and friends along the way. On arriving in Milwaukee, we temporarily moved in with our kids' friends Mandy and Matthew. We'd met them only once before, and they didn't really know us when they opened their home to us. The parents of two young girls, Mandy is a special education school-teacher and Matthew a visual artist. From the start, the couple integrated us into the grocery shopping, cooking, dishwashing, and housekeeping rotations. They helped us hose off the trailer before returning it to the rental center and learn our way around so we could shop and keep our car fueled. They introduced us to their neighbors, and with spring coming, we even were invited to a block party while they were traveling. When we were finally permitted to move into our new home, a crew of people from Mandy and Matthew's church helped us get settled.

When Cleopas and his companion invited Jesus to spend the evening with them, I am sure they were thinking of more than the hospitality of providing Him with safe comfortable lodging for the night. As they walked from Jerusalem to their home in the village of Emmaus, Jesus had engaged them in fascinating conversation about God's unexpected way of accomplishing His redemptive plan. I am sure they were as hungry for that discussion to continue as they were for food. At the evening meal Jesus took the role of the host. As He blessed the bread, broke it, and gave it to them, they recognized that Jesus had been with them all along.

> *Anyone who welcomes you welcomes me, and anyone who welcomes me welcomes the one who sent me.*
>
> MATTHEW 10:40 (NIV)

Each evening at Mandy and Matthew's home, we gathered around the dinner table from our scattered activities of the day. These evening meals cemented the cohesive core of our connection. We'd become a small community. The little girls, Izzy and Emma, entered right in, recounting both delights and challenges in their relationships with other children and even adults. Mandy shared the joy she felt when her students achieved goals they had thought of as out of reach, as well as the stress she experienced when a student was stuck in the doldrums.

Matthew elicited our responses to imagery he was considering for his commissioned art. They all listened patiently as Candy and I rehearsed the uncertainties of our unfamiliar journey to a new life in Milwaukee.

No one said it out loud, but we were all aware that Jesus also had a seat at the dinner table those evenings. He was a contributor to those conversations, not just a topic for discussion or a resource to quote. Jesus was a magnet who drew us together and oriented us to each other around the table each evening. Never intrusive nor domineering, He was always present and participating. Nor was Jesus a pious overlay for the evening. He just infused the atmosphere.

Candy and I have been settled in the duplex for four years now, but our relationships with these friends continue to be an

Connected by Grace

Psalm 85:8–11 (NIV) tells of the intimate connection between God's steadfast love and faithfulness.

I will listen to what God the LORD says;
he promises peace to his people, his faithful servants—
but let them not turn to folly.
Surely his salvation is near those who fear him,
that his glory may dwell in our land.
Love and faithfulness meet together;
Righteousness and peace kiss each other.
Faithfulness springs forth from the earth,
and righteousness looks down from heaven.

extension of those evenings we spent together with Jesus around the dinner table. Jesus was both guest and host with His friends in Emmaus. Perhaps you can recall times you were a guest and realized that Jesus was enriching you as you received your host's hospitality. Or maybe you can remember having extended hospitality to someone who brought Jesus with them.

Jesus, You are both our host and our guest. Speak to us through those with whom we share hospitality. Thank You for welcoming us, dining with us, and helping us find a safe refuge.

Lessons from Home

LOGAN ELIASEN

And Jesus grew in wisdom and stature,
and in favor with God and man.

LUKE 2:52 (NIV)

"I can't believe the house sold after all this time," I said. I finished taping a cardboard box closed, then hefted it from the floor.

"Me neither," my dad said.

My parents' home had been on the market for the past three years, but they had owned it for nearly twenty. I couldn't imagine them living anywhere but here.

"It's time for us to move forward," my dad said. "We don't need this much room now that most of your brothers are grown. And I don't have the time to maintain this old house."

He was right. The house was a century and a half old and needed constant repairs. The house holds a pivotal place in the community, but it also held a pivotal place in my life. It was where many of my favorite memories had taken place. Though I had moved out a decade ago, I still thought of it as my home. A town had grown up around this house. But I had grown up in it. It wouldn't be easy for me to say goodbye.

I carried the box to the minivan and loaded it inside.

"That's enough for today," my dad said. "Let's take this load to the new house."

I slammed the back door of the vehicle closed. Getting into the passenger seat, I avoided looking up at the house.

The days passed quickly as the closing approached. I continued to help them clear out our old home. Soon, the interior was barely recognizable. The house felt like an empty photo frame.

The day before closing, I took a final trip through the home. I ran my hand over the curved banister of the staircase as I walked toward my childhood room. I stood in the window, looking down over the Mississippi Valley one last time. The river looked calm and steady—much different from the way I felt. From up here, I could see the neighbor's lawn I had mowed as my first summer job. I could see Main Street, where I had helped organize the homecoming parade. Just out of sight was the bench where I had let go of the first girl I loved. Saying goodbye had always been difficult for me. I stepped away and closed the door to my room for the last time.

> *Our lives begin to end the day we become silent about things that matter.*
>
> MARTIN LUTHER KING JR.

Later that afternoon, I sat with my mom in her new living room, drinking a cup of coffee. We were both quiet. I knew letting go of the house was even more difficult for her than for me.

"Are you OK?" my mom asked.

"Yeah," I said. I looked deep into my mug. "But so many of my memories are tied to the house. It's hard to leave it behind."

"A lot of living happened there," she said.

She was right. When they first bought the house, I had been twelve years old. So much had changed since then.

"Remember how I was bullied in high school?" I asked. "That house was the only place I felt safe during that time."

My mom nodded.

"The back swing is where I sat when I decided to change my major to theology," I said.

"I know," my mom said.

"The driveway is where I messed up the Explorer's engine while changing its oil." I chuckled. "I was so scared to tell Dad."

"That house was the place where you became who you are," my mom said. "It's where you learned endurance, honesty, and how to love Jesus."

I looked up. I hadn't thought about it that way.

I had been so focused on what I was letting go of that I had forgotten what I could hold on to and what remained. The house would no longer belong to my family, but the values I learned under its roof would stay with me for my entire life.

Letting go of the house would be difficult. But I was no longer the young boy who had once moved to the house on the river. During my time in that home, I had become the kind of man who could do difficult things—things like saying goodbye.

Jesus, thank You for providing me with opportunities to grow and mature. In this world of change, thank You for being unchanging and faithful.

Let the Stones Shout

RICK HAMLIN

"Blessed is the king who comes in the name of the Lord! Peace in heaven, and glory in the highest heaven!" Some of the Pharisees in the crowd said to him, "Teacher, order your disciples to stop." He answered, "I tell you, if these were silent, the stones would shout out."

LUKE 19:38–40 (NRSV)

In the fall of 1986, my wife, Carol, and I had just moved into our new apartment in upper Manhattan. Expecting our first child, we'd look out onto the sidewalk below our place at the people passing by—especially anyone pushing a stroller. We wondered what it would be like to be parents ourselves. We felt expectant, apprehensive, and even a bit unmoored to be living in this new place, on the cusp of a new experience in life.

One night, a few months before Carol's due date, I remember being lost in my thoughts, looking out the apartment window, seeing a bright sliver of the Hudson River and the reflected glow of the George Washington Bridge. Later, we trundled into bed, read a few pages from our respective books, kissed each other goodnight, then shut off the lights. We left the window slightly ajar on that warm autumn night. The darkness felt welcome, comforting even. We both fell soundly asleep.

Sometime later, all at once, a loud clamor woke us up. It was the sound of clapping, shouting, and people banging pots outside our window. Why was everyone making such a racket at this hour? I looked at the clock; it was after midnight. Then I heard it: "Go Mets!" The Mets had won the World Series! It was a cause for universal—or at least local—celebration.

Although sleep is precious, there are moments when being awakened in the middle of the night is worth it. Carol and I were caught up in the joy of that night. After that, we felt part of the neighborhood in a new way. We'd experienced something special, something communal, there.

Five months later, in the wee hours of the morning, I walked the more than a dozen blocks home from the hospital after the birth of our first son. I felt overwhelmed, overjoyed, and eager to tell someone the good news. I rushed home to call my family

Meditation Creates Positivity

Meditating is helpful in so many aspects of life, but it can create positivity and reduce stress.

Meditating might just mean taking five minutes to check in with yourself after a stressful encounter or a rough day. Close your eyes, focus on your breathing, clear your mind, and be at peace. Or meditate for longer intervals, more regularly, or while practicing guided imagery, which is when you create peaceful scenarios to help calm your mind.

If you're just starting out, or if meditating doesn't come easily to you, try committing five minutes to sitting with yourself and tuning into your body's natural rhythm.

back home in California. It would be well after midnight there, but this couldn't wait.

Mom answered the phone, her voice groggy.

"Mom," I practically shouted. "It's a boy!" A baby boy, our first son! Would that I could have banged a pot out a window to herald the good news. It sounded to me like Mom and Dad wanted to do the same thing. We were filled with joy.

The word *Gospel* means good news. And the Good News of Christ is cause for celebration! Even the stones would shout out, as Jesus said, if our hearts weren't lifted in praise. Since that time, when good news comes my way, whether it's about the love of God or something else that's wonderful in my life, I share it.

As I write this, dozens of years after that life-changing night, my life is about to be filled with joy and celebration again. Soon I expect to hear good news coming from that same hospital in New York City. Carol and I wait, expectantly, for the birth of our first grandchild. If it comes by means of a phone call in the middle of the night, we'll receive it with true gratitude and joy.

Dear Lord, thank You for the Good News of Your love and grace. I end this day remembering what it feels like to be full of joy. As I drift off to sleep, I thank You for the many blessings in my life.

Waves of Thanksgiving

LAWRENCE W. WILSON

When I consider your heavens, the work of your fingers, the moon and the stars, which you have set in place, what is mankind that you are mindful of them, human beings that you care for them?

PSALM 8:3–4 (NIV)

I love my work, but it had been incredibly busy for weeks. During intense periods of productivity, it's difficult for me to find rest, even during off hours. I know I'm not alone in that.

The day after I finished a large and consuming project, I left for a beach vacation with my daughter, Lydia, and son-in-law, Andy. We'd been planning the trip for two years. It had been scheduled for the previous summer but cancelled due to illness, and I'd had to forfeit a deposit on a cottage. My desire to get away from work and clear my mind, my growing sense of urgency to keep connected to my adult children, and my determination to make up for the loss of the previous year's trip created a perfect storm of heightened expectations.

As we drove south toward the Gulf Coast, I found myself growing more tense rather than more relaxed. My mind refused to surrender the stress of the previous weeks. The drive was long and tiring. The weather report predicted thunderstorms all week.

By the time we arrived, the sky had grown overcast. We hastily prepared a meal and ate in silence. I imagined a rainy week ahead with little to do.

I felt keen disappointment in the situation and in myself. I'd staked too much on this trip, and a week on the beach—even in good weather—could never have carried the weight I'd placed on it. Renewing my mind, redeeming past losses, reconnecting with my children. It was just seven days. Sun or no sun, this vacation was bound to collapse under the weight of my expectations.

"We should go to the grocery store tonight," I said. "We'll need some things for the week and probably won't feel like going in the morning."

"What time is sunset?" Lydia asked. We'd always kept a first-night ritual of walking on the beach at sunset.

I looked at the weather app on my phone.

"Seven thirty-seven," I said. "That's twenty-two minutes from now. But the way the sky's been, I'm afraid it'll be a disappointment."

Secretly, I hoped she'd give up the idea, but Lydia guards family traditions more fiercely than does the British royal family.

"We need to go now," she said. And so we did.

Minutes later we walked to the staircase that goes down to the beach. Andy and Lydia paused at the top to take a selfie. I heard the surf breaking for the first time and couldn't help but smile at their smiles. We descended the steps and felt the snow-white sand between our toes, the tension in me melted further. Like baby sea turtles, we moved instinctively toward the water. The waves lapped over our toes, cool and refreshing.

I looked to the sea and saw that the sky had cleared a bit. The view was clear and expansive. Then I turned to the right, and there it was, the huge red ball, sinking slowly toward the horizon. Families paused their walk, parents pointing out the sight to their children. Couples sat on blankets, snuggling and enjoying the moment together. Andy and Lydia stood arm in arm, foreheads touching, as if renewing their sacred bond before Jesus.

As the sun drew closer to its exit, I could see the Florida Panhandle nearly from stem to stern. Panama Beach was outlined behind me, Destin before me, Navarre just a dot on the horizon, all joined by this beautiful emerald-green shore. And there was I, a dot within a dot, a mere speck upon this glorious landscape. Yet Christ's love shone on me too, in these last moments of a most hectic day.

> *The whole earth is filled with awe at your wonders; where morning dawns, where evening fades, you call forth songs of joy.*
>
> PSALM 65:8 (NIV)

Standing there, I recalled the reason for our little family tradition, that evening walk on the beach. There is something spiritual, even mystical, about the sunset. It resets not only the day but all of creation. It refreshes the soul. Sunset is an act of creative destruction. One day is erased. All its pain and all its triumphs are erased with a ball of fire. And from that little death, the new day rises. This miracle is repeated every day when I am willing to notice. In fact, this gift is unending. At this very moment, the sun is setting somewhere, washing the fatigue from weary souls and replacing it with the promise of rest and strength for a new day.

Gratitude lapped at my soul as gently as the ocean's foam. Now I could think only of good things. My daughter and son-in-law, gloriously happy in their marriage. Truly this was a gift given from Jesus to them, and also a gift to me. My work fulfills a

Make Time for Nature

Have you ever had the good fortune of standing on a beach, gazing into the majestic vastness of the ocean, on a cold winter's day? The effect of being in such a beautiful natural space can be instantaneous and powerful, connecting that deep-seated human need to feel a sense of awe, our smallness in the presence of something vast.

Most forays into nature, like gazing out at the ocean or walking in the woods, are journeys into a special kind of silence that provides an ideal opportunity to be overcome with gratitude, presence, and peace.

Tomorrow, spend time in nature, which reveals God's power, wisdom, creativity, and lovingkindness. Thank Him for reminding you of His loving presence through the beauty of His creation.

lifetime ambition. It challenges and delights me, two gifts in one. I am alive. And I have the privilege of watching the sun set over one of the most beautiful places on earth. I am truly blessed.

Lord Jesus, thank You for caring for us, refreshing us with the promise of a new day tomorrow. Thank You for taking our weary minds and hearts and giving us rest.

Respite for My Soul

BRENDA YODER

*Then he said to them, "My soul is
overwhelmed with sorrow to the point of death.
Stay here and keep watch with me."*

MATTHEW 26:38 (NIV)

I drove home from school that day with a headache, my eyes heavy. My heart was even heavier: It had been one of the toughest days I'd ever had as a school counselor. As I provided services for fifth- and sixth-graders, my days were always busy with classroom lessons, helping kids resolve conflict, screening reports of bullying, and supporting teachers and students with behavioral interventions. I loved the energy I got from working with students and the variety of things I did each day. I was accustomed to dealing with stressful situations, including explosive students and irate parents.

This particular school day, however, was particularly draining in every sense—physically, mentally, and emotionally. That day, I dealt with one difficult and heartbreaking issue after another. In meeting after meeting, students shared their struggles, and the details were difficult to hear. I prayed that Jesus would comfort them; I prayed that He would comfort me. I longed to go home and curl up into the comforting lap of Jesus. The verse from Psalm 23:2 ran through my mind, "He makes me lie down in green pastures."

I am adamant and proactive about self-care and professional boundaries, so I try never to bring the stress of my workday home. Upbeat music or prayerful silence often lightens the emotional or mental load during my evening commute. Even the ritual of driving past our family farm to the driveway of our house is therapeutic. It's like I physically leave the day's events at the mile marker before home, creating a physical boundary along with a mental one.

Unfortunately, none of these tactics worked that day.

I walked in my kitchen, put my purse on the counter, then told my husband and kids, "I've had a really rough day. I need to be by myself. You'll have to make dinner." I went into my bedroom, shut the door, and cried.

For a moment, I felt guilty that I couldn't switch to a more cheerful demeanor for the sake of my family, but then I remembered the example Jesus set, both withdrawing from other people when He needed to and also asking His disciples for their support. He asked them to sit with Him, to pray with Him, and He expressed His true emotions. I began to feel a sense of comfort, knowing Jesus spoke up for His needs in His most difficult hour. I felt invited to share the burdens of my heart with Him.

"Come to me," Jesus says, "all you who are weary and burdened, and I will give you rest. Take my yoke upon you and learn from me, for I am gentle and humble in heart, and you will find

> *It is a common experience that a problem difficult at night is resolved in the morning after the committee of sleep has worked on it.*
>
> JOHN STEINBECK

rest for your souls" (Matthew 11:28–29, NIV). In the quiet of my bedroom, my heart open to Jesus, I felt His gentle and loving heart. I knew He was giving me rest for my soul.

Jesus, thank You loving me. Thank You for always keeping Your promise to give me rest for my soul. Thank You that I don't have to bear my burdens alone. Tonight, while I sleep, I ask for renewal and gentle rest.

A Hairy Choice

JEANETTE LEVELLIE

*And when you are old, I will still be there,
carrying you. When your limbs grow tired,
your eyes are weak, and your hair a silvery
gray, I will carry you as I always have.
I will carry you and save you.*

ISAIAH 46:4 (VOICE)

"How do you like your hair color, honey?" my husband Kevin asked. He's a preacher, not a hair stylist, but he always seemed to gain a feeling of satisfaction after transforming my faded auburn to strawberry blonde.

"It's lovely," I said. "You did a great job, as always. But I'm so tired of doing this."

We'd been slopping this goo on my scalp since I was thirty-five, three decades earlier. And to keep up with the encroaching white roots, we needed to do it every three weeks!

"I'm not sure I want to go natural, though," I admitted. "I'd hate to look older than I am. Besides, I love being a redhead. It matches my personality."

Kev was smart enough not to give me advice of any kind. "Whatever you decide, sweetheart, you'll be beautiful," he said.

I'd been diligent in taking good care of my hair and skin, ever trying to avoid signs of aging. But those white hairs showed up anyway! You hear about "fine lines" and "crow's feet," but when I am being hardest on myself, I see my wrinkles in much less elegant terms. Think motorcycle ruts and ostrich feet!

In the midst of wondering about letting my hair go naturally white, I saw a photo of my fellow redhead and friend Peggy on a social media site. Her hair had grown into angelic white. When I told Peg how stunning she looked, she said it took months to grow it out. I couldn't bear the thought of white roots with red hair. I asked several friends for their input. Half of them said keep it red. The other half said let it go natural. I was back where I started.

> *As the Father has loved me, so have I loved you. Now remain in my love.*
>
> JOHN 15:9 (NIV)

Finally, I did the best thing I've ever learned to do when I'm at an impasse: I consulted with the Lord.

"Jesus," I prayed. "I don't know if this is vain or silly of me to obsess over the color of my hair. But please show me Your will."

I used to feel embarrassed to ask for the Lord's help with little things like what to order at a restaurant or the best time to call someone until I heard a preacher say, "Nothing is too little for God. And nothing is too big for Him either." Clearly, my "hairy" dilemma was a small issue, but not too small to take to Jesus.

My answer came when I saw a verse from Isaiah that references God's abiding love for us—including when our hair is "silvery gray" (Isaiah 46:4). I came across that verse, seemingly by accident, three times over the course of two days.

Make Love Your Job

Watch what God does, and then you do it, like children who learn proper behavior from their parents. Mostly what God does is love you. Keep company with him and learn a life of love. Observe how Christ loved us. His love was not cautious but extravagant. He didn't love in order to get something from us but to give everything of himself to us. Love like that.
—Ephesians 5:1–2 (MSG)

"OK, Lord, I get it," I answered. "My heart—not the color of my hair—measures my worth. I will trust You to see myself through Your eyes of love."

I settled on a plan to have my stylist add white highlights over a few months, so I could gradually go natural. I've been surprised at the compliments I've received. And I've discovered something else: As long as I smile when I look in the mirror, my white hair and wrinkles look softer and more attractive.

Besides, both Jesus and my husband Kevin love me and tell me I'm beautiful. And that's what truly matters.

Dear Jesus, thank You for Your enduring love for me. As I move toward sleep tonight, help me to remember, with gratitude, all the blessings and protections of this life. Help me, too, to see myself through Your eyes of love.

Two Burglars

DURWOOD SMITH

Therefore I say unto you, Take no thought for
your life, what ye shall eat, or what ye shall drink;
nor yet for your body, what ye shall put on.

MATTHEW 6:25 (KJV)

In early November, a month before my wedding, I applied for a church pastorate in a small coastal town and was voted in, the congregation assuming correctly that I would be married by the time I preached my first sermon. My fiancée and I had already secured a furnished apartment but were out of money to stock the cupboards. Maybe a rocky road ahead? We had college debt, an old car, and empty stomachs. I was to be paid monthly, so a paycheck was thirty days out from the day I'd begin work in December.

While our honeymoon was simple and brief, we promised ourselves we would "do it up right" sometime later, someday. Until my first weekend at the new church, we stayed in our parents' spare bedrooms and ate at their tables. We truly had no money to our name, and the gifts of meals from our families meant all the world to us. I knew that God always provided, and He was providing for us through their kindness. And I trusted that Jesus would take care of our needs. Didn't He feed the 5,000 with a few loaves and fish? Hadn't Jesus provided drink at a lengthy wedding festival? Didn't Jesus cook a campfire breakfast for the disciples after the resurrection? Old and New Testaments proved that God would provide. We were looking to Jesus to carry us through. Armed with a theology degree and a marriage certificate, my wife and I embarked on a life together in a town of lumberjacks and mill workers. We were happy, but hungry. How would we make it to our first paycheck?

One night, a few days before my job started, with nothing in the house to eat and no invitations to dinner, we toyed with just using a credit card to buy food. But with no assets and a load of college debt hanging over us, we had been warned about using credit cards, especially early on in our marriage.

"We could use the card just this once," my wife said.

"No, let's hold off," I said. "I have twelve dollars in my wallet. We can use that."

"But it won't last long enough."

"Jesus knows our need," I said, trying to sound full of faith. Privately, though, I was worried. "What are our other options? Could we drop in on your sister and her husband? Surely they'd feed us dinner."

"You can't just drop in on relatives and ask, 'What's on the menu tonight,'" my wife said. "They've already been so kind. I don't feel like I can keep asking."

"Maybe I could call the Board of Trustees chairman and ask for an advance," I suggested.

"Wouldn't that be embarrassing and start us off on a questionable foot with the congregation?"

"Well, I'm out of ideas," I said, anguished. "We could blow our last twelve dollars and then where would we be? I'm so sorry, I feel like I didn't plan very well."

"Don't you think we should pray?" my wife asked.

"Yes, God will provide," I said. *But how?*

On the couch in our little apartment, we held hands and bowed to pray. "Dear Jesus," I said. "Here we are. You see us. Our money won't last through the month. We don't want to go further in debt. You have proven faithful to us in the past. We don't have anywhere to turn except to You. We are depending on You. Thank you in advance for your answer. Please show us what to do."

The twelve dollars was gone in the next two days. Saturday evening, before our first official Sunday as pastor and wife, we visited the empty church, letting ourselves in. In order to move into the church study with my books and supplies, I had been given a set of keys. Traversing the long stairway to the second-floor sanctuary, we ended at the top landing to have a look, walk the auditorium, step behind the pulpit, get the feel of it all. Tomorrow was our "big day." Entering back out into the landing of the stairs, we spied grocery bags full of food. Canned goods, flour, twenty pounds of potatoes, sugar, canned ham, bread, and vegetables. Written on the sacks was our name: "The Smiths." What generosity!

> *But my God shall supply all your need according to His riches in glory by Christ Jesus.*
>
> PHILIPPIANS 4:19 (KJV)

"Wow, these must be for us. "Thank You, Jesus!" we rejoiced. Gratefully, we carried armloads of groceries down the stairs and out to the car. Buoyed with our bonanza, we smiled all the way back to the apartment, threw open the cupboard doors and went to work carefully putting things away. We enjoyed a beautiful dinner together that night, full of joy and gratitude.

Sunday morning, we arrived at the church ahead of the service and were met by the chairman of the board.

"I'm so sorry to have to tell you this," he said, "But we meant to give you a food shower this morning during the service. But, somebody broke into the church last night and stole all the grocery bags full of food. So, we'll have to plan it for later."

I looked at my wife. *Oops,* I thought.

"Uh, Fred, I confess, there was no burglar, it was us. We saw our name on the sacks, and we thought we were meant to take them. Please forgive us," I pleaded. It was kindly overlooked, but the awkward moment lingered in our minds for years. Later, of course, we learned to laugh about it.

Looking back on that period in my life, one of such uncertainty and financial instability, I remember the feeling of ease and gratitude for the gifts others gave us, whether a bag of groceries, a home-cooked meal, or the gift of accepting us, mistakes and all.

*Lord, thank You for all the ways
You've met my needs, over the course of my
whole life. You are a generous God, ever giving
me good things. I thank You, Jesus, tonight.*

As He Loves Us

RANDY PETERSEN

*By this everyone will know that you are
my disciples, if you love one another.*

JOHN 13:35 (NIV)

I knew, with all the conviction my four-year-old heart could summon, that I did *not* pick Mr. Miller's flowers. Several decades later, I still maintain my innocence.

Our next-door neighbor prided himself on his gardening skills. My mom had often commented on the gorgeous array of color leading up to his front door. But now Mr. Miller had called her with a problem. He had seen me in his front yard, along with my friend Robby, picking some of his flowers.

"Mr. Miller wants you to apologize," Mom said.

"But I didn't do it," I said.

"He says he saw you and Robby picking his flowers," Mom said.

"Maybe Robby did, but I did not!" I insisted.

Mr. Miller could be grumpy sometimes, but he wasn't mean. Looking back, I think he just saw this as a teachable moment, one that might protect his precious garden in the future. And it *was* a teachable moment—just not in the way anyone expected.

Looking back, I imagine Mom was in a quite a quandary. She would have known that I was a good kid with a tender conscience, not the sort to misbehave and lie about it. The more I maintained my innocence, the more uncertain she must have felt. Should she believe her son or the accusing neighbor? She might have thought that I had just blocked the misdeed from my memory or maybe that Mr. Miller's eyesight was failing. I bet she wondered how she'd keep the peace in this situation.

Personal Change through God's Grace

When we self-reflect, we can't help but notice areas in our life that we would like to change—like weight, job, or finances. In seeking change, many of us turn to self-help books, podcasts, articles, seminars, and life coaches. While these resources may provide great insight on how to work towards changing these areas, we tend to forget the most powerful resource of all: grace.

God's grace can take us places that no book or person can. It was grace that transformed Paul into a preacher. It was grace that brought Mary Magdalene to witness Jesus's crucifixion and resurrection.

The list of men and women whose lives were transformed by God's grace is never ending. In order to truly change, it takes more than willpower and hard work. It takes God's grace. Through God's grace and our faith in Him, all things are possible. He can change how we think, live, and love.

"I believe you," Mom finally said, "but Mr. Miller thinks he saw you do this, and we want to keep being friends with him. We want to be good neighbors. He wants you to say you're sorry and promise never to do it again."

"But, I didn't do it *this* time," I said.

"I know, but he wants to be sure it won't happen ever again," Mom said. "Maybe you could help make sure Robby doesn't pick his flowers. You know that Mr. Miller really loves his garden."

"I promise not to pick his flowers."

"So you'll say you're sorry?" Mom asked.

"You want me to tell a lie about picking his flowers?" I asked.

"No, I want you to make peace with him," she answered. And then she told me, again, that I needed to apologize. We practiced my apology a few times, and she walked me over to his house. As I recall, I said what our neighbor needed to hear, that I was sorry and wouldn't do it again. I wanted to blurt out the truth, but I didn't. In hindsight, I realize that Mom was trying her best to follow Jesus's injunction to "Love your neighbor." She may have believed that I was innocent, but what she knew was that, until he received an apology, Mr. Miller would be unhappy.

Some might have a problem with the way my mom resolved that situation. Shouldn't truth win out? If I didn't pick the flowers, why should I be made to apologize? Don't the facts matter? Sure, they do, but as Mom probably realized, there's always a margin of error. Our perception of the facts might be amiss. She taught me that it's always best to lean toward love.

Over the course of my life, I've tried to do that. Maintaining a relationship, whether it's with a neighbor, friend, or family member, matters greatly to me, so I try to meet the other person halfway. I use what I call the "55 percent error" and the "60 percent solution."

Let me explain. You see, I think, in most relationships, people overestimate their own contributions and underestimate those of the other person. For instance, you might think you're doing

55 percent of the work in your marriage, and you might begrudge your spouse for only doing 45 percent. But *both* partners may see things this way, each assuming *they're* doing more than their share of the housework, hands-on raising of children, emotional support, or a myriad of domestic responsibilities. That perception can end up leaving both people in a marriage feeling bitter, but Jesus asks us to *love* not *resent* one another!

But if both partners plan to put in 60 percent of the effort—if they *both* see that as an acceptable contribution to maintaining their relationship—then the acrimony vanishes. This widens the margin of error, so even if both of them are overestimating their contributions, they're still give more than required. When this becomes a normal way to live together, they stop keeping score, and they both lean toward love.

Compassion is the basis of morality.

ARTHUR SCHOPENHAUER

I'm only human, of course, and won't pretend that I *always* follow this strategy with important people in my life, but when I do, I feel closer to them and also to Jesus.

I try to remember it's better to be loving than to be right. That little phrase is stunning in its simplicity. Sometimes, when my convictions clash with someone else's, I repeat that in my mind. *It's better to be loving than to be right.* And sometimes the words trouble me: *Is love really better?* Then an array of Bible verses sweep through my mind—like the beginning of the famous "love chapter," 1 Corinthians 13. "Though I speak with the tongues of men and of angels . . ." The stately language in the King James Version might distract us from the fact that a series of highly religious, eminently righteous activities are described, and each of them is declared *pointless* without love. This includes understanding "all mysteries, and all knowledge" and faith that can "remove mountains." Without love, they are nothing.

Elsewhere, Scripture calls love "the fulfillment of the law" (Romans 13:10, NIV). Within a culture that viewed biblical law as the ultimate authority of what was right, this passage sets up an even more ultimate consideration: love. It was the "new command" Jesus gave his closest followers and gives to us. He told us to love one another, as He has loved us (John 13:34–35).

We can argue for decades over who's right about certain issues or who's working harder or even about who wronged whom, but Jesus teaches us that it's better to be loving than right. And isn't that the value I learned at age four, when my wise mother dared me to swallow my pride and make peace with my flower-loving neighbor? I believe it is!

Dear Jesus, thank You for showing me what love looks like. Tonight, as I prepare for sleep, I thank You for the reminder that it's better to be loving than right. Thank You for all the people in my life who have loved me so well.

My Charging Station

BOB HOSTETLER

*Come to me, all you who are weary and
burdened, and I will give you rest.*

MATTHEW 11:28 (NIV)

Throughout my adult life I've had trouble falling asleep at night. Sometimes I attribute this problem to external circumstances. A neighbor's barking dog. The pop and bang of fireworks. Or, when I'm traveling, unfamiliar beds, pillows, and heating or air-conditioning units throw off my ability to settle down to sleep. Sometimes, however, the source of my sleeplessness is internal. Maybe I'm anticipating an early morning flight or important appointment the next day. Or perhaps I've got leftover adrenaline after watching a late-night baseball game.

I've tried many things to improve my sleep habits. I've reduced my caffeine intake, added a cup of hot chamomile tea to my evening routine, and refrained from using my computer, or any screen for that matter, after dinner. Those may have had some

> *To fall in love with God is the greatest romance; to seek him the greatest adventure; to find him, the greatest human achievement.*
>
> SAINT AUGUSTINE

impact, but one part of my going-to-bed routine has been much more beneficial.

I started my bedtime preparations one night in much the same way as I always did, walking to my nightstand and plugging in all my devices so they'd charge overnight. But, in that perfectly ordinary moment, I had an epiphany. Whether I'm in my own bedroom, a hotel room, or somewhere else, I connect my devices to the power source that will enable them to begin the next day fully recharged. But what I'd lost sight of is that my mind and heart require something similar every night. A connection. Not to electricity, but to something—or, rather, to Someone.

When Jesus says, "Come to me, all you who are weary and burdened, and I will give you rest" (Matthew 11:28, NIV), He invites us to become His followers and to learn from Him. He continues: "Take my yoke upon you and learn from me, for I am gentle and humble in heart, and you will find rest for your souls. For my yoke is easy and my burden is light" (Matthew 11:29–30, NIV).

But what if that invitation applies also to those of us who have already become His followers? What if He's extending a daily offer to us to keep us charged? What if I understood my personal connection with Jesus to be like a recharging station—a nightly habit that is indispensable if I want to get the rest I need?

I've long made Bible reading and prayer a regular part of my evening routine, but I must admit at times it's been, well, *routine.* Yet I've come to understand that it's not my effort that fosters rest; it's the coming, the connection, the spark, the flow of mercy, love, and grace from Jesus to me that quiets my mind, calms my heart, and soothes my soul.

Since that realization, I do my best to make sure that, first and foremost, my evening routine includes connecting with Jesus. It

Praying with Compassion for Others

The Gospel compels us to carry out what many consider to be Jesus's impractical principles: Love our enemies and pray for those who persecute us, forgive others as He forgives us, do not judge, love your neighbor as yourself and so forth. These principles provide a roadmap for how we are to live, love, and pray for others.

A compassionate Jesus took great interest and concern in the needs of others. He extended justice, kindness, and love to all He encountered. He reached out to the despised tax collectors, healed lepers, and forgave a woman caught in adultery. He repeatedly demonstrated His compassion to all.

How do these acts teach us to pray compassionately for others? They remind us that people and their needs matter to Jesus. It means that we, too, need to embody that spirit in our prayers.

When we pray with compassion for others, we seek to connect to them—to feel their pain, understand their struggles, place ourselves in their shoes. Praying with compassion requires us to remove judgment and be merciful.

Let us remember that we pray to a compassionate Jesus, whose heart is open to our very own needs, a Jesus who weeps with us and is merciful when our actions miss the mark. This same Jesus who hears our prayers also hears the pleas of others.

may happen through singing a hymn or from a Gospel reading. It may spring from reading a tender poem or devotional essay. It's sometimes unplanned and unexpected, but it never fails to bring rest, fulfilling the promise, "I will refresh the weary and satisfy the faint" (Jeremiah 31:25, NIV).

Jesus, night after night, You promise to release me from the weights and burdens of the day. Tonight, I come to You with gratitude, trusting that You recharge my heart, mind, and soul through this night, as I repose in Your embrace.

Gathering Together

BETH GORMONG

*There is no doubt that it is around the family
and the home that all the greatest virtues ... are
created, strengthened, and maintained.*

WINSTON CHURCHILL

The first thing I saw when my husband, Jeff, and I walked in Dad's back door was his dining room table carefully set for a special family meal. Four china plates, four stemware glasses, a freshly ironed tablecloth, and a vase of daffodils from his flower garden awaited us. It was a welcoming way to celebrate the day.

"You're here! Happy Easter," he said, getting up from his recliner.

"Happy Easter to you too. The table looks beautiful," I said.

I saw a blush of pleasure creep up his face as I wrapped him in a quick hug before rushing my chicken casserole, Mom's recipe, to the kitchen. I slid it onto the middle rack, thankful that Dad had preheated the oven for me. A white Depression glass pitcher filled with water sat on the kitchen counter. We sat around the table catching up while we waited for the casserole to cook and our daughter, Jess, to arrive.

An hour later, Jess knocked on the screen door, holding a family dessert, calypso pie. My sister-in-law usually contributed this ice cream–and-Oreo-smothered dessert to family gatherings. But not this year. Instead of squeezing twenty-five or more people around tables, it was just Dad, Jess, Jeff, and me. My siblings were visiting their children and grandchildren in various states, leaving the four of us to carry on the family tradition.

We sat down, clasped hands, and Dad asked Jeff to pray. I looked at all the food on the table, enough for a huge crowd, all the family favorites: corn and green beans from Dad's garden, Jell-O salad, the chicken casserole, green salad, and rolls. The only thing missing was the rest of the family.

But as we passed the food and conversation flowed, I noticed how easy it was to hear each other

It is not joy that makes us grateful; it is gratitude that makes us joyful.

DAVID STEINDL-RAST

and how much elbow room I had, instead of dealing with the normal crush of bodies and raucous gathering. With such a small group, we could give each other our undivided attention. It was a peaceful, intimate Easter dinner.

After clearing the table, dividing up the leftovers, and washing the dishes, we sat in the living room and discussed plans for Jess's graduation a few weeks later. We ended our time together as we always do, with a family prayer hug. Standing in a circle, arms around each other, like a sports team getting ready for a game, Dad prayed and asked for Jesus's blessing over us. Then Jess, Jeff, and I left, loaded down with leftovers and packets of flower seeds from Dad's and my sister's flower gardens.

On the way home, I reflected on the day. It wasn't perfect. I missed my brother's big laugh, my sister-in-law's flashing camera, and my own absent children. But Dad had worked hard to make it special, like he and Mom had always done at holidays. We each did our part to keep our family's cherished rituals alive. I was reminded of 1 Thessalonians 5:16–18 (NIV): "Rejoice always, pray continually, give thanks in all circumstances; for this is God's will for you in Christ Jesus."

Dear Jesus, may I be thankful for each precious moment I spend with those I love. Help me to accept the changes that happen in life, and help me to preserve the traditions that echo and reflect Your love for us.

In His Image

RICK HAMLIN

*Make your face shine on your servant
and teach me your decrees.*

PSALM 119:135 (NIV)

Sometimes when I pray, I hold an image in my mind. It might be a hoped-for outcome, like when I pictured a friend, who had just had hip replacement surgery, up and walking without a cane. Sometimes it's a positive change for people who are yearning for one, like when I've imagined a couple who has been struggling in their relationship smiling together and holding hands. I also envision changes I want to see in *myself*. I picture myself as becoming more loving, caring, and less judgmental. I spend time in prayer imagining I'm more like Jesus.

A few days ago, I had a surprising conversation about mental imagery with my good friend Lee, an art historian and critic. When we spoke, I learned that in addition to reviewing the exhibitions that she attends in different galleries and museums, critiquing art with an eagle eye and appreciative gaze, Lee also has a practice of loading specific images from the world of art into her phone to represent each of her friends. When one of us calls, a picture she associates with that person appears on the screen.

Before I tell you about the image she chose for me, I'll share that she explained that for one friend, the image is that person's favorite flower. For another, it is a statue they both liked in a museum. Some of these pictures recall a happy memory or places she's visited with someone in her life. Lee is a world traveler; she spent much of her childhood in Italy and Spain because her father was an international businessman. Her husband is retired from the foreign service, and they have lived all over the world together—from Brussels to Zagreb to Madras. Her travels have shaped her and, of course, inform her work as an art critic. She has knowledge and insights that boggle my mind. If I had to choose a picture to represent her, it might be an iconic landmark from one of those distant places—the Taj Mahal in India, say, or the Spanish Steps in Rome.

It's not enough to have lived. We should be determined to live for something.

WINSTON CHURCHILL

The other day, when I called Lee and identified myself, she said, "Oh, I knew it was you. There's a picture that pops up on my phone whenever you call." And then she explained her practice of choosing images to represent her friends.

Of course, I was very curious to hear what she'd chosen for me. When Lee told me that it is a portrait of Jesus, I was startled. She said that there is a beautiful rendering of Christ painted on an antique urn in her home and, to my surprise, she thinks of me when she sees it. I was speechless; I didn't dare ask her why.

But... what an honor and, truly, what a *challenge* to know that she associates me with Jesus. How humbling that someone would see the Lord in anything I've said or done or written. To

Infuse Your Life with Purpose and Meaning

Look for ways to share the love of Jesus through the work He has given you to do.

Mother Teresa said, "Many people mistake our work for our vocation. Our vocation is the love of Jesus." What she's saying is that the work, no matter what it is, is secondary. Our vocation—what we do—our fundamental focus and calling—is the love of Jesus. His love informs whatever daily tasks there are to perform and infuses them with purpose and meaning.

be like Jesus—to have His face shine upon me—is life's greatest opportunity and gift.

Ever since that revelation, I've used Lee's imagery in my bedtime prayers. Sure, I still picture outcomes like a friend recovering in the hospital or a couple making it to the other side of a rocky spot in their marriage. But now I picture someone else coming alongside them, entering the scene. I picture Jesus there with them, as close as their breath.

Thank You for making Your face shine upon me, Jesus. May I be more like You, Lord, in all that I do.

United in Love

LORI HATCHER

*You are no longer foreigners and aliens, but fellow citizens
with God's people and members of God's household…
a dwelling in which God lives by his Spirit.*

EPHESIANS 2:19, 22 (NIV)

Furnished with sixty folding chairs, two microphones, and a portable lectern, the room bustled with people. Women waved fans and blotted damp foreheads. Music emanating from two guitars and a tambourine competed with the traffic noise outside. This was Comunidad la Bíblica, a church that met in a storefront in the Mexican Baja peninsula.

It was impossible for me not to notice the contrast between this worship space and the one I was accustomed to back in the U.S. At home, my church has a 1,000-seat sanctuary with padded pews, an orchestra, and air conditioning. But, although the creature comforts were simpler at this house of worship, my family and I immediately knew that it was the same Holy Spirit who lived in our hearts and moved among us all, and although our cultures and the languages we spoke were vastly different, we all worshipped and were loved by the same Jesus.

We'd traveled from Columbia, South Carolina to the farthest tip of Mexico—Land's End—to minister alongside friends who'd planted a church there. I knew the fledgling church met in two rented rooms in a retail building, but I wasn't prepared for the Golden Palace, a three-story structure with open doors and a steady flow of shoppers.

On entering the building, Carlos, our missionary friend, pointed upstairs where the church assembled on the second floor. Adults crowded into the largest room for Sunday school and worship. Thirty or so children sat on carpet squares in the smaller room. Youth reclined on the floor of the breezeway that separated the church's space from a barber shop and a clothing store.

I'm not a Spanish speaker, but I listened intently while the pastor made opening announcements. I was able to recognize only a few words: *Señor, la Biblia, los misionarios.* I resigned myself to a lengthy church service where I would understand little that was spoken, but perhaps understand the spirit of what was being said.

> *A friend is someone who knows the song in your heart and can sing it back to you when you have forgotten the words.*
>
> C.S. LEWIS

At one point, the worship leader stood, walked to the microphone, and invited the congregation to stand. I expected the musicians to play music unfamiliar to myself. Instead, the notes of the beloved hymn "Great Is Thy Faithfulness" reached my culture-shocked ears.

All around me, my Mexican brothers and sisters in Christ lifted their hands and closed their eyes.

"*Oh Dios eterno, Tu misericordia,*" they sang, their voices swelling, blending, and soaring.

I joined in, in English: "There is no shadow of turning with thee."

As they sang in their native tongue and I in mine, our voices united in a concert for Jesus, our Lord.

"Thou changest not, Thy compassions, they fail not, as thou hast been, Thou forever wilt be."

We spoke two different languages and lived in two different cultures, but the same Holy Spirit lived in our hearts and moved among us. The same Jesus loved us. As the music swelled around me, I closed my eyes and pictured the sound of our voices floating up to heaven and reaching God's ears.

Surrounded by my brothers and sisters in Christ, united by God's Spirit and joining our voices in praise to Him, I glimpsed what heaven will be like one day. There, people from every tribe, tongue, and nation will gather around the throne of Jesus and sing, "Holy, Holy, Holy is the Lord God Almighty." Singing in Spanish and English, German and Russian, Portuguese and Azerbaijani, and countless other languages, our voices will blend, swell, and soar, filling God's ears with the sound of our worship.

Quiet Time

Regular quiet time will help you stay connected to Jesus throughout the day. Think of Him when you wake up, offer brief prayers of gratitude as you notice things, pray with friends on the phone or via email. Walking with Him all day will make it easier to step aside from life and savor His presence for a focused time.

When you begin to look for Him in every situation, He will show you more about Himself.

That day, I caught a glimpse of the beauty of God's people, and my heart overflowed. Tears of wonder and awe spilled from my eyes and ran down my cheeks. In an instant, I understood that we weren't strangers separated by geography and language. We were *family* united by Jesus and His love.

Jesus, thank You for welcoming me into Your beautiful, diverse family. Help me to see my brothers and sisters in You with Your eyes, appreciating our differences and marveling at the unity we enjoy through the power of Your Holy Spirit. Tonight, I pray for believers around the world that You would comfort and protect us. In the strong name of Jesus I pray.

Wasting Time

NORM STOLPE

Come with me by yourselves to a
quiet place and get some rest.

MARK 6:31 (NIV)

During my pastoral career, I took an annual three-day personal retreat. I remember my first one at Francis House of Prayer in Westampton, New Jersey. It took two or three trips to lug my suitcase, attaché case, and a couple of tote bags of books up to my second-floor room. I was met by a Sister who welcomed me cordially enough but suggested that all I would need would be a Bible, a notebook and pen, and maybe a hymnal.

"Oh, but I'm wanting to dig into some things I think Jesus has been telling me lately," I said.

She smiled and replied, "I'm sure that if you are quiet enough to listen, He'll tell you whatever you need to hear."

Determined to accomplish something valuable in these special days, I plunged into my books that first day. But the second day, I gave myself permission to walk around the grounds and enjoy the woodsy surroundings. By my second night, I had packed away my books and just chose to relish sitting in the garden listening to the wind chime. The Sister had been right; I could best hear Jesus speaking to me when I kept silent.

After that retreat, I began to wean myself off of all of the books I'd carry around to fill free moments. I started to relinquish my self-assigned quest for each retreat. Initially, I'd felt compelled to have something concrete to share with the congregations I served: insights for teaching and preaching, ideas for ministry ventures, pithy quotes from esteemed authors. After all, these were paid workdays and the costs were covered by my study leave allowance. At the very least, I'd hoped my congregation would think that I returned more energized to serve them. I felt obligated to assure them that I wasn't wasting my time.

Eventually I was able to, as it were, sit on a bench overlooking a lake with Jesus at my side. Together we watched the sun set. As dusk faded into dark, stars began to glow, and I gradually recognized constellations. I always felt joy identifying Orion's Belt. On some occasions, depending on the season, watching those three stars slip below the horizon was a gentle reminder to retire for the evening. I became increasingly comfortable just wasting time with Jesus. Just being with Him.

> He says, "Be still, and know that I am God; I will be exalted among the nations, I will be exalted in the earth."
>
> PSALM 46:10 (NIV)

When I started doing interim pastorates at the conclusion of my career, and then after I retired, the annual retreats were not practical. But I still craved "wasting time" with Jesus. Now I build a twenty-minute silent time with Jesus into almost every day's schedule. My adult children, and sometimes even my wife, will gently tease me about staring into the flame of my oil lamp, but they also know not to disturb the silence when the lamp is lit. But perhaps the best opportunities for wasting time with Jesus come in the evenings after the supper dishes are washed and put away. My wife and I play a game, get in our pajamas, and read to each other aloud from devotional books. The point is not winning the games or learning lessons from the devotionals. Rather, they are our way of wasting time with each other and with Jesus each evening.

To be sure, most people do not have careers that allow for an annual three-day retreat. Tasks such as housekeeping and childcare may preclude a daily window of silence. Besides, prolonged silence doesn't suit everyone's temperament. Yet, I suggest that Jesus does invite us into a rhythm of spending some time with Him every day, much as friends and loved ones crave just being together. Jesus affirms that rest in our daily rhythm is not wasting time. He invites us to be with Him.

Thank You, Jesus, for being present with me tonight and always. As I quiet down after a busy day, let me hear Your voice, sense Your presence, and relax with You.

The Third Voice

BOB HOSTETLER

Jesus said, "Have the people sit down."

JOHN 6:10 (NIV)

Our family was visiting Red Rock Canyon National Conservation Area, a few miles west of Las Vegas. My granddaughter Avery, then four years old, was the youngest in our group. When we stopped off at a promising trailhead, her two older siblings and two older cousins jumped at the chance to climb the imposing rocks alongside the steep trail while the adults waited nearby.

Avery halted. She saw the other kids gleefully scrambling up the hillside, but her eyes widened as she scanned the giant rock formations.

"I'm scared," she said, her voice trembling. A few seconds later, however, Avery made her hands into fists, thrust them onto her hips, and exclaimed, "But I'm doing this!" With those words, she bounded up the trail and onto the rocks and soon overtook her sister, brother, and cousins.

Avery's determination in that moment has come to characterize her approach to life. She faces challenges with a positive attitude. She may be afraid at times—as we all are—but she doesn't let fear hold her back. She overcomes limitations with fiery determination.

In the days of Jesus's earthly ministry, He met many people who let fear hold them back. Once as He sat on a hillside to teach, a crowd of thousands of people gathered to hear Him. He turned to one of his closest followers, Philip.

"Where shall we buy bread for these people to eat?" Jesus asked him.

Philip was apparently taken aback by the question.

"Eight months' wages would not buy enough bread for each one to have a bite!" he said, looking at the vast number of hungry people. Philip saw an impossible situation and voiced despair.

> *We should certainly count our blessings, but we should also make our blessings count.*
>
> NEAL A. MAXWELL

Another of Jesus's disciples was standing close enough to hear the conversation. This man, Andrew, said, "Here is a boy with five small barley loaves and two small fish, but how far will they go among so many?"

Andrew didn't echo Philip's abject fear, but he did express doubt, wondering how so little food could feed so many people. But Andrew had been there when Jesus had turned water into wine. He'd heard Jesus say to the nobleman whose son was dying, "Go, your son will live" (John 4:50, NIV). He'd watched as Jesus healed the man at the pool of Bethesda, telling him to pick up his mat and walk. But Andrew still couldn't help doubt.

Neither voice won that day, however, because the third voice belonged to Jesus, who said, "Have the people sit down."

His was the voice of fiery determination. Fearful Philip thought the task was insurmountable. Andrew was full of doubt. Jesus, however, knew something that those two were still figuring out: God was with them, and with God, all things are possible. Informed faith such as this can work miracles, as it did that day, when Jesus fed more than 5,000 people and there were leftovers to spare (see John 6:1–15).

Like my granddaughter Avery, I'm occasionally scared by the obstacles I face, and I'm often intimidated by the success

Train Your Brain to Combat Negativity

Psychologists and brain scientists call our propensity to focus more on negative thoughts, feelings, and events, and less on positive ones, the "negativity bias."

Yet we don't need to reject or avoid so-called "negative" emotions like fear, sadness, and anger to live with meaning and optimism. In fact, accepting and processing the fullness of your life's experiences is a required component of positive living.

One neuropsychologist offers a simple technique for changing the way one's brain processes positive experiences. Bring to mind someone you know who cares about you and visualize yourself in a positive situation together with that person (or pet!). Hold onto these thoughts for 10 to 20 seconds.

This technique is effective because as brain scientists say, "Neurons that fire together wire together," meaning that associating positive memories with tolerable negative ones can deploy the feel-good brain chemicals to soothe and tame the stress-induced ones.

The gradual, cumulative impact of this practice can help our brains decide how to feel and how to respond when positive or challenging moments arise.

of others who seem to take big challenges in stride. But I want determination to characterize my approach to life. I want to face hurdles and hindrances with a positive attitude. I don't want fear to hold me back.

As Jesus was with that hillside crowd that day and gave them plenty to eat, He is with me. Not that my task will always be easy, but God is with me, and with God, all things are possible.

Jesus, thank You for reminding me that You are always with me. When I'm faced with what seems to be an impossible task, help me to stay positive and determined, knowing that because You are in my life, all things are possible.

A Generous Spirit

SUSANNA FOTH AUGHTMON

Give, and it will be given to you. A good measure,
pressed down, shaken together and running over,
will be poured into your lap. For with the measure
you use, it will be measured to you.

LUKE 6:38 (NIV)

One of my favorite things in the world is giving gifts. Planning for birthdays is fun for me, and I just love Christmas gift shopping. I love the process of finding something special that will bring my friends and family joy. It doesn't have to be big. It just has to be thoughtful. A marketing book for my husband Scott. A Hershey bar with almonds for my mom. A magazine for my mother-in-law. A tube of shiny lip gloss for my cousin. When we have guests come to stay at our house, I like to have little treats waiting in the guest room. Crisp Granny Smith apples. Juicy clementine oranges. Wedges of chocolate. Bottles of water. These are simply little delights that bring a smile and let my people know they are welcome and truly and deeply loved.

Generosity is a value that has passed down through the generations of my family. My mom and dad are some of the most giving people I know. Money hasn't always been plentiful for them, living a life in Christian ministry. But what they had, they always shared. They have sacrificed their time, energy, and love so that my siblings and I could thrive. Mom and Dad say that they love investing in us. They have funded dreams, helped in times of crisis, and have a habit of sending their kids and grand-kids "fun" money. This money often comes with the directive, "Make sure you go out for ice cream."

My mom's parents also modeled this generous behavior—both in terms of ice cream *and* money. When we'd arrive at their house, Grandpa would ask his grandkids if we would like a choc-olate milkshake. We rarely turned that offer down. As pastors and farmers, my grandparents' lives were spent investing in peo-ple. The kind of returns they were looking for weren't monetary. They wanted to see things around them grow. People. Projects. Almond trees. They accomplished this by sharing what they had with others. They rarely spent money on themselves—not on clothes or furniture or big trips. They saw money as a means to an end—and that end was loving others.

> *As we express our gratitude, we must never forget that the highest appreciation is not to utter words but to live by them.*
>
> JOHN F. KENNEDY

Grandpa liked to say, "Get rid of that filthy lucre!" "Lucre" is an antiquated way to describe money that has been made dis-honestly. But I think Grandpa meant if you have money in your pocket, you need to start spreading it around. He and Grandma had made the decision that they wanted to tithe 50 percent of their income and live off the rest. Being generous with others meant being thrifty with themselves. They didn't just share their money, however. They shared their lives. In his years of pastor-ing, Grandpa planted a church, founded a K–12 Christian school, and established a retirement home for the elderly. Grandma held down the home front raising five kids.

When Grandpa retired from pastoring, he and Grandma simply shifted their focus. They started sponsoring Vietnamese and Russian refugee families in their community of Modesto, California. They often bought grocery staples from the Army surplus to share with people in need. They hand-delivered these to the families they knew needed a little extra. They recognized that they weren't just meeting people's material needs: They were giving hope. The goodness of Jesus had transformed their lives, and it transformed others in the process. I know this because it transformed me.

Even with all that they were doing, Grandma and Grandpa always found time to invest in our family. When my parents had the opportunity to build their first home, Grandma and Grandpa showed up to help. I was in high school. While we kids stained wood window frames and painted bedroom walls, Grandpa Blakely, in his checked shirt and Modesto Christian School baseball cap, got down on his knees and helped lay tile. Grandma, in her long-sleeved flowered blouse, wiped down all the dusty windows. They wanted

> *Hope does not disappoint, because the love of God has been poured out within our hearts through the Holy Spirit who was given to us.*
>
> ROMANS 5:5 (NASB)

to see us flourish and thrive in our new home. Our joy was their joy. Our success was their success.

Their generosity didn't stop with their time, it overflowed into the words they spoke. Every time I showed up at their house, from when I was a little girl to a young adult, an exchange would take place between my grandparents, one that always made me smile.

Grandpa would say, "Mother, did you know that I really like that Susanna?"

Grandma, smiling, would respond, "Oh, yes, Daddy, I like her too."

Grandpa: "She is pretty special."

Grandma: "We love her the most."

I would stand there feeling a combination of embarrassment and delight. In their presence, I was seen. I was accepted. I was cherished. "We love you the most" was the banner that my grandparents flew over every child and grandchild that entered

Practice Deep Kindness

"Confetti kindness"—things like paying for a person's coffee in line and sending a card—is important. While these kinds of acts are significant and far from trivial, they can make us think that kindness is easy.

Deep kindness requires more work—listening, sacrifice, intentionality, and discipline. It forces us to move past the pleasantries with our kindness. Deep kindness calls on us to lean into the unpleasantries to actually solve problems. It requires that we allow ourselves to be vulnerable and humble and causes us to invest in listening and giving people what they need.

Nearly 45 percent of our day is spent in habitual behavior. To help make deep kindness a habit, we need to be intentional and consistent in our practice.

their home. When you were around them, you knew you were loved.

My grandparents looked a whole lot like Jesus because Jesus is the most generous One of all. There is nothing that He wouldn't give in order to see me thrive and flourish. He invested His life for me. My joy is His joy. My success is His success. He is generous with His forgiveness. He welcomes me into His presence and flies a banner of love over me. He sees me. He accepts me. He cherishes me. His generosity anchors me in a place of peace.

Dear Jesus, tonight, I thank You for Your endless kindness. I can rest well, knowing that Your boundless love surrounds me. You give me grace. You offer me mercy. Your great love for me anchors me in a place of peace.

The Joy of Counting Gifts

CRYSTAL STORMS

O give thanks to the Lord; call upon his name:
make known his deeds among the people.

PSALM 105:1 (KJV)

The previous day had been full of challenges. My husband,
Tim, is a truck driver and was out on the road. Not only did I
have the arduous job of clearing out the house on my own before
a visit from a pest company, but I missed him. I worked hard to
get everything done, but it was one of those times when each
small task took longer and was more complicated than expected.
And I had a speech to give!

Finally, I finished loading my car with the food from our pan-
try, the contents of our medicine cabinet, and provisions for our
Yorkie, Minnie, and me for the next few days. I showered and
squeezed in a few minutes to practice my Toastmasters speech
one final time as I dried my hair. I made what I hoped would be
a quick phone call to my mom as I applied makeup and straight-
ened my hair. I could hear in her voice, however, that Mom
needed help, so I made plans to drive to her house after my
speech.

On my drive to the meeting, I prayed for Jesus to calm my
spirit and take care of Mom. Finally, my speech done and my visit

with Mom completed, and after a day that felt more like a week, I crawled into bed.

The next morning, I stared at the top of my journal page. I have a daily practice of writing three things I am grateful for that happened the day before. Looking back on that hectic day, I wondered if I could identify three good things. Surely a day like that had nothing good to reflect on.

But, I soon realized I was wrong. There were wonderful things about that long day. I'd won "speaker of the night" at Toastmasters. I also received a celebratory ribbon from the month before. And, driving home from my mom's later that night, I had a few "bunny sightings," which always delight me and make me smile. Looking over my short list, I realized I had a fourth thing to be grateful for: My friend Karen had attended the meeting and had recorded my speech. On that difficult, tiring day, Jesus had blessed me with three gifts—and a bonus!

Every good gift and every perfect gift is from above, and comes down from the Father of lights, with whom there is no variation or shadow of turning.

JAMES 1:17 (NKJV)

Counting gifts and writing them in my journal keeps me aware of how Jesus is with me, each and every day. It reminds and assures me of His love. Had I not jotted those gifts down, I wouldn't have noticed them or reflected on how Jesus blessed me throughout that day. I would have missed the evidence of His fingerprints in my life. I would have just kept my focus on what had been hard the day before. Packing the car. Missing Tim. Making a late-night visit to Mom's.

I started my "counting gifts" habit after reading Ann Voskamp's book *One Thousand Gifts*. In her "Joy Dare," she

Replay Happy Moments

Remembering joyful life events and savoring how they make you feel imprints them in your emotional brain. The next time something wonderful happens—a vacation, a fun day with a friend, a spectacular visit to nature—write it down soon after. Note exactly what made you so thrilled. You'll get to re-live it while you write it, and you'll have specific memories preserved that you can look at when you need a boost.

challenges readers to write down 1,000 things for which they're grateful. I listed the first hundred gifts or so with ease. Home. People I love. Blessings I see around me. But then, as my list grew longer, I had to be more intentional. I needed to focus on how Jesus was present with me, in small graces and in significant ways. Counting gifts helps me to appreciate the sweetness of an orange at lunch. The warmth of the sun on my cheek when the temperatures drop. The pops of purple and pink blossoms on the trees as I drive down the road. A smile from a friend.

In counting gifts, I see the fingerprints of Jesus in my life. I recognize every good thing I see as a blessing from His hand. A sign of His goodness, a testament of His love, a promise of His presence.

Jesus, I thank You for all the evidence,
day after day, that shows me You are with me.
Give me grace to notice the good gifts
You have given me.

Alone but Not Lonely

JEANETTE LEVELLIE

And never forget that I am with you every day,
even to the completion of this age.

MATTHEW 28:20 (TPT)

"How is Kevin?" my friend Beth asked. "And tell me how *you're* holding up!"

"He still sleeps twenty-two out of twenty-four hours, and as for me, I'm so lonely!" I said.

My husband, Kevin, usually bursting with plans and purposes, had caught a strange virus. For a week, he was flat on his back in the guest bedroom, fast asleep. I only interacted with him when he woke up long enough for me to spoon some applesauce or a poached egg into his mouth. Afterwards he'd drop back onto the pillow, exhausted. The next week, Kevin was strong enough only to get up and take a shower. Then he'd lie down again and drift off to sleep. Our conversations, usually electric with ideas, were brief and mundane.

"Take these vitamins," I'd say.

"Uggh. Again?" he'd respond.

"Yes," I'd say. "You really must. They'll speed up your healing."

I poured out my heart to Jesus: "Lord, I never realized how knit together Kevin's and my lives are. He's here, but still I miss him so much. Please heal him and please be with me in my loneliness!"

This reality check, Kevin's illness, forced me to see how dependent I was on my husband. The jar of grape jelly I'd recently purchased to feed orioles sat unused in my fridge because my tiny hands weren't strong enough to open it. I had to drag the full trash bag the fifty yards across our lawn to the barrel. Kev would have carried it out with no trouble. But the worst part of those weeks he was laid up was the sense of abandonment and emptiness I felt. I missed talking and laughing and praying with my partner.

One night during the second week of Kevin's illness, I discovered a new habit that helped me overcome loneliness: I began praying myself to sleep. As I lay in the darkness trying to relax and trusting that God would help Kevin recover, my mind went over everyone I knew who needed prayer. I prayed for friends who were ill or discouraged. I prayed prayers of thanks for those who were celebrating good fortune like a new baby, a new job, or a recovery to health. I prayed for people in my life who needed discernment and guidance. I prayed grateful prayers for beauty in nature—for the trees outside my window that gave us shade or the flowers that, year after year, came up in the spring. And Jesus listened to me. I felt His presence with me, nodding and affirming my best hopes and prayers for those in need. Hearing my pain. Understanding my fear.

But when you pray, go into your room, close the door and pray to your Father, who is unseen. Then your Father, who sees what is done in secret, will reward you.

MATTHEW 6:6 (NIV)

Talking to Jesus during those hours in the dark comforted my soul. His sweet presence embraced me until I drifted off. Before then, I'd always prayed in the mornings, but I found that adding extra time with Jesus at the end of the day deepened my friendship with Him.

Inch by inch, Kevin recovered. We now enjoy the same sweet fellowship we had before he got sick. More than ever, I appreciate all he does to keep our household running smoothly. And I appreciate our conversation, laughter, and mutual support even more than before he became ill.

But the fellowship I have with Jesus—blossomed from a lonely time—is sweeter to me still.

Thank You, Jesus, for never leaving me. No matter how I feel, You are always with me, helping and healing. Thank You for the gift of prayer and of Your listening heart. I ask for a restful night tonight and thank You for the peace You bring.

An Intentional Life

LOGAN ELIASEN

There is a time for everything, and a season
for every activity under the heavens.

ECCLESIASTES 3:1 (NIV)

"All right, show me what we're working with," I said, hefting a big bag of dirt onto the patio.

My friend Xuan set a sprawling pothos plant onto the table. Its tangled mess of vines fell nearly to the ground, the foliage so thick that I couldn't see its pot. At the beginning of the summer, Xuan had asked for my help managing this overgrown plant. As a plant hobbyist, I was happy to help my friend. But I was busy, and the better part of summer had slipped by before I had time to help him.

"First, we are going to have to repot this," I said.

I went to the shed and returned with a large terracotta pot. I directed Xuan to start filling it with dirt while I removed the pothos from its plastic planter. The roots were dense and matted, so I began loosening them.

"What are you doing?" Xuan asked.

"The plant is rootbound," I said. "If we don't separate the roots, the plant's growth will be stunted."

I worked to untangle the mess of roots. The smell of earth was refreshing. I had always loved working with plants, it feels restorative to care for something green and growing. Most summers, I grew tomatoes or herbs, but this year I had been too busy.

Satisfied with the roots, I set the pothos in its new pot. In the bigger pot, the plant didn't seem nearly as large. The vines of the plant were spread apart—finally distinguishable. Some of them were strong and leafy. Others were sparse and leggy.

The best way to lengthen out our days is to walk steadily and with a purpose.

CHARLES DICKENS

"We need to do some pruning," I said. I pointed to a spindly vine. "Let's trim off the branches that look like this."

Xuan peered at the plant. "There are quite a few of them," he said. "Will it damage the plant to cut so much off?"

"Nope," I said. "Right now, the plant is wasting its energy on these weak branches. By pruning it, we are redirecting the plant. We're showing it which branches are important."

Problems Have Purpose

Norman Vincent Peale said, "God knew what He was doing when He constructed this world so that there was difficulty in it. That is what makes it possible for us to grow in strength and understanding. There is conflict in the universe and that is what makes life go." The next time you feel pulled apart by a challenge, recognize how rich your life story is becoming by experiencing the hurdles and bumps on the road of life's journey.

Tonight, as you pray, thank God: Mighty God, because of You, I can overcome even the greatest difficulties.

"I get it," Xuan said. "We're making its growth more intentional."

"Exactly," I said.

I handed Xuan a pair of clippers. Together we trimmed off the spindly branches. As the pile of trimmings grew, I thought about the word Xuan had used. *Intentional.* Was I being intentional with my schedule? Was I being a good steward of the time the Lord had given me? All summer, I had felt overwhelmed. I had been trying to just make it through the days. Meanwhile, months had slipped by. And so had opportunities. I hadn't gardened. I hadn't even had time to help my friend. Those were meaningful parts of my life—activities that brought me joy. They were important to me. I needed to set aside time for them. They required intentionality.

Xuan and I finished pruning the plant. It was no longer wild and overgrown. It was intentional. And that's just the way I wanted to start living my life.

Tonight, I thank You, Jesus, for the gift of life that You have given me. Help me to live intentionally and to invest my time and attention into the parts of my life that are most important to You.

Wow! God Really Is Here!

NORM STOLPE

*Where two or three gather in
my name, there am I with them.*

MATTHEW 18:20 (NIV)

"**W**ow! God is really here!" one of the adolescent boys would break the reverent hush of evening prayer. But the truth of his words landed on our hearts, almost like a reminder from Jesus Himself that He was with us.

Earlier that Friday night, about twenty-five high schoolers gathered together after spending a week in Syracuse, New York, working with Habitat for Humanity. Teamed with an adult group from a church in another community, the high schoolers had framed two houses and gotten the exterior walls secured. The homes were ready for the roofing crew to come the following week.

Supper dishes were washed, and the teams assembled for the final Vespers of the week. A culminating group activity would be followed by singing together before retiring for the night, anticipating an amusement park excursion on Saturday before the Sunday drive back to New Jersey.

As pastor in charge of Vespers, I formed four groups of the young people. Each one was to plan and present a summary of their experiences that week, in whatever manner or style they desired. The first group did a comedy sketch of new skills, ones they'd learned by correcting their own mistakes. Improvised costumes and over-the-top makeup evoked knowing laughter from us all as the flubs of the week were dramatized. The second group recreated conversations with some of the adults from the other church, who had affirmed the value of our group's work. The third group enacted a tour of the houses with future residents who thanked them and Habitat for Humanity for enabling them to become homeowners—something that had been beyond their wildest dreams. The mood had naturally shifted from vigorous humor to serious reflection before the fourth group began.

> *Grace, mercy and peace from God the Father and from Jesus Christ, the Father's Son, will be with us in truth and love.*
>
> 2 JOHN 1:3 (NIV)

The fourth group wanted to act out the lesson they had learned about how, by serving other people, the prospective owners of these houses, they were acting on Jesus's behalf in this neighborhood. They read the story of Jesus washing His disciples' feet at the Last Supper from John 13:3–17 aloud. One of the girls took the role of Jesus and washed the feet of the others in their group. Just as it seemed they were finished, each young person in that fourth group produced a previously unseen towel and bowl of water. They went around the circle, each one washing the feet of several youth and the adults. The sacredness of that quiet moment was evident to everyone.

This was one young man's, Shane's, first work trip experience. When his turn came to have his feet washed, Shane exclaimed, "Wow! God is really here!" He blushed and muttered an apology. A number of affirming smiles were flashed his way.

After all the feet had been washed, shoes and socks put back on, towels and bowls put away, I asked if anyone wanted to say anything. Several immediately offered that Shane got it right. God really *was* there. And, in the four groups' presentations, we had gone from humor to reflection to gratitude to the holy. God must have planned that sequencing because we sure didn't. And it was Shane, not one of the veterans of previous work trips, who pointed that out. Several others affirmed him. "Don't be embarrassed," they said. "Jesus used you to tell us He was there and that we should pay attention."

I'll never forget that joyful proclamation that Jesus was with us. And, I'm comforted to know, He always is and He always will be.

Jesus, thank You for stirring my heart and giving me gentle—and sometimes enthusiastic—reminders of Your presence. Thank You for the example You set for us, of serving one another, washing one another's feet, and being in loving communion with Your friends. Tonight, as I go to sleep, I thank You for the moments in my life when I felt You, close as anyone else in the room, right beside me.

A Quiet Retreat

LORI HATCHER

Then, because so many people were coming and going that they did not even have a chance to eat, he said to them, "Come with me by yourselves to a quiet place and get some rest."

MARK 6:31 (NIV)

I was thrilled when Sue, my writing mentor and friend, accepted the invitation to join me on an impromptu writers retreat. I would be staying at a mountain cabin that belonged to my boss, and I was happy for her excellent company. As a busy homeschooler, I'd been struggling to find time to finish my first book, and Sue was writing her third. Although Sue's kids were grown, I suspected she, too, would benefit from a few days of uninterrupted writing time.

"It's quiet and beautiful," I said. "We can write to our hearts' content with no interruptions. There are four bedrooms, so you can stay up late or get up early without worrying about bothering anyone. And the view is amazing. It's guaranteed to inspire creativity."

I also invited two other writer friends to join us. Julie, a mother of four, was working on an editing project. Sarah was starting to work on a blog. The four of us chatted and laughed our way to

Asheville, North Carolina on the drive. As the Blue Ridge mountains appeared in the distance, I shouted, "Woohoo! Mountains, here we come!"

Soon we were parked on the gravel drive overlooking the valley. Giggling like teenage girls at a sleepover, we hauled our laptops, bookbags, and even a printer up the wooden steps to the cabin. Sarah had brought a crate full of writing books, and Julie brought her copy of *The Chicago Manual of Style*.

We all got up early the next morning, eager to get to work. By eight, we were seated in our respective corners, tapping away on our keyboards. I watched Sue out of the corner of my eye, curious to know how a "real" writer ordered her days. At lunchtime, we broke for a quick sandwich, then we all returned to work. All of us except Sue, I should say. She went for a walk.

"I saw a flock of turkey hens down the road a ways," she told us when she returned. "And the most beautiful field of wildflowers. About a quarter of a mile away, down the hill, is a waterfall. I found a flat rock and just sat there listening."

We nodded politely, then got back to work.

The next morning, Sue joined the rest of us at the dining room table but closed her laptop after an hour and went outside to the porch. I assumed she was changing writing locations, and I stopped to stretch my aching shoulder and neck muscles and glanced her way.

In contrast to our flying fingers, her hands lay clasped in her lap and her eyes were closed. *Has she fallen asleep? No, her lips are moving.* Soon she opened her eyes, drinking in the beauty of the blue-green valley, dotted with whipped cream clouds.

On our third day, Julie announced, "I'm halfway through my edit!" She'd taken the loft bedroom because it was set apart from the others and quieter. I'd seen her light on well past midnight both nights.

Sarah shared her progress. "I've written three blog posts already," she said. "Today I'll format them and get them scheduled."

"I'm making headway too," I said. "Only twelve more devotions to write."

Sue smiled, rose from the table, and carried her coffee mug to the sink. That morning, she didn't write at all.

> *A day of rest yields a hundred days of progress.*
>
> ADRIENNE POSEY

She must have writer's block. Poor thing. How terrible to have five uninterrupted days to write and be stuck like that, I thought.

While we pounded away at our computers, Sue sat on the porch swing, watched the hummingbirds swoop and flutter at the feeders, and took a nap.

At dinner that night we asked her about being a professional writer.

"How do you come up with such wonderful plotlines?" I asked.

"How do you deal with writer's block?" Sarah asked.

"How do you know what God wants you to write?" Julie wondered.

Sue smiled and answered our questions by telling us a story. "One of the most acclaimed writers of the nineteenth century left London and moved to a tiny town on the outskirts of Sheffield," she began. "Word got out that a famous author was living there. Every day someone would walk past her cottage, hoping to catch a glimpse of her. One day, a resident found her strolling the fragrant hills, arms full of wildflowers, hair blown wildly by the

Dim the Lights and Listen

Nighttime is the perfect time to relax and listen to Jesus.

First, let yourself experience the dark. Turn off the lights and become aware of how soothing a dim place is. Next, get quiet and consciously connect to your body. Then take a deep breath and say, "Speak, Lord, for Your servant is listening."

Although you can speak to Jesus at any time, connecting with Him in the evening allows you to just be in His presence. Make yourself present as you spend ten or fifteen minutes listening to Him. Being alone with Him can renew you, body and soul.

wind. 'I thought you were supposed to be writing,' the woman said in surprise. The writer smiled, glanced at the rolling hills, and said, 'I am.'"

In the years since our time together, I've come to appreciate Sue's example and wise counsel. She taught me that while hard work is crucial to success, so is rest and relaxation. Whether we're writing books, managing households, raising children, or caring for sick loved ones, our minds and bodies can't work efficiently without time to reflect and renew.

Sue learned this from Jesus's example. He often went off by Himself, withdrawing to quiet places or the wilderness to pray. Looking back, I realize that Sue could have filled our ears with warnings about burnout and exhaustion or listing off her favorite writing tips. Instead, she modeled Jesus's wise formula for success by resting, relaxing, and praying.

Jesus, help me remember that even You chose to rest and relax. God the Creator modeled it on the seventh day of creation, and You often retreated to quiet places to find renewal. Guide me as I seek to find the balance between work and rest, effort and trust. In the strong name of Jesus I ask.

No Empty Seats

BRENDA YODER

*There is a time . . . to scatter stones
and a time to gather them.*

ECCLESIASTES 3:5 (NIV)

In the past, I used my wedding china only on special occasions, like Christmas and Thanksgiving. In recent years, however, I get it out on what might look like ordinary occasions to others, but are significant for me. I use the fancy dishes when all four of our young adult and adult children are home for a meal. Such dinners have been a rarity since our firstborn left home to attend a university eleven hours away from home. After graduation, she went to the mission field for several years.

It's been a transition for me, moving from a full house to an empty nest. It's been hard for me as a mom in a small, rural community where most families have their children and grandchildren near them. It's common here for extended families to live within minutes of each other. This was true for my husband and me: We lived near both sets of parents while we were raising our family.

Our own kids' lives have been very different, but that's all right. When we were raising them, we made it a priority to encourage our kids to follow their dreams and goals. When they were little, I prayed that each child would follow God's call, wherever He might take them. As they've gone through high school, college, and life after school, we've encouraged them to take opportunities if they believed they were what Jesus had for them.

Our firstborn and only daughter took us up on this. She lived both in Guatemala and Mexico for several years working for ministries that served orphaned and vulnerable children. Because she lived so far from home, she missed a lot of family events as her three younger brothers grew up. When she'd come home during those years, I sometimes felt awkwardly emotional when the kids were all together under my roof again. Though I was happy my daughter was serving God, I felt wistful when I saw families in my community who were able to share Sunday dinners and go on family outings regularly.

Gratitude can transform common days into thanksgivings, turn routine jobs into joy, and change ordinary opportunities into blessings.

WILLIAM ARTHUR WARD

On a recent spring day, however, our dinner table was fuller than it had ever been. Each of our kids was home, including our first grandchild and new dating partners that accompanied our son and daughter. I put the wedding china and heirloom dishes on the dining room table and called the family to eat. We all took our seats, and my husband prayed.

After the prayer, I wanted to say a few words to welcome our guests, but tears came instead. I couldn't stop them from falling. I refrained from talking so I could catch my breath and not speak without sobbing. Embarrassing my kids was the last thing I wanted to do. My family thought I was full of emotion because of the new additions to the family, but I wanted them to know it was something different.

I told them the tears sprung from profound gratitude. It was so good to have our daughter stateside after living out of the country. It had been such a long time since we had a simple

Sing Praise to the Lord

Henry Williams Baker

Sing praise to the Lord! Praise Him in the height;
Rejoice in His Word, you angels of light.
You heavens, adore Him by Whom you were made,
And worship before Him in brightness arrayed.

Sing praise to the Lord! Praise Him on the earth
In tuneful accord, you saints of new birth.
Praise Him Who has brought you His grace from above;
Praise Him Who has taught you to sing of His love.

Sing praise to the Lord! All things that give sound,
Each jubilant chord, re-echo around.
Loud organs, His glory tell forth in deep tone,
And trumpets, the story of what He has done.

Sing praise to the Lord! Thanksgiving and song
To Him be outpoured all ages along!
For love in creation, for Heaven restored,
For grace of salvation, sing praise to the Lord!

meal in springtime with everyone there. It was something other friends may have taken for granted, but to me it felt like a precious gift.

The full house didn't last long, and there were empty seats once again. But my heart felt full. That night, I crawled into bed and thanked Jesus for a simple meal with my family. I cried, again, thanking Him for the few hours where there were no empty chairs.

Jesus, thank You for our families, whether our loved ones live far or near. Fill us with gratitude for the time we have together. Please protect and bless our family members who live far from us and bring us back together again.

Adversity Transformed

RANDY PETERSEN

We know that suffering produces perseverance;
perseverance, character; and character, hope. And
hope does not put us to shame, because God's love
has been poured out into our hearts.

ROMANS 5:3–5 (NIV)

"Oh, good!" my mother said, holding up an envelope. "A letter from Aunt Dottie!"

I was ten years old, and this was a time long before email. Mom loved bringing in the mail in those days, especially when there was a letter from a friend.

"Who's Aunt Dottie?" I asked.

Mom tried to explain the connection, but it was complicated. This distant aunt wrote a wonderful letter to my mother every year or two. Mom said that one of the things she loved about Dottie was how she could turn any catastrophe into a celebration.

"Things are fine here now," Mom read, with humor in her voice. "Of course a few months ago I was crossing the street and got hit by an Army truck, but everyone was really nice about it. I had to go to the hospital, but that was a good thing, because they discovered the problem with my gallbladder. They had to take it

~305~

out, and there were some complications, but that gave me more time to get to know my roommate."

Dottie listed one problem after another, but each became a blessing in her mind. Put anyone else in those same situations—a traffic accident, a health crisis, a hospital stay—and they'd probably be complaining about how terrible life is. They might moan, "How could God let this happen to me?" But Aunt Dottie greeted each event with a sweet spirit and a profound understanding of the love of Jesus. Over the years, I was always glad when one of her letters arrived and my mother read it aloud to me. In her odd way, she was presenting a very healthy approach to life.

Dottie's transforming vision lines up with what Jesus said about sparrows. He did not say that God prevents sparrows from falling. But there's something more important to trust and to understand: He cares. Even the death of a discounted sparrow matters to Him. And so, like Dottie, when my circumstances take a turn for the worse, I know that it matters to Jesus. Adversity doesn't mean He has forgotten me. It means He has a new plan.

Blessed are the poor in spirit, for theirs is the kingdom of heaven. Blessed are those who mourn, for they will be comforted. Blessed are the meek, for they will inherit the earth. Blessed are those who hunger and thirst for righteousness, for they will be filled.

MATTHEW 5:3–6 (NIV)

If I expect God to keep everything bad from happening, I'll be constantly disappointed. Or else I'll deny whatever bad things occur. But what Jesus promises is that He will honor His

Improve Your Physical Health with Positive Thinking

Recent studies are confirming that optimism supports physical well being.

In one study, researchers found that those who reported optimistic and positive thought patterns were less likely to have a heart attack or other cardiac condition than others who were more pessimistic in their outlook. They observed that optimists tend to take better care of their health. They're more likely to exercise and eat better and are less likely to smoke.

In even more good news, the research also supports the notion that optimism can have a positive impact on health and well being at any age. One researcher noted that it's never too early, and it's never too late to foster optimism.

relationship with me through thick and thin. This is a transformational reality. Because of my relationship with Jesus, I see that positivity is not just a good mood. Positivity is a deep recognition of Jesus's love and power that permeates all circumstances.

As I settle down each evening, I try to look for moments when Jesus has shown up for me during the day: the positive encounters, the kind words and deeds, the times when I felt motivation to do the right thing. Through these, I understand, Jesus is deepening a relationship with me, beckoning to me to move ever closer to Him.

Thank You, Jesus, for the many good things You've brought into my life. Thank You for You— for the relationship we have through good times and bad. I trust You to be with me as I lie down to sleep tonight and know You will be with me when I awake in the morning.

The Phases of Forgiveness

ERYN LYNUM

*Therefore, if anyone is in Christ, the new creation
has come: The old has gone, the new is here!*

2 CORINTHIANS 5:17 (NIV)

As soon as I see his red eyes and tear-streaked cheeks, I know I am in the wrong. Two of my three sons wear their hearts on their sleeves, but this son rarely communicates his emotions to me. Yet here he stands, overtaken by sorrow. I know, in that moment, that my accusation was wrong. He hadn't, in fact, hit his brother and lied to me, but instead, as he reported, his brother was accidentally hurt when he jumped off the countertop. My own jump to a wrongful conclusion has left his spirit bruised.

In nine years of parenting, I have made countless mistakes. Tonight, my son readily forgives me, not only the first time I ask, but also after I've apologized twice more. I have found my kids quick to forgive. Forgiving myself, on the other hand, is difficult.

Coming face to face with my failures, I've seen the story of forgiveness in Matthew 18 in a new light. Peter approached Jesus and asked Him, "'Lord, how many times shall I forgive my brother or sister who sins against me? Up to seven times?' Jesus answered, 'I tell you, not seven times, but seventy-seven times.'" The number itself is rather arbitrary, but Jesus compels

His followers toward extending complete grace to others—the same grace He shows us. That evening with my son, I recognized Jesus's call to total forgiveness not only extends to those we need to forgive but also to ourselves.

A few days before the incident with my son, we'd wandered a two-mile nature trail, stopping to observe caterpillars and marveling at the butterflies flittering across the grasslands. That morning, we'd read how caterpillars undergo four phases. During these stages of development, the caterpillar molts and discards its old skin. After four phases, it enters the pupa, or cocoon, state. Once swaddled in a protective shell, its muscles liquefy and organs reorganize so that the caterpillar can soon emerge as a new creature. This process is one of the many wonders and engineered designs of our wonderful Creator that we cannot fully grasp!

I marvel at how this process reflects our transformation and new life in Christ. Each time I practice forgiveness, whether toward another human or in forgiving myself for mistakes made, it's as if I shed my skin, like a caterpillar. I let go of what once was—my sinful state—and move closer to the new life Christ has in store for me. I know, of course, that my redemption and new life are secure in Him. Yet while I walk this earth, Jesus is continuously making all things new, including me.

Dear Jesus, Thank You for the way You transform my heart and mind to reflect Your own, through all the phases of my life.

You Can Stop Now

LAWRENCE W. WILSON

*Jesus said to them, "Come with me by yourselves
to a quiet place and get some rest."*

MARK 6:31 (NIV)

To say I was feeling smug about my volunteer work would be a major understatement. At the time, I actually felt like one of God's Marines—one of the few, the proud—and, like a Marine, I saw myself as *Semper Fidelis*, "always faithful." Others at church seemed lukewarm in their commitment to service. They may not have been willing to sacrifice themselves, but I certainly was! That self-righteous pride was more than enough compensation for a few evenings of my time.

My self-satisfaction only grew when a friend compared me to others, saying he knew he could always count on me. We'd been working on organizing a missions festival one or two evenings a week for about a month. The pace was demanding, but the need was great, and I was more than willing to do my part for Jesus.

I pinned that moment in my mind for a couple of reasons. One was that I felt a bit of satisfaction at knowing that I had exceptional passion for "the Lord's work." The other was that my sacrifice had been noticed by someone else. That was proof I was doing my part, and more, to advance the Gospel.

Through the fall and winter, I kept that same pace. After the missions event, a leaders retreat, the Christmas program, the annual stewardship campaign, a couples banquet, the youth quiz team, and the preschool fundraiser all demanded my time. And I gave it. During one particularly busy stretch, I noticed that my calendar was filled with various types of church events for seventeen straight evenings. Between Bible studies, worship services, committee work, and service projects, I'd spent more than a fortnight away from my wife and young children.

The truth is, though, I'd spent much of that time away from Jesus as well. I ran from morning until evening, nearly every day of the week. There was barely time for dinner with my family and no time for relaxation. Who had time for meditation or prayer? Besides, I felt guilty whenever I slowed down. There was simply too much work to be done.

"Work, for the night is coming," goes the old gospel song. *Work, work, work.* That's virtually all I did for months. And it was His work. Christ's work. Certainly, He understood that I had to be busy. Certainly, my wife did, and my children. And they did seem to understand, or at least they were tolerant of my frequent absences. There was no reproach from my family, and none from the Lord that I was aware of. Everyone seemed to accept my need to save the world at any cost. Everyone, that is, except my own body and mind.

Things came to a head the next spring, around Easter. My friend, the missions committee volunteer, decided to take a break and declined to organize the sunrise service and pancake breakfast. It should have been a small thing, especially between comrades in service. Heaven knows he'd earned a rest. But I was too exhausted—physically, emotionally, and spiritually—to deal with the least disappointment. I felt abandoned by a close ally. My frustration turned to anger, then resentment, all of which I internalized.

With Easter less than a week away, I began to panic. There was so much to be done, and it was all on me, so it seemed. My mind rambled through my list of grievances, vaguely directed toward the One I'd been serving. I've done so much, sacrificed so much. I've had no hobbies, no interests, no friends outside of church. I've had no time off. It's not fair, Jesus!

I dreaded Easter Day. Yet it came, of course. Remarkably, the celebration of Christ's resurrection was joyful and meaningful, despite our minimal preparation.

A few days later, I was able to relax and enjoy a quiet spring evening. As I sat on the front step enjoying a cup of tea, the sun casting colorful streaks along the horizon, He spoke to me. I was finally able to sit quietly and listen. With body and mind finally relaxed, I was at last able to enter His presence. In the waning moments of the day, an epiphany came.

It wasn't Jesus who'd demanded that I grind myself to dust. I'd done that on my own, to satisfy my own need for recognition and achievement. Jesus had never asked me to skip meals, go without sleep, or become a stranger to my children. He wasn't pushing me to be a Marine for Him, but instead inviting me to live fully in Him. And that requires spending some time in quiet

> *Rest time is not waste time. It is economy to gather fresh strength.... It is wisdom to take occasional furlough. In the long run, we shall do more by sometimes doing less.*
>
> CHARLES SPURGEON

~313~

prayer, just watching the evening sky. Even He took time away to eat, to pray, to rest. I took a deep breath and released all my tangled feelings slowly, and He gently received them. What relief!

Jesus, thank You for knowing me and patiently waiting for me when I fill my life too full and don't come to You. Thank You for the good work You do through me, despite my limitations. Thank You for the rest You offer Your servants.

Grace upon Grace

SUSANNA FOTH AUGHTMON

For it is by grace you have been saved, through faith—and this is not from yourselves, it is the gift of God—not by works, so that no one can boast.

EPHESIANS 2:8–9 (NIV)

I have always loved taking a deeper dive into the meaning and history of words. Maybe it's because I am a writer. Or because I am a reader. Either way, I like checking the etymology of different terms to figure out where and when they hail from. Latin? French? Anglo-Saxon? I find it fascinating. I am a bit of a word nerd, and I love how the words *grace* and *gratitude* have the same Latin root. One means "favor" and the other means "grateful." This makes perfect sense to me. The more grace I receive, the more grateful I am.

I have known Jesus's grace in so many different ways throughout my life. But when I became a mom, the reality of His goodness and grace seemed to grow exponentially. I began to understand the concepts of grace and gratitude on a more concrete level. The bigger my belly got, the more grateful I was. I was caught up in the marvel of new life at work within me. What began as a hope and dream was becoming a reality: I was going to be a mom. The thought of it left me awash in gratitude.

I would drive in the car and sing, knowing that my baby was hearing my voice. My favorite song to sing during my pregnancy with my first, Jack, was the song "I Am Blessed" by Jaci Velasquez. I couldn't hold back my joy and thankfulness. Often, I would be so overwhelmed by the gift of becoming a mom that I would cry while I sang. (Those pregnancy hormones are strong!) I loved knowing that soon I would be holding the most beautiful baby in my arms.

When Jack was born and the nurse handed him to me in the delivery room, both my husband, Scott, and I cried. We were so bowled over by this little bundle, we could hardly speak. His red, scrunched-up face was perfection. I loved the weight of him resting against me. His tiny hands balled into fists. His dark hair framed his face. He was beautiful. We were beyond grateful to be his parents.

> *A thankful heart is not only the greatest virtue, but the parent of all the other virtues.*
>
> CICERO

When our sons Will and Addison were born, we had the same reaction. Tears. Joy. Gratitude. Will's blonde hair looked like it had been frosted at the tips. Addison had a sprinkling of hair that capped his sweet round head. Each son was so different, yet also so uniquely themselves from birth. But Scott and I, grateful to Jesus, responded in the same way. *Thank You. Thank You. Thank You.*

One of the things that I loved best about being a mom to young babies was getting to rock them and sing to them. Along with the gift of motherhood, however, came the gift of full-body fatigue. My goal each afternoon was to get them down for a nap—so that I could take a nap. Rocking Will was more of a

Tips to Brighten Your Mood

When you are stuck in negative ruminations, consider the following tips to brighten your mood.

- Pay attention to the little things that make life better. Gratitude is about noticing that there is always something positive, regardless of how difficult circumstances are at the time.
- When you can't stop dwelling on bad things that have happened, think of a negative event that ended up with a surprisingly positive outcome.
- Remind yourself of things you do for others and wish to do for others to give yourself a boost.
- Recall the joyful and fun times you have spent with loved ones and allow yourself to bask in the warmth of the memory of those moments.

wrestling match. He was wired to *move*. But if I could get his wiry little body tucked tightly against mine and start to rock and sing, he would begin to relax. Addie would hum along with me as I rocked him. I sang a handful of worship songs, and my favorite was "Thank You, Lord." That phrase is repeated over and over in that one. When my boys got older, they would invite me to lie down with them at bedtime and ask, "Can you sing to us, Mom?" I always said yes. Being close to them was my joy.

Now in the throes of my boys' burgeoning adulthoods, I am still thankful to be Jack, Will, and Addison's mom. I am thankful for who they are and for the young men they are becoming. I am thankful that these three grace my life. I didn't do anything to deserve them. Even in the wildest moments and most hectic and upside-down days, they are a gift. Plain and simple. Grace upon grace. And I am grateful.

Jesus offers me the gift of His grace at every turn. Not because I deserve it, but because He loves me. He not only gives me good gifts, He also forgives my sins. He offers me His grace in my weakest moments and when I am confused or unsure of my future. He sets me free from fear and anxiety. Grace upon grace upon grace. Being close to Him is my joy. He gives me favor when I don't deserve it. His grace is all that I need, in any and every situation. Plain and simple. My only response can be gratitude. Thank You. Thank You. Thank You.

Jesus, tonight I thank You for Your powerful grace. Thank You for the way You are at work in my life. I know that Your love and mercy is offered to me, not because of what I have done, but what You have done for me. I can rest in the fullness of Your grace tonight.

Without a Word

LORI ROELEVELD

*My little children, let us not love in word
or in tongue, but in deed and in truth.*

1 JOHN 3:18 (NKJV)

My dad, a firefighter, didn't love me with a lot of words. It took years for me to come to appreciate that he connected with me by buying dinner, sending flowers, and fixing my car. It wasn't until I watched him try to express his love with words and then dissolve into tears that I recognized the deep feelings that were often behind actions I'd taken for granted.

Similarly, my husband isn't a man of many words. Once I mentioned to him that it had been weeks since he'd offered me a compliment. He insisted he'd done so just a few nights earlier.

"When?" I asked.

"Don't you remember?" he asked. "You said you thought those pants made you look fat. I said, 'No, they don't.'"

No surprise that greeting-card creators aren't beating a path to his door.

While he's short on words, my husband expresses his love richly through his actions. He works long hours, fixes whatever breaks in our house, and helps me keep the house clean, taking on extra responsibilities, especially when I'm on deadline. His acts of service to our family, church, and community are well known. His actions reveal his steadfast love for Jesus.

1 John reminds us that God doesn't just listen to what we say—He watches what we do. This is a caution to us "word" people to be sure we're backing up what we say or write with our actions, and it can be a strong comfort and affirmation for those who demonstrate love mostly by what they do. With Jesus, words and actions are fully integrated; they are one. Jesus is the Word made flesh (John 1:14) who came and dwelled with us. He is the living Word who acted on our behalf when He laid down His life on the cross. He spoke words of hope, forgiveness, and

Scripture for Better Relationships

In chapter twelve of Romans, Paul tells us the "secrets" to establishing and maintaining good relationships by connecting more deeply with others. Here is how part of that passage reads, as translated by Eugene H. Peterson in *The Message*:

- Take your everyday, ordinary life...and place it before God as an offering. Be what we were made to be, without enviously or pridefully comparing ourselves with each other or trying to be something we aren't.
- If you help, don't take over.... If you give guidance, be careful that you don't get bossy; if you're put in charge, don't manipulate; if you're called to give aid to people in distress, keep your eyes open and be quick to respond.
- Love from the center of who you are. Be a good friend who loves deeply; practice playing second fiddle. Make friends with nobodies; don't be the great somebody.

affirmation. He also healed the sick, fed the hungry, and grieved with those who grieved.

What we do bears witness to who we are; our actions testify on our behalf. How we live and serve tell a profound story. What we give, share, provide, and contribute does not go unseen by Jesus, and often it's not unnoticed or unappreciated by those around us. Even if they wait until we're gone to acknowledge it.

One of the younger fire chiefs my dad trained shared some rare words over social media after Dad died. This chief recalled that at major incidents such as fires, accidents, and rescues, Dad would come up behind him and just stand. Often he wouldn't say anything, but he would squeeze the younger man's shoulder and let him know that he was there. After Dad became ill, this chief faced the biggest fire of his career. All throughout the incident, he kept waiting for that hand on his shoulder, knowing it wouldn't come. Remembering the times that it had been there, though, strengthened him to do what had to be done.

God designed us with a need for connection, community, and relationship. At the same time, He created a variety of personalities that express love in many ways. Jesus is the Living Word but He lived a life of loving actions, deeds that testify, touches that ministered, and service that endures. He is the hand on our shoulder, letting us know He's there and that He loves us.

Jesus, Your love of variety is evident in all creation. Help me recognize the many different ways people in my life express their love. Help them to recognize mine.

God's Handiwork

BRENDA YODER

*For we are God's handiwork, created in
Christ Jesus to do good works, which God
prepared in advance for us to do.*

EPHESIANS 2:10 (NIV)

When I was forty, I started graduate school. After working full-time as a high school history teacher for many years, I decided to pursue a new career in counseling. Although teaching was a passion and I loved the relationships I built with my students, I felt that working instead as a counselor would better fit the needs of our busy family. At that time, our four children were still all at home, and I was looking for part-time work. Counseling fit my skill set, interests, and career goals—and I thought it might give me more time with my kids.

The only problem was that, sometimes, I felt like an impostor in my graduate program. While my classmates were clear and passionate about their shared goal to become therapists, I honestly didn't feel that calling. I knew I'd be lying to others and to myself if I said I did. Other than teaching, the only other occupation that felt like a true calling for me was Christian ministry. I loved teaching the Bible and caring for people. But there weren't options for such a profession for me in my small, conservative, rural community.

Sometimes I felt like Jacob in Genesis 32 as I "wrestled" with God about His purpose and plan for my life. I wanted to be sure I was making the right decisions, but also—like Jacob—I longed for a clear sense of God's blessing on my life.

One afternoon, over coffee, I came clean and shared my struggles and doubts with a classmate. Her response not only surprised me, but it turned out to be a pivotal one in my life.

"Brenda, what's your *ministry*?" she asked.

No one had ever before asked me that question, and it would take me weeks to formulate an answer. Before she asked it, I thought of "ministry" as a formal position or title, like "pastor." But her question set me on a path toward new understanding of what ministry really means.

I prayed, and I wrestled with God for quite a while after that conversation. I wanted someone—

> *Many are the plans in a person's heart, but it is the LORD's purpose that prevails.*
>
> PROVERBS 19:21 (NIV)

preferably Jesus Himself—to tell me what God's plan and purpose was for my life. I wanted to be handed a clear job description: teacher or therapist . . . or even something else entirely.

But after a time, I felt like Jesus was beginning to answer my questions and give me clarity about my future. I reflected on the fact that I love teaching, encouraging others, and building relationships with people like I did as an educator both at school and at my church. I was happy when I connected people with resources to meet their physical, mental, and emotional needs. These things felt like ministry, but I wondered how they all could fit together.

I felt prompted to look up the word *minister*. As a verb, it means to attend to the needs of someone. Reading those words,

~323~

I felt a sense of calm and knew that ministry was my purpose, even though it didn't come with a formal job description or my own pulpit. God's plan for me, I realized, is to meet the needs of others in a variety of ways. Some days that means teaching a workshop or a Bible study. At other times, my ministry is encouraging people, counseling them, or helping to meet their needs by connecting them with resources or other professionals.

It was a gift to realize that "ministry" isn't defined by a specific checklist. I saw that I didn't need to go to seminary to fulfill God's purpose and calling. I could complete the counseling program and use that training, along with my teaching skills, to minister to people. I felt more peaceful and confident when I realized that God's plan for me will continue to morph and change over the course of my life. I love knowing that I've been called to a life of ministry, wherever and however God leads me to fulfill it.

Jesus, thank You for the calling You have for me. Help me to be aware of opportunities to minister to other people, wherever they arise. I ask that the rest I have tonight will result in my ability, tomorrow, to be attuned to how I can serve others, showing them Your love.

Praying through the Alphabet

RICK HAMLIN

If you abide in me, and my words abide in you, ask for whatever you wish, and it will be done for you.

JOHN 15:7 (ESV)

I don't count sheep before I go to sleep. I prefer to do something I learned years ago from the late Norman Vincent Peale. Following his advice, I pray through the alphabet to settle my mind before sleep, praying for someone or some need for every letter.

I like to tell my niece Addie that she gets more of my prayers than anybody else in the family because her name starts with an "A." I might, you see, find myself nodding off by the time I get to "T" or "W" when I pray for my sons Timothy and William. No matter, there's always something I wish for them, the verse from Psalms floating through my head, "As a father has compassion on his children, so the LORD has compassion on those who fear him" (Psalm 103:13, NIV).

The thing about working through the alphabet this way is that on different nights, different names or needs will come to mind. When someone asks me to pray for them, I always do it right then and there, but then later, as I'm falling asleep, their names will fit into my prayer.

Some people are constants. "C" is always for my wife, Carol, although her needs, of course, change from day to day. "H" is for my brother Howard. Two years apart, we shared the same bedroom for years, and I can still hear his snoring in my dreams. What about "I"? I'll pause there, until I think, *Pray for yourself, Rick! You have needs and worries, not to mention hopes and dreams.* If the psalmist could bring a host of issues to the Lord, why should I be hesitant about asking God for my heart's delight? "J" either evokes my sister-in-law Julie or our youngest niece, Janna, who is currently in graduate school, studying to become a clinical psychologist. "M" reminds me of my beloved niece Marcie, a high school counselor.

Take my yoke upon you and learn from me, for I am gentle and humble in heart, and you will find rest for your souls.

MATTHEW 11:29 (NIV)

Some letters pull up concerns for whole groups of people. The letter "F," for instance, brings to mind people with unmet financial needs. When I get to "P," I pray for the poor and destitute, the hungry and homeless. My prayer at the letter "U" is usually for the unemployed, that they may find meaningful work that will help them provide for themselves and their families.

There are certain letters of the alphabet that used to have me stumped. "X" was a particular problem, until one night I thought of "X-ray technicians." Now, I often pray for those professionals and all of the healthcare workers at the large urban hospital only 15 blocks away from my home. I spend a few moments on "X," imagining these nurses, technicians, doctors, and others. I ask God to protect and bless them in their work.

Resting On My Saviour's Love

by Eliza E. Hewitt

My heart is sweetly resting
Upon my Saviour's love,
Upon the grace that saves me,
For mansions bright above.

Afar I need not seek him,
He dwells within my soul,
And from the living fountains
Rich waves of blessing roll.

While thus on him I'm resting,
My heart from care is free,
To labor in his vineyard,
And serve him faithfully.

The more I lean upon him,
The more I learn his power,
And find his grace sufficient,
To meet life's every hour.

Resting, resting,
Resting on my Saviour's love,
Resting, resting,
On my Saviour's love.

This bedtime ritual of praying through the alphabet is a chance to clear out my worrying mind, empty it of all that might weigh me down, putting into God's hands what should be there in the first place.

By now, though, you might be wondering what I do for "Z" if, indeed, I'm ever awake by the time I get to it. That one is a no-brainer. "Z" is for good, sound sleep, for myself and for all of those who need rest.

Thank You for hearing my prayers, day after day and night after night, Lord. Thank You for Your presence and Your loving care. Please give me rest tonight, Jesus, and the secure sense that You have me covered and hear all of my concerns, from A to Z.

A Place of Grace

RANDY PETERSEN

Give thanks to the LORD, for he is good;
his love endures forever

PSALM 107:1 (NIV)

There's a curious story in the Gospel of Luke about Jesus healing ten lepers. Because of their disfiguring skin disease, lepers were barred from public worship and excluded from society in general. Yet Jesus often reached out to outcasts, literally touching "untouchables" and healing them. After cleansing the ten from their disease, Jesus sends them off to the local priests so they could be declared fit to re-enter society. They rush off to get this clearance.

But one of the people Jesus heals comes back to thank Him, and Luke's report includes an important detail: This man was a Samaritan. Why does his ethnic identity matter? Why did Luke mention it? As you may know from other Gospel stories, in that time and place, Samaritans were often considered second-class citizens. I have to think that, while the others hurried off to regain their rightful place in society, the Samaritan received the gift of healing with a deeper sense of humility. Not only had Jesus broken health protocols, but He had crossed social barriers to make this man whole. I believe this Samaritan humbly received his healing as a *gift*, something he did not deserve.

Jesus tells him, simply, "Your faith has made you well" (Luke 17:19, NIV).

This story teaches us something about faith and also about the importance of gratitude. All ten lepers exhibited *faith* when they asked Jesus for help, but the Samaritan stands out from the rest because he returns and thanks Jesus. He was not only trusting in Jesus's power to cure him, he was trusting in Jesus's kindness and love.

The word *grace* comes from the Latin *gratia*, meaning favor. When it was first used in the late twelfth century, it was defined as "God's unmerited favor, love, or help." The word *gratitude* is related; from the Latin word *gratus*, it means "thankful" and "pleasing."

> *And whatever you do, whether in word or deed, do it all in the name of the Lord Jesus, giving thanks to God the Father through him.*
>
> COLOSSIANS 3:17 (NIV)

Both words have to do with gifts, or undeserved favors that bring us pleasure. The thankful person says, in essence, "You have freely chosen to give me something of value—whether it's time, attention, kind words, or even a lovely sweater—which I do not deserve. I appreciate your generosity." This statement puts both people in a place of grace. Gratitude is offered freely, in appreciation for a kindness received. When I express my gratitude to Jesus for the gift of grace, healing, and love He gives me—I do so not because I have earned or deserved it, but because He loves me and I love Him.

As this day draws to a close, I take a little time to thank Jesus for all the blessings He has freely given me. He has answered my prayers. He has touched me and healed my body over and over

~330~

during the course of my life. He accepts me, even when I am feeling weary, misunderstood, or out of place—when I feel the way that Samaritan did. I know in my own life, when I focus on Jesus and bring my gratitude to Him for the astonishing, undeserved grace of God, I feel that all is well with my soul.

Thank You, dear Lord, for the many blessings, relationships, and joys You've given me. I am most thankful for the life-sustaining connection I have with You.

He Who Laughs Lives Well

LORI ROELEVELD

A cheerful heart is good medicine.

PROVERBS 17:22 (NIV)

My father and I both chose to work in high-stress profes-sions. He spent over fifty-one years as a fire chief, one of only two paid firefighters in our small-town volunteer fire de-partment. I've spent my career in child abuse prevention, work-ing with families in crisis. Both jobs have their rewards. We gain satisfaction from knowing we've made a positive impact on our community. We love the new challenges each day brings. There's rich camaraderie with our coworkers, great joy when things go well, and the reward of knowing we help others through life's worst moments. The flip side is that often we see and hear things too painful to share with others at days' end.

Dad let me in on his key strategy for coping with work stress. For him, maintaining humor in grim situations was his secret weapon against stress and sadness. "Take the job seriously, but don't take yourself too seriously," he would always say.

This was powerful guidance from a man who struggled with occasional depression associated with PTSD. Dad was deadly serious about firefighting, rescues, and community safety. His department had high standards for training. But every firefighter remembers the cartoons Dad would post on the bulletin boards or mail to individual members whenever they needed a boost.

In his later years, Dad and I had a nightly appointment to watch one hour of sitcoms or funny movies. A favorite was *M*A*S*H,* a comedy set in a U.S. Army mobile medical unit stationed in Korea during the war. Watching those fictional soldiers find opportunities for joy while enduring conflict was exactly the medicine Dad prescribed for coping with our jobs. Dad's favorite funny movie was *Home Alone,* a slapstick comedy featuring a young boy left to his own devices who outwits two would-be burglars during Christmas. It was as much fun to watch Dad belly-laugh as it was to watch the movie.

> *Consider it pure joy, my brothers and sisters, whenever you face trials of many kinds.*
>
> JAMES 1:2 (NIV)

Dad enforced this value of maintaining positivity on the job. Every person affected by an emergency was held in the highest regard and treated with care and respect, not only in their presence but afterward. Debriefing after tough calls, though, Dad would tell stories of his own follies that would have the firefighters in stitches— like his brief but memorable ride on the front of a rescued bull or the time he was in the garage when my mom yelled, "Fire." Dad was halfway down the driveway before he realized the smoke was coming from his own kitchen! A pan of grease had gotten away from Mom. It was quickly extinguished, but she never let him forget that he almost drove away from his own housefire.

In James 1:2 (NIV), we're told to "Consider it pure joy, my brothers and sisters, whenever you face trials of many kinds."

It was certainly harder to do that as Dad's health began to fail, but even then, he would rise from his chair and do a couple of silly dance moves just to make me laugh. A cheerful heart surely is good medicine. Dad was proof of that. I'm sure it's the reason that despite the doctor's initial prognosis of six months, Dad enjoyed four years beyond that, full of laughter and love.

When firefighters and family gathered after Dad's funeral, the stories flowed and the room filled with cheer, even as our tears fell. Each of us had plenty to tell of the times he'd made us smile amid hard but necessary work. We knew our laughter rising over plates full of great food is exactly how he wanted his life to be celebrated. His legacy is one of sacrifice and community service but also one of relentless joy.

My family and I carry on his tradition of taking time at the end of every day to laugh, whether telling stories around the fire, watching a great sitcom, or busting out a couple of silly dance moves. And we always remember Dad.

What a wonderful gift from our Heavenly Father that we have joy to heal us and laughter to buoy our spirits as we serve one another, even through hard times. Good cheer is indeed medicine for our hearts!

Jesus, thank You for laughter and for joy.
Help me not only to seize the opportunity
for joy despite challenging situations, help me
also to share it with those around me.

We Don't Walk Alone

LORI HATCHER

Therefore, since we are surrounded by such a great cloud of witnesses, let us throw off everything that hinders and the sin that so easily entangles. And let us run with perseverance the race marked out for us, fixing our eyes on Jesus, the pioneer and perfecter of our faith.

HEBREWS 12:1–2 (NIV)

Our family was camping in upstate South Carolina. As my daughter and son-in-law pitched the tent and got our site organized, my grandkids and I explored the woods. Bursting with new growth, the forest paraded its spring wardrobe. Verdant greens formed the backdrop for pink azaleas and white dogwoods. Wild blueberry bushes, dotted with teardrop-shaped blossoms, flourished under a canopy of oak and pine. In the shallows of the lake, along the edge of the campground, buggy-eyed spring peepers sang their off-key chorus while the kids and I threw rocks into the water.

At the back of the campsite, I spied a fallen tree trunk, white against the leaf-covered ground. It extended an invitation I couldn't resist.

"Hey guys," I called, "Let's go walk on that log."

My oldest two granddaughters didn't need a second invitation. They raced to the fallen tree and clambered up onto it. The victim of a storm years ago, the pine had lain there so long the insects had stripped off its bark, leaving behind a smooth white core. Seven-year-old Lauren and five-year-old Caroline started to walk across it, their arms extended like gymnasts on a balance beam.

> *You will find as you look back upon your life that the moments when you have truly lived are the moments when you have done things in the spirit of love.*
>
> HENRY DRUMMOND

The thirty-foot log spanned a shallow depression where erosion had dug a channel in the soft earth. When the girls reached the halfway point, they paused and looked down.

"Look at us, Gigi," Caroline called. "We're up high!"

"Yes, you are," I called. And then, in typical grandma fashion, I added, "Be careful!" Of course, they were only a few feet off the ground, but from their perspective, it probably felt like ten!

I then turned my attention back to Collin, my one-and-a-half-year-old grandson. Fourth-born children are known for following the pack, and this little guy was no exception. He wanted to do everything his sisters did.

But walk across a fallen log spanning a ditch taller than he was? I wasn't so sure he'd be up for it, but he was determined. He pulled himself up onto the log and watched his sisters tiptoe across ahead of him. He pointed toward them, then looked up at me, now standing beside him.

"You want to go across, Collie?"

He nodded his head.

"Let's go," I said, extending my hand. "Gigi will help you."

Carefully, one tiny step at a time, he set off, his hand clinging to mine.

"Look at you!" I said. "What a big boy!"

His sisters reached the end and cheered, jumping up and down like gold medalists. Collie looked at them, grinned, then continued his careful steps. His sisters, done with their celebration, turned to face him. It was then that he hesitated.

"You've got this!" Caroline called.

He took a brave step and laughed, which disturbed his balance. He wobbled and, clutching my hand, glanced down at the ground below and whimpered.

Connection Practices

A study conducted at the State University of New York and Florida State University found that people don't like to be cold—they will seek out ways to warm themselves, physically and emotionally.

Warmth describes the emotions associated with connection, comfort, and mutual appreciation. Here are a few suggestions for connecting practices:

- Reach out to your house of worship or other community organizations for programs or volunteer opportunities.
- Reach out to a friend to share some quality time together, perhaps with a walk or a get-together where you can share some laughs.
- Bask in the warmth of your own good company, remembering there's joy to be found in solitude.

"Come on, Collie. You can do it! Hold onto Gigi," Lauren shouted. "You'll make it across."

"Don't be afraid," I said, tightening my grip. "Gigi's got you. I won't let you fall. We're walking together."

He looked again at his sisters and took a step. Then another. And another. When he reached the end of the log, they scooped him into their arms and swung him in a happy circle.

"You did it!" they said. "We knew you could."

His grin stretched from ear to ear.

Collin's journey is a lot like mine. I began my Christian life carefree and confident that I could do anything. The path was smooth and easy, and Jesus walked beside me. Life, though, grows more challenging as we age. The firm ground of youth, health, and invincibility shifts. Circumstances cause me to forget that Jesus walks beside me, and my faith wobbles.

When I cry out in fear, I feel the strong grip of Jesus holding my hand.

"Don't be afraid," He whispers to my anxious heart. "I've got you. I won't let you fall. We're walking together." I remember the promise of Hebrews 13:5 (NIV), "Never will I leave you; never will I forsake you."

Ahead of me a great cloud of witnesses cheers me on. "You can do it!" they call, just like Caroline and Lauren shouted out to their little brother when he faltered. "Hold onto Jesus, and you'll make it across."

And I do—one wobbly step at a time, clinging to Jesus's hand and looking toward the finish line. There my brothers and sisters await, eager to wrap me in a heavenly hug and celebrate my victory.

"You did it!" they'll say. "We knew you could."

As my faith matures, I'm learning that Jesus never abandons me in the valleys of my life. No matter what trial I face or what circumstances make my heart race and my steps uncertain, I'm not alone. My brothers and sisters in the faith cheer me on. The great cloud of witnesses waits to welcome me home, and Jesus walks beside me every step of the way.

Jesus, I thank You! You promise to be with me always, even in life's most challenging moments. Tonight, help me to relax and rest, knowing You hold and protect me. I will hold tight to You tonight and always. In the strong name of Jesus, I pray.

Creating Room for Margin

CRYSTAL STORMS

This is what the LORD says: "Stand at the crossroads and look; ask for the ancient paths, ask where the good way is, and walk in it, and you will find rest for your souls."

JEREMIAH 6:16 (NIV)

A hurried day and rush to an afternoon service at church left me feeling cranky and stressed. That day, I worked diligently through my to-do list. In the morning I'd completed a few writing assignments. After a quick lunch, I tidied the house to prepare for the guests who'd arrive the next day. I then prepped our dinner before my husband, Tim, and I left for church. I snapped at Tim as we climbed in the car. I also encouraged him to hit the gas when the light turned yellow.

That day, I'd left no room for margin. Margin to breathe. Margin for my husband to get the knot right on his tie. Margin to get stuck at a red light. Margin to reflect on the gifts of the day. But Jesus invites me on a different path. He invites me to slow down, to be still, and to know that He is God. He welcomes me to reflect on who I am in Christ. He encourages me to move forward and do the work I have to do from a place of rest.

Jeremiah 6:16 reminds me I don't have to guess what His best is for me. I can ask Him. When faced with a decision, I can seek

His guidance. His counsel helps me choose between better and best. I can look to the Shepherd to direct my steps. And when I follow His leading, Jesus promises rest for my soul.

So, since that hectic day, I've begun to let some things go and to create more margins. I've begun to accept that things often take longer than we anticipate. That we need extra time for the unexpected. To acknowledge that although something might fit on the calendar, it still may not belong there. To recognize that I don't need to automatically say yes—even when I have nothing else going on.

Leaving space in my days makes room for Christ's peace. It provides space for me to hear His voice. It allows me to receive

Choose Peace

Are you longing for rest, for peacefulness? Maybe the restfulness you seek is a choice. Maybe it comes from asking for what you know you need.

Take a moment. Whisper, *Lord, I want peace.*

The Lord knows your heart. He knows your desire is to walk in living-breathing peace, both the kind you hope to find in slumber as well as that soul-claiming kind of rest. The kind that's present in the wakeful hours. The kind that washes into the spirit as a gentle tide that pulls back uncertainties and leaves a smooth surface of serenity.

The kind that overrides worry and fear.

Take another moment and whisper, *Lord, I choose to trust You with the weight of my worries. Please show me how.*

Choose trust. Choose peace. The Spirit will help you.

His guidance. He's modeled this for me. When I read the Scriptures and examine how Jesus lived, I recognize that not all things are mine to do. The Gospels don't depict a Jesus who's always rushing about. Jesus walked at a pace that allowed Him to get away with His Father. He left things undone so He could do what He was called to do. He withdrew to the wilderness to pray so He could move forward in calm wisdom.

It takes trust to let go of the good and reach for His best. Trust to follow Christ's example. Trust that I am who He says I am, and I don't need to prove my worth. Trust that my value isn't determined by how much I accomplish every day.

When I pause to ask Jesus what His best is for me, I find rest for my soul. Rest that leaves room for margin. Rest that allows me to respond in kindness. Rest that gives and receives His grace.

That day, so long ago now, I apologized to Tim for my harsh tone and the stress I'd put on him to get to church on time. He forgave me and reached for my hand. We said yes to enjoying the evening and savoring the presence of the people around us. Yes to walking in peace. Yes to leaving space in our days so we had room for His grace.

Jesus, show me what I can release so I can walk in Your peace. Thank You for leading me in Your good way and giving me rest for my soul.

Trust and Obey

LORI HATCHER

Instead, speaking the truth in love, we will grow to become in every respect the mature body of him who is the head, that is, Christ.

EPHESIANS 4:15 (NIV)

Tooth Morphology, a third-semester class for dental hygienists, was almost over. Our final project, designed to demonstrate that we understood basic tooth design, involved carving an incisor, a premolar, and a molar—to scale—out of a bar of Ivory soap. And carving teeth out of soap put me in a terrible mood.

I've never been a fan of complicated projects or tedious detail work. I don't sew or put puzzles together for fun, and this project taxed my patience. I knew if I shaved off millimeter too much from any surface, I'd have to start all over again. The pressure of perfection was affecting my normally sunnier disposition.

"I hate this," I said to classmates seated near me. "This is a waste of time. Why should I spend hours of my life carving soap when I could be in the clinic learning a skill I'll actually use one day?"

"Lori."

I jumped at my instructor's voice. Dr. H. was the director of the program, and although small of stature, he was formidable.

"Come into my office," Dr. H. said. "I need to speak with you."

I rose and followed him down the hall. He indicated that I should sit down. I sat, my eyes focused on my tightly clenched hands.

"Lori," he began. "You've been grumbling about this project for a week, and I've had enough. It brings me no pleasure to tell you this: Frankly, I doubt you have what it takes to graduate. Would you like to quit now and make it easier on all of us?"

"No, sir," I said. I might have mumbled an apology, but truly, I didn't know what to say. Dr. H. quickly dismissed me, and I slunk back to class.

After that harsh reprimand, I realized that I'd lost my grasp on *why* I was there and what I wanted to accomplish after graduating. I needed to stay focused on completing the requirements of the program. Fortunately, I turned things around and did graduate.

> *The mystery of human existence lies not in just staying alive, but in finding something to live for.*
>
> FYODOR DOSTOYEVSKY

And of course, my professors knew what they were doing. Contrary to my short-sighted assessment that carving teeth out of soap was a worthless pursuit, I've used my knowledge of tooth contours *every single day* as I care for my patients.

Although Dr. H.'s words and tone were harsh, they were necessary. From that point on, I trusted that the projects and assignments we were given were carefully chosen and worth my full attention and time. And I stopped complaining.

Still, one semester later, I again sat in one of my instructors' office because of something I'd said.

"Lori," Ms. T. said. "I've overheard a few conversations this week. I understand you're worried about your tuition."

"That's right," I said. "I just don't know how I'm going to do it next year."

Ms. T. was a fellow Christian. She knew I loved Jesus too.

"Do you believe the Lord called you to this program?" she asked.

I nodded.

"I want to remind you of Jesus's words in Matthew 6:31–32," she said. "Therefore do not be anxious, saying, 'What shall we eat?' or 'What shall we drink?' or 'What shall we wear?' Your heavenly Father knows that you need them all."

"Do you believe He can provide what you need to finish?" she asked.

I nodded again.

Tears filled my eyes. In that short interaction, Ms. T. brought truth into my life, and I felt my worry slip away.

A month later, I received a student aid award that enabled me to finish school debt-free. On the day of my graduation, I walked across the stage with a smile on my face—and three perfectly carved soap teeth in my pocket.

Both instructors' words were timely, and Jesus spoke to me through them. They addressed attitudes that needed correction. As I mentioned, I've used my knowledge of tooth contours daily. I've also continued to apply Ms. T.'s reminder that if Jesus calls me to do something, He'll provide everything I need to accomplish it.

Lord Jesus, thank You for the ways You speak to me through the words of others. Give me rest tonight, Lord, and help me to begin the day tomorrow with a sense of trust and purpose.

Puzzled

JEANETTE LEVELLIE

But he said to me, "My grace is sufficient for you,
for my power is made perfect in weakness." Therefore
I will boast all the more gladly about my weaknesses,
so that Christ's power may rest on me.

2 CORINTHIANS 12:9 (NIV)

I sighed as I perused the table filled with jigsaw puzzle pieces. "Are we still missing that turquoise edge piece?" I asked my husband, Kevin. "I bet one of the cats knocked it under the fridge or took it down to the basement."

Kevin and I had almost finished assembling this serene picture of brightly colored birds perched on lavender hydrangea bushes. The edge pieces came together fast. All but one. We finally gave up looking and started putting together the inside. I hated the thought of finishing the puzzle with a piece missing. Especially an edge. Then I remembered an incident that took place many years ago.

When our daughter Esther was ten, she beckoned me to see a puzzle she'd just completed. "I'm so excited because all but two pieces are here!" she said. "I thought I'd lost more than that."

I looked at her in amazement. *What a great attitude!* I thought. *If that happened to me, I'd throw the whole puzzle away. Esther is thrilled that* only two *pieces are missing.*

Sometimes I look at myself with similar perfectionism. *Why can't I listen more than I talk? Why can't I have more self-control when it comes to eating sweets? Why can't I more consistently obey Jesus?* I find myself focusing only on the missing pieces in the puzzle that is my character or the gaps in my own life. Some pieces are missing because of past hurts caused by other people. Others are broken or absent because of poor choices I've made. When I focus only on what's missing or imperfect in me, I begin to feel discouraged.

> *See what great love the Father has lavished on us, that we should be called children of God! And that is what we are!*
>
> 1 JOHN 3:1 (NIV)

What brings me back on track is remembering and acknowledging that Jesus sees me with His grace-filled and tender gaze. Like Esther rejoicing about her beautiful, incomplete puzzle, Jesus rejoices over me. He's thrilled that, in spite all the holes in my heart, I trust Him as much as I do. He sees the pieces that fit together and the colorful picture they make. He sees the way my life reflects His love. It calms me to contemplate the fact that Jesus looks at me—and all of His children—with a heart full of unconditional and unending love.

Jesus was fully divine and fully human, making Him a realist. He's realistic enough to accept that we won't be fully grown and "all together" until we meet Him face-to-face. On that day, He will change us into His image. No missing pieces. No brokenness. Nothing incomplete.

When Kevin and I were almost done with our bird puzzle and there were only a few pieces left on the table, that final edge piece appeared, as if out of nowhere.

"Well, how did we overlook this?" I asked.

What Makes a Grateful Person?

Someone said, "It is not happy people who are thankful. It is thankful people who are happy."

These are some of the attributes that make up grateful people:

- Express their joy.
- Celebrate all of God's blessings.
- Remember who and what helped their lives turn for the best.
- Endure hardships with grateful hearts.
- Serve others with their talent, time, and money.
- Value the small things in life.
- Spend time with loved ones and friends.

Kev smiled wide and said, "We just needed to get to the end to find it."

When I lay my head on my pillow tonight, I will thank Jesus for His unconditional love and the fact that I am becoming closer to Him each day.

Lord Jesus, I'm grateful that You see me complete in You, with nothing missing and nothing broken. Please help me accept and love myself, just as I am, this evening. I end this day imagining the healing calm of Your loving gaze.

Without Guile

NORM STOLPE

*Jesus saw Nathanael coming to him, and saith of him,
Behold an Israelite indeed, in whom is no guile!*

JOHN 1:47 (KJV)

To describe my wife, Candy, as "trusting" would be an understatement—you might even say she's gullible. She's always taken people at their word; sarcasm, exaggeration, and even some humor just doesn't resonate with her. When they were teenagers, our boys would laugh when their mother didn't get a joke that relied on the twisting of logic and language. They often had to tell her, point blank, when they were kidding or teasing her in a friendly way. I've often commented that Candy is like Nathanael when Jesus met him, someone in whom there is no guile. Though she sometimes misses out on a punchline, we all consider the fact that her thoughts and words are always characterized by trust, sincerity, and grace quite admirable.

When thinking of my wife, I prefer the way the King James Version translates Jesus's words about Nathanael as being a person "in whom is no *guile*," rather than having no "deceit," as used by other translations. "No guile" suggests to me the purity of heart which is much more than mere honesty. I see that, too, in Candy who has always been able to find ways to recognize the best in people.

Jeanie is a widow who lives across the street from us. When Milwaukee weather permits, she sits on the steps of her front walk in the afternoons, smoking cigarettes and passing out treats to the dogs whose humans walk them by her house. If by chance Jeanie is not there, many of the dogs stop and sit in hopes she will come out. From her living room recliner, Candy can see when Jeanie comes out, and often Candy heads down our front steps and across the street to chat with her friend. Having lived her life in a tobacco-free environment, Candy has an aversion to cigarette smoke, but Candy has never mentioned this to Jeanie. She simply stands upwind of the smoke. Over the years, Jeanie and Candy have become prayer partners, for which Candy is so grateful.

Of course, clueless responses to humor and ignoring cigarette smoke are not complete indicators of being guileless or pure of heart. But I love ending the day talking with Jesus about what Candy's gracious temperament and trusting nature teach me about Him. I end the day in prayer, reviewing with Jesus my observations not only of my wife, but others who reflect His love. I'm nourished spiritually when I think about people who are models for me, and I yearn to be a person of character too.

Jesus, thank You for the people You place in our lives, people who show us how to live and love the way You did. Thank You for helping us to mature in faith and to live in a way that honors You.

Light in the Darkness

BRENDA YODER

Then you will shine among them like stars in the sky.

PHILIPPIANS 2:15 (NIV)

When I was growing up, my family and I watched the nightly news during dinner. I was fascinated by current events and happenings around the world. When I had a family of my own, watching the news was a relaxing transition at the end of the day. Current events helped me feel connected to the bigger world. I later was a U.S. history, government, and sociology teacher. The nightly news informed both my classroom instruction and my professional growth.

Now I am a therapist and school counselor. The evening news rarely feels relaxing to me because it mirrors the painful events in the lives of students and families with whom I work.

After watching one particular news segment, I clicked off the TV and shared my angst with Jesus. Did He see the pain in this world? Why did He let it be so hard for so many? As I prayed, I remembered the lyrics from an old Sunday School song about letting your light shine. Those lines coming to mind seemed to me like Jesus answering my prayer, asking me to concentrate on being a bright spot in people's day. By doing so, His light would shine.

What were small things I could do to spread positivity and to reflect Jesus's love? I started at a drive-through window by asking a teen employee about his post–high school plans. I told him how responsible he was for working while going to school. He flashed a big smile and said thank you.

At a drugstore, I started talking with the cashier. When I left, she said our conversation was the highlight of her day; I felt the same way.

I've started seeking even more positive interactions every day. I turn off the news when it's negative. I text people who are on my mind to let them know I'm thinking of them. I smile a lot more at people and post cheerful photos on social media. I try to leave positive footprints wherever I am, whether it's online or in person. And I'm on the lookout for the loving and positive messages from other people too.

I used to believe that one person can't make a difference in the larger scheme of broken systems and an off-kilter world. But Jesus has showed me that I was wrong about that. More than once I've gone to bed with more good news than bad in my day. Not because the world is changing, but because the brightness of Christ, when illuminated, shines brilliantly, like the stars.

> *Let gratitude be the pillow upon which you kneel to say your nightly prayer. And let faith be the bridge you build to overcome evil and welcome good.*
>
> MAYA ANGELOU

Jesus, help me to see where I can share Your love and light with others. Tonight, as I drift off to sleep, I thank You for shining like the stars.

Every Part of My Story

ERYN LYNUM

Let us therefore come boldly to the throne of grace, that we may obtain mercy and find grace to help in time of need.

HEBREWS 4:16 (NKJV)

The week was marked by exceptional beauty. We'd glimpsed the massive summits of Colorado, played in crystal-clear lakes, and hiked aspen-lined trails, but this was a different category of allure. The pine forests and rolling green hills were less dramatic than other sights that week, alluding to a humble beauty.

Dotting the trail were petrified stumps—massive remnants of a forest fallen long ago. It's a well-known fact that a tree's age is revealed by the rings of its stump. Yet it's not only the years we can observe, but what those years held. We can see evidence of drought and storms, and even scars from wildfire. As I walked among the stumps, I considered my own life and what the "concentric circles" of my story might one day reveal.

Just as the lines of a tree tell the narrative of its life, Jesus knows my story. He knows my entire story, including the events yet to take place, and He's capable of using the rough seasons for extraordinary purposes. I can view the difficult seasons in the positive light of His redemption.

In John 10:14 (ESV), I see how intimately Jesus knows me. "I am the good shepherd, and I know my own, and my own know me." Not only is He intimately familiar with my story, but He empathizes with seasons of adversity. As I consider the concentric circles of Jesus's own life, I discover many scars. He chose to take on flesh and acquaint Himself with my sorrows, ultimately giving His life so I would be redeemed.

> *When we work for a bigger purpose, we find an endless supply of happiness at work.*
>
> JON GORDON

Jesus's life wasn't perfect. In the words of John 11:35, "Jesus wept," I see Him suffering from grief. In John 4:6 (NASB), I find Him tired, "Jesus, being wearied from His journey, was sitting thus by the well." John 6:66 (NASB) finds Him abandoned by companions, "As a result of this many of His disciples left and would no longer walk with Him." His story is marked up by hardships and pain, all so that my story can be made new in Him.

Jesus sees every line of my story, and He can relate to what I feel. He has already redeemed each detail for my good and His glory. I don't know the end of the story yet, or how it will all work out. But I know it's going to be a good one—scars and all.

Dear Jesus, You see the hurts and failures of my past, You know what I'm facing presently, and You are fully aware of the days ahead of me. I trust you, Jesus, with everything my life holds. You are redeeming each scar and writing a magnificent story.

Through the Night

DURWOOD SMITH

*The L*ORD *is thy keeper: the L*ORD *is thy shade upon thy right hand. The sun shall not smite thee by day, nor the moon by night. The L*ORD *shall preserve thee from all evil: He shall preserve thy soul.*

PSALM 121:5–7 (KJV)

Sometimes he wore a Samoan sarong, but most of the time he dressed like a typical young American man. His hands were massive, his shoulders like mountain foothills. His voice was as quiet as the rumblings of a nearly extinct volcano. Dark eyes hid thoughts that seldom surfaced into speech. You could easily be misled by his appearance or demeanor. You might even be afraid of him, but there was no need: James was a protector.

Bedded down in a sleeping bag on the concrete floor of an open-air church in the tiny hillside village of Dupuy, Haiti, I wasn't quite asleep. I'd traveled together with my church's "work and witness" team of fifteen, including James, from the U.S. We were hushed in slumber beneath roof trusses that tomorrow would support a new sheet metal roof but tonight were open to the Caribbean night sky. Thunder rumbling in the distant hills echoed the low beat of nightly voodoo drums. I felt safe because of James, the carpenter, my big Samoan friend.

I also felt safe because I was on mission for the Savior. We were "called" to this project because of need. Wasn't it Jesus who went to where the need was? "I must go and preach in other towns also, for thereto was I called," Jesus said. These villagers had no resources to build a new church, a clinic, or a school as this church soon would be. I was doing the work of God so villagers could also do the will of God.

The thunder clapped closer, and the sky was no longer starry. Lightning flashed. Rain poured in earnest. The Caribbean overcast was letting loose. Hushed slumber broke into shouts, "We're getting wet! My bedding is soaked." Plastic tarps rustled into action. People dashed about looking for shelter. "How long is this going to last?" someone shouted. At age sixty-five, I wasn't the spryest team member, so I gave in to staying put and settled for a soggy night.

> *Then (Jesus) arose and rebuked the wind and the raging of the water: and they ceased, and there was a calm.*
>
> LUKE 8:24 (KJV)

In the dark between flashes of lightning, a figure loomed over me. "Quiet! Be still, I'm covering you with a plastic tarp. No need to get up. You'll be dry." I drifted into calm, my sleeping bag, a cocoon of rest. I thought of Jesus stilling the storm when disciples were about to drown, and took comfort in the words, "Peace, be still." The storm moved on.

The next morning, rising at 6:00 to work, we got a jump on the tropical sun. After two hours, a meager breakfast was served just ahead of the 100-degree heat and humidity. I had to inquire about the night before.

"Whoa, wasn't that a night!" exclaimed half our crew. "I was soaked. Didn't sleep much after that. Is that what we're in for every night?"

"No, we'll fasten half the roof panels on by tonight. We'll all sleep under those. Today we'll need all the construction guys on the roof," instructed our leader. The tasks of our roof crew were gruelingly tough. Because of heat and exhaustion issues older people can experience, I was given a job in the shade where it was only ninety-eight degrees. *So much better than the blazing sun,* I mused in gratitude. *The sun shall not smite thee by day.*

We finished the project and two days later flew out of Port-au-Prince back to the U.S. Crowded next to James on the flight home, I asked, "Was that you, that night covering me up with a tarp in the rainstorm?"

"Yes, you needed protection. I could see that you were exhausted by the work and the heat of the day. You needed rest," he explained.

In the hill village of Dupuy, it was Jesus at work in James, sheltering me from the storm.

Lord, You know my exhaustion and the heat of my day. Tonight, I lie down to rest with a calm heart because I know You are my protector. Rise in the night, speak to my storm, Carpenter of Nazareth, Prince of Peace.

ENTRIES BY TOPIC

ENTRIES BY WRITER

CONTRIBUTORS

Susanna Foth Aughtmon is an author and speaker who loves to use humor, Scripture, and personal stories to explore how God's grace and truth intersect with her daily life. Susanna lives in Idaho with her funny, creative husband, marketer/pastor Scott Aughtmon. She is mom to three fantastic young men, Jack, Will, and Addison, who bring her a whole lot of joy. Susanna likes to connect with her readers through her blog, Confessions of a Tired Supergirl, and her Good Things Newsletter. You can catch up with her on Facebook and her website, www.sfaughtmon.com.

Logan Eliasen grew up with four brothers on the banks of the Mississippi River. He and his Labrador Old Sport now live in Des Moines, Iowa. Logan has a B.A. in Biblical and Theological Studies from Wheaton College and a Juris Doctor from the University of Iowa. In addition to writing for *Evenings with Jesus*, Logan has been writing for *Daily Guideposts* for a number of years. In his free time, Logan enjoys reading, cycling, and camping.

Beth Gormong is the co-author (along with fellow *Evenings with Jesus* contributor Jeanette Levellie) of two women's devotional books, *Hello, Beautiful! Finally Love Yourself Just as You Are* and *Yes, You Can! Overcome Crises with God's Help*.

She is a *Guideposts* magazine contributor, Parish Administrator for Trinity Lutheran Church in Terre Haute, Indiana, and maker behind the GreenGableStudio Etsy shop. Beth is the wife of a farmer, mother of three adult daughters, and devotee of two crazy cats and one beagle. She lives in a 100-year-old farmhouse in rural Indiana. You can find more information about Beth Gormong at bgormong.com

Rick Hamlin is the author of numerous books on prayer, including *Even Silence Is Praise, Pray for Me, Ten Prayers You Can't Live Without, Finding God on the A Train*, and novels such as *Reading Between the Lines* and *Mixed Blessings*. A longtime editor at *Guideposts* magazine, he's written several op-eds for *The New York Times*. His wife, the writer Carol Wallace, wrote the book *To Marry an English Lord*, which became the inspiration for the series *Downton Abbey*. They live in New York City and both sing in their church choir. They are the parents of two grown children and look forward to becoming grandparents. Rick also writes weekly blogs on Guideposts.org. He is currently in training to become a spiritual director.

Lori Hatcher is a transplanted Yankee living happily in the South with her pastor husband, David. She's the author of *Refresh Your Faith: Uncommon Devotions from Every Book of the Bible* and *Refresh Your Prayers: Uncommon Devotions to Restore Power and Praise*. Her devotions have appeared in *All God's Creatures* and *Guideposts One-Minute Daily Devotional*, and she's written for ReviveOurHearts.com, *Our Daily Bread*, and *Upper Room*.

Lori shares hope and encouragement as a women's ministry speaker, Bible teacher, writing instructor, and healthcare professional. A lover of chocolate, small children, and puppies, Lori can be found pondering the marvelous and the mundane on her blog, Hungry for God... Starving for Time, Five-Minute Devotions for Busy Women (www.LoriHatcher.com).

Bob Hostetler is an award-winning author, literary agent, and international speaker from Nevada. His more than fifty books, which include the award-winning *Don't Check Your Brains at the Door* (co-authored with Josh McDowell) and *The Bard and the Bible: A Shakespeare Devotional*, have sold millions of copies. Bob is an agent with the Steve Laube Agency (www.stevelaube.com) and the executive director of the Christian Writers Institute (www.christianwritersinstitute.com). Bob was also the founding pastor of Cobblestone Community Church in Oxford, Ohio. He and his lovely wife, Robin, have two grown children, who have given them five perfect grandchildren.

Former newspaper columnist Jeanette Levellie moved from L.A. to southern Illinois in 1999 with her pastor husband, Kevin. Surrounded by corn and soybean fields, Jeanette relishes waking to birdsong and watching squirrels and chipmunks play in her backyard. She has one husband, two grown kids, three grandchildren, and four spoiled babies disguised as cats. Jeanette has authored and published six books and hundreds of stories, articles, calendar poems, and greeting card verses. She has written for *Guideposts* publications since 2018. Other writing credits include *Focus on the Family*, *Woman's World*, and *Country* magazines. Her hobbies include watching black-and-white movies, gardening, and reading novels.

Eryn Lynum is a certified Master Naturalist, speaker, and the author of the book *936 Pennies: Discovering the Joy of Intentional Parenting* (Bethany House Publishers). She is a contributor to five Guideposts books and a freelance writer for several ministries and businesses. She holds a degree in Biblical studies and systematic theology. Her passion is to combine the two fields of nature and Bible study, sharing profound Biblical truths through vivid imagery in creation. Eryn, her husband, Grayson, and their four kids enjoy hiking, camping, and exploring God's vast creation in the Rocky Mountains they call home. Eryn has been featured on Focus on the Family, FamilyLife, Proverbs31 Ministries, MOPS International, Bible Gateway, Her View from Home, and For Every Mom. She shares her adventures at www.ErynLynum.com.

Randy Petersen has written more than sixty books about the Bible, history, worship, music, and relationships. In the heart of the pandemic, he collaborated with friends on an e-book, *The Joy of Working at Home* (Credo, 2020). He also contributed to the Guideposts book *Messages from Heaven* (2021). Besides his religious writing, Randy works as a marketing copywriter and messaging consultant. As a playwright, Randy has had a number of plays produced in the Philadelphia and Chicago areas. He has taught acting and public speaking at the college level. He preaches occasionally at his church and has served there in many roles, including that of softball coach.

Lori Roeleveld is a blogger, speaker, and disturber of hobbits. She enjoys inviting comfortable Christians into Christ-centered adventures (like Tolkien's hobbits). Lori has authored four award-winning books, with a fifth in the works. She speaks regularly at women's events and retreats across the country. Though she has degrees in Psychology and Biblical Studies, Lori learned the most from studying her Bible in life's trenches. She speaks her mind at www.loriroeleveld.com.

Twelve years as a pastor and a thirty-year architectural career specializing in luxury residences in three states fulfilled Durwood Smith's professional life until his retirement. Life as a husband, father of two sons, and grandfather of nine grandchildren enriches his days, often in unexpected ways. Durwood volunteers in his local church and serves abroad in world missions, adding enjoyment to his life and moving his heart. Durwood is a member of the Northwest Christian Writers Association, and he enjoys classical music, live drama, gardening, art collecting, car shopping, and visiting small historic towns of the U.S. He and his wife make their home in the Pacific Northwest.

After beginning his career developing church education curriculum, Norm Stolpe enjoyed over forty years of pastoral ministry. Since his wife Candy's Alzheimer's diagnosis in 2016, the Stolpes have shared a duplex in Milwaukee with their middle son, David, and his family. Their oldest son, Jon, and his family live in Pennsylvania. Erik, their youngest, lives in Texas. The Stolpes care for Candy's ninety-four-old father, who moved to a nearby assisted living facility to be close to them. Norm contributes devotionals to Guideposts' *Strength and Grace*. In 2018, he published *Ripples*, a book of stories from his time as a pastor. He credits his experiences as a pastor and caregiver and his lifelong personal journey with Jesus for the insights in his writing.

Crystal Storms is an award-winning author, watercolor artist, and speaker. She has been featured in Guideposts' *All God's Creatures* and *One-Minute Daily Devotional, Focus on the Family*, and more. Drawing from her personal faith and her love of God's Word, Crystal shares her honest struggles so others know they are not alone. She wants the words and art that she shares to encourage hearts and help others in their journey in Christ. Crystal loves coffee, chocolate, tea, good books, and most of all, Jesus. When she's not creating, you can find her exploring God's creation, snuggling with her husband, Tim, or working through her long list of books to read. Crystal and Tim have been married since 1995 and live in Florida with their Yorkie, Minnie. You can connect with her at CrystalStorms.me.